Changing Maps:
Governing in a World of Rapid Change

Changing Maps:
Governing in a World of Rapid Change

Steven A. Rosell, *et al.*

The Second Report of the Project on
Governing in an Information Society

CARLETON UNIVERSITY PRESS
in collaboration with
THE MERIDIAN INTERNATIONAL INSTITUTE
and
THE PARLIAMENTARY CENTRE

Published by Carleton University Press in collaboration with The
Meridian International Institute and The Parliamentary Centre.

Printed and bound in Canada.

Cover art, Illustration & Design by Soren Henrich.

Published by:
Carleton University Press
1125 Colonel By Drive
Ottawa, ON
Canada K1S 5B6

Distributed by:
Oxford University Press
77 Wynford Drive
Don Mills, ON
Canada M3C 1J9

CANADIAN CATALOGUING IN PUBLICATION DATA

Main entry under title:
    Changing maps : governing in a world of rapid change

Includes bibliographical reference and index.
ISBN 0-88629-264-6

1. Policy sciences – Methodology.   2. Public administration.
3. Management.   4. Information society.   I. Rosell, Steven A.

HD58.8C46 1995   658.8'06   C95-900144-1

Contents

Governing in a World of Rapid Change

HOW CAN WE ORGANIZE AND GOVERN ourselves successfully in a world of rapid change and increasing interconnection? Today that is a critical challenge facing all sectors of society, both public and private. In jurisdictions around the world, the emergence of a global information society is accelerating the pace of change and overwhelming established methods of organizing and governing that were developed for a world of more limited information flow, greater stability and clearer boundaries. Gradually, we are coming to understand that, to be effective in this world of rapid change, we need to develop learning-based approaches to how we organize and govern.

This book represents one chapter in that search. It describes the second phase[1] of an effort by a roundtable of senior Canadian public servants and private-sector executives, working with researchers and international authorities, to make sense of the implications for governance of the emergence of a global information society, and to develop more effective, learning-based approaches to governing in this new context.[2]

The idea for this project began to take shape in a series of conversations I had with senior government officials, private-sector

---

1 The first phase of this effort is described in Steven A. Rosell et al., *Governing in an Information Society* (Montreal: Institute for Research on Public Policy, 1992).

2 Governance (as will be elaborated in the introductory chapter) is the process by which groups, organizations and societies steer themselves. While the work of the project has focused on issues of governance at the national level, comparable governance challenges increasingly are being faced by groups and organizations (both public and private) at all levels of society, from local to global.

executives, researchers and others involved in governance in Canada, the United States, Europe and the developing world. What was striking about those discussions were the similarities in the dilemmas voiced, in the perceived crisis in governance described, even though those conversations were about very different political, economic and cultural systems. Many of those dilemmas seemed to have roots in the complex of social, economic and technological changes that has come to be called the "information society."

We developed this project as one means to enable practitioners to examine more systematically those fundamental changes underway in the information society, and their implications for the process of governance. Those changes are very difficult to perceive, much less address, because they cut across organizational boundaries, and their time horizon exceeds that of most planning. Generally, they are not captured within the mental maps and models that we use to make sense of the world. This project was conceived as an effort to broaden those mental maps, and to enable us to re-perceive the more specific issues we face in the context of those deeper changes. It is an effort to rethink the questions we ask and, in that context, to encourage the development of more effective responses.

This project is not primarily about problem solving. There are many groups, within government, in the private sector, and throughout society, far better equipped to design solutions to particular problems in particular contexts. This project is about broadening the ways in which we frame those problems, about broadening the context within which groups, with greater expertise, resources and authority on particular issues, pursue their responsibilities. In the concluding chapter of this report, there are some suggestions on how those groups might continue the work begun by the project, and apply it to the more specific issues they face.

One strong conclusion of the project has been that, in the rapidly changing environment of the information society, the life cycle of any particular "solution" is likely to be short. In that environment, we need to focus more on strengthening the ongoing process by which we construct shared mental maps, shared values, objectives and frameworks of interpretation, in the context of which a multiplying range of players can devise a continuing succession of more particular "solutions," and mutually can coordinate their actions. That process of constructing shared mental maps is central to the learning-based approaches to organizing and governing we seek.

In a world of rapid and continuing change, eroding boundaries, multiplying interest groups, and fragmenting institutions and belief systems, we need to invest more time and energy in the continuing process of constructing shared frameworks of goals and values, in developing a shared understanding of where we want to go. And we need more effective leadership to provide direction to that process, and then to encourage a wide range of players to innovate and learn better ways to achieve those objectives.

While government retains an essential responsibility for providing that leadership, business, labour, social groups, academics, the media and more all are playing increasing roles in the information society. It is from them that much innovation and leadership can come. We need to learn better ways in which this more distributed system of governance can be made to work.[3]

This project has been designed to be one prototype of the sort of learning process, the sort of ongoing strategic conversation, that we require in order to construct those shared frameworks and to update our mental maps. For that reason, the report that

---

3 We also need to learn from the successes and failures of other jurisdictions around the world in this regard. In April of 1994, the Organization for Economic Cooperation and Development (OECD) convened a meeting of member states in Paris to discuss many of the issues and challenges raised in the initial report of this project. In the course of those discussions, senior practitioners from some 20 governments compared the ways in which the emergence of a global information society is changing the practice of governance in their countries. I hope that meeting will prove to be one step toward a continuing international dialogue on these issues.

follows is as much about the process we undertook, as it is about our substantive findings. Descriptions of the process are interspersed throughout the narrative.[4] In the continually changing and more interconnected world of the information society, this sort of learning process needs to become a much more important and normal part of the ways in which we organize and govern ourselves. And it needs to be broadened to include those far beyond the necessarily limited group who have undertaken this experimental project.

In its second phase, the project was supported by nineteen federal government departments and three private-sector organizations. It was organized as an experiment in participatory action research, in which the subjects of the research (the senior Canadian government officials and private-sector executives in this case) become an active part of the research team. This second phase of our work also focused, in particular, on the construction of a set of scenarios for how the information society may reshape the environment for governance over the next ten years. That scenario process was intended to be an experiment in defining shared frameworks, in developing shared mental maps.

In the course of the project we met with a wide range of international experts who greatly assisted our work. Members of the roundtable set the agenda of issues to be pursued in those sessions, tested the presentations of those experts against their own experience and judgement, and used the results to focus and to further our inquiry. While I coordinated the work of the project, and drafted the report, this very much was a collective effort in which the direction of the research, the definition of the scenarios, the conclusions drawn and the content of the report all were determined by a roundtable of all participants.

---

4   For those readers who are particularly interested in understanding (or ignoring!) the process we followed, the major discussions of that process can be found in the sections of Chapter 1 headed "An Infrastructure for Learning" and "Beginning the Process," in the section of Chapter 3 headed "The Scenario Workshop," and in the sections of Chapter 5 headed "Summary" and "On the Importance of Process."

The members of that roundtable were:

Howard Balloch	Jim Lahey
Michael Binder	Harvey Lazar
Robert G. Blackburn	Peter Liebel
Robert F. Bourgeois	Norman Moyer
Anthony Campbell	Mary J. Murphy
Mel Cappe	Kathy O'Hara
Jeff Carruthers	François Pouliot
Allan J. Darling	Victor Rabinovitch
Mary Dawson	Pierre Racicot
Greg Fyffe	Ken Stein
Moya Greene	Richard Stursberg

They are very much co-authors of this report, but final responsibility for what appears in the text and, in particular, for any errors or omissions, rests with me. Special mention should be made of the role played, at the inception of phase II, by Ian Clark and Mel Cappe (who were, at the time, the Secretary and Deputy Secretary of the Treasury Board respectively). Without their understanding and support, it is unlikely that the second phase of this project could have been undertaken.

The substantive work of the project was supported by a secretariat composed of Arthur Cordell (senior advisor at the Department of Industry and a leading Canadian authority on the information society), Roberto Gualtieri (a former senior public servant now teaching at Carleton University), Prof. Geoffrey Oldham (Special Advisor, Science and Technology, at the International Development Research Centre), James Taylor (Professor and Chairman of the Department of Communications at the Université de Montréal), and myself. In addition, Ian Stewart (formerly Deputy Minister of Finance) acted as a special advisor, participating in all roundtables and consistently offering much insight, wisdom and thought-provoking comment.

My colleagues at the Meridian International Institute provided ongoing assistance and sound counsel throughout the project.

Meridian is a non-profit research organization, established to work with leaders from all sectors of society to frame emerging issues, and to address the revolution in governance that we are experiencing. At different stages of the project, especially helpful contributions have been made by a range of Meridian Fellows, including Walter Truett Anderson, Harlan Cleveland, Daniel Coates, Napier Collyns, Alexis Halley, Robert E. Horn, Donald N. Michael, Ruben Nelson, Elsa Porter and Edgar H. Schein.

The administrative home of the project (in its second phase) has been the Parliamentary Centre. The Director of the Centre, Peter Dobell, provided welcome support and encouragement throughout the project, and participated actively in a number of our roundtable meetings.

The organizational skills, initiative and administrative support of Leigh McGowan kept this complex undertaking running smoothly against all odds. Lois Johnston looked after financial administration and also provided valuable editorial help in the preparation of the book.

Governing, in the world of rapid change that is the information society, requires a continuing process of learning, both within government and across society. This project can be seen as a microcosm of the sort of learning process we require, a process that now needs to be broadened to include a wider range of participants (from government at all levels, the private sector, labour, social organizations, the academic community, the media and more). I hope that the publication of this report will be a step in that direction.

Steven A. Rosell
January, 1995

Part I

Report of the Roundtable

1 Introduction

"Every few hundred years in Western history there occurs a sharp transformation. Within a few short decades, society – its world view, its basic values, its social and political structure, its arts, its key institutions – rearranges itself. Fifty years later there is a new world. And the people born then cannot even imagine the world in which their grandparents lived and into which their own parents were born. We are currently living through such a transformation."[5]

WE ARE IN THE MIDST OF A FUNDAMENTAL SOCIAL and economic transformation whose extent and implications we only partially grasp. The magnitude of those changes is calling into question many of the mental maps and models we use to make sense of the world, and to underpin the ways we organize and govern ourselves.

We use those mental maps to look for pattern amidst what William James called the "buzzing, blooming confusion" of sense data. That ability to separate the important pattern from the noise is essential to our survival and development, and our culture and experience provide us with a set of tested maps that tell us what to look for and what to ignore. Those maps are embedded in the stories we tell, the language we use and the myths we share. They are what we teach our children. We see what fits that map, what has meaning in that context. Those maps become the lens through which we see. Amidst the fundamental social and economic changes we now face, however, those lenses can become

5 Peter F. Drucker, "The post-capitalist world," *The Public Interest* (Fall 1992).

blinders, leaving us to make our way in one world, using maps designed for another.

Shared mental maps and models provide the basis for our ability to communicate and work together, and for how we organize and govern ourselves. As we have started to perceive that those maps no longer correspond well to the world of our experience, practitioners in many fields have begun a search for new maps, and for new ways of organizing and governing, more appropriate to the new context.

This book reports on one such effort, undertaken by a group of senior Canadian government officials, private-sector executives and researchers over the last four years. This volume focuses on the second phase of that work, on our efforts to explore the fundamental changes in the economy, in culture and values and in the social contract that characterize the emergence of a global information society, and what that may mean for how we organize and govern ourselves. It describes how we used that exploration to construct a set of alternative scenarios, alternative maps, of how the emergence of a global information society may reshape the environment for governance in the coming decade. And it tells how those scenarios led us to conclude that we need to balance the relationship between the economic and the social in a different way, to give greater emphasis to building social cohesion and the capacity to learn together in the information society, and to rethink the role of government in that context.

This is the story of a learning process that still is underway, a learning process that, itself, is at least as important as any particular substantive findings. As one participant phrased it, toward the end of the second phase of our work:

> The process is an important product for us. In fact, in many ways, it is a primary product.... Part of what we are trying to do is to communicate findings about process as well as about more substantive ideas.

For this reason, throughout this report, substantive discussions are interspersed with descriptions of the process we followed. To begin that story, we need to summarize how this project came to be, and what we learned in its initial phase.[6]

The project grew out of a series of informal conversations, among senior government officials and researchers, about a growing crisis in governance,[7] a crisis that is not unique to Canada, but that seems to be occurring in very different political, economic and cultural systems around the world. In those conversations we discussed many examples where the traditional apparatus of government seemed less and less capable of responding to new challenges, so that, in the end, the only way to generate any response was to bypass that apparatus. We discussed the multiplication of special interests, the fragmentation of decision-making, and the effects of the media. And we discussed the growing loss of public confidence in government, and the diminishing legitimacy of the system.

More broadly, we shared the sense that the models and understanding we had of how the governance system should operate, seemed to correspond less and less to our experience. In the words of one official:

> ... it's like trying to fly a plane in which the gauges and controls have been rewired in ways you don't understand.

As our conversations proceeded, we began to identify the complex of social, economic and technological changes, that has

---

6 For a more complete account of the work and findings of the first phase of the project, see Steven A. Rosell et al., op. cit.

7 From the outset of the project our focus was not just on "government" but on "governance." "Governance" derives from the Greek "kybernan" and "kybernetes," which mean "to steer" and "pilot or helmsman" respectively (the same Greek root from which "cybernetics" is derived). The process of governance is the process whereby an organization or society steers itself, and the dynamics of communication and control are central to that process. While the role of government is (and remains) central to the process of governance, in the information society more and more players – voluntary organizations, interest groups, the private sector, the media and so on – become involved in that process.

come to be called the "information society,"[8] as a critical factor shaping a new environment for governance, an environment not adequately comprehended by our existing mental maps.[9] To test that idea, we convened a more formal meeting of senior officials and researchers. In advance of that session, all participants received a brief discussion paper on some implications for governance of the information society, along with a number of relevant journal articles. In the intense discussion that followed, participants recounted personal experiences of how the information society was changing the process of governance in their areas of responsibility, and began to explore some of the consequences of those changes. In that process we started to construct a shared perception of the nature and effects of the information society, and of the resulting challenges.

The Information Society

What is the information society? The view we began to construct, at the initial meeting, saw the information society not just as the product of, or equivalent to, information technology, but rather

8   See, for example: D. Bell, "The Social Framework of the Information Society" in T. Forester (ed) *The Microelectronics Revolution* (Oxford: Basil Blackwell, 1980); H. Cleveland, "The Twilight of Hierarchy: Speculations on the Global Information Society," *Public Administration Review* (January/February 1985); Conklin and Deschênes (ed) *Canada's Information Revolution* (Ottawa: Supply and Services Canada, 1991); A. Cordell, *The Uneasy Eighties: The Transition to an Information Society* (Ottawa: Science Council of Canada, 1985); D.M. Michael, "Too Much of a Good Thing? Dilemmas of an Information Society," *Technological Forecasting and Social Change* (1984), 25:347–54; S. Nora and A. Minc, *L'informatisation de la societé* (Paris: Le Seuil, 1978); Donald A. Schon, *Beyond the Stable State* (New York: Norton, 1971); J.R. Taylor and E.J. Van Every, *The Vulnerable Fortress* (Toronto: University of Toronto Press, 1993); and the various issues of the journal *The Information Society*.

9   While we recognized that many factors, in addition to the entry into an information society, may contribute to the fundamental changes in the context and process of governance we are experiencing, we thought that trying to interpret those changes through the lens of the information society could provide a valuable perspective and new insight.

as the product of an interplay of social and technological dynamics including:

- developments in information processing and telecommunications, and the increasing links between those technologies;
- the emergence of a more educated and informed population, and the development of a wide range of groups organized to assert a role in the governance process;
- the increasing role and reach of the mass media;
- higher degrees of specialization in a more knowledge-based economy, and consequent changes in the structure of work;
- a much richer infrastructure of public and private organizations and a stronger degree of interaction (both collaboration and contention) among those organizations.

The "information society" that results is experienced as more richly interconnected and complex (everything seems connected to everything else). It is characterized by a vast increase in information availability (along with greater overload, filtering and denial), a compression of both time and space, and growing turbulence and unpredictability. As our meeting progressed, we identified what we thought were some of the most important effects of the information society, relevant to the process of governance:

- *Globalization:* For example, globalization of the economy (interconnected stock exchanges, frontierless capital markets, globalization of technology, production and marketing, and a rationalization of business on a regional and, increasingly, on a global basis), the pervasive influence of globalized science and technology, the beginnings of a global popular culture, and the growing requirement to handle issues, from trade to the environment, to human rights and more, in supranational fora, networks and organizations.
- *Atomization, democratization, and fragmentation.* Are reflected in the increasing power of sub-national governments, in growing regionalism and the fragmentation of multinational states, and in the proliferation of "multiple voices;" that is, an increase in the

number and influence of groups organizing to assert a role in the process of governance.

- *A breakdown of the bureaucratic/industrial model of organizing.* Both public and private sectors are downsizing, stripping away middle management, contracting out work (and, in the public sector, privatizing functions), and relying more on networks and task forces and other more flexible, decentralized "client-centered" ways of organizing.
- *The growing importance of human resources.* In both the public and private sectors, well-qualified staff are becoming a key asset (with their ability to manage large amounts of information, establish effective working relationships within and outside the organization, make judgements and innovate).
- *A loss of boundaries and a fundamental restructuring.* There is a breakdown in the historical distinctions between industries, between the public and private sectors and even between states, accompanied by a search for new relationships and alliances between those entities, and the need to rethink some basic conceptual distinctions.
- *The decreasing possibility of secrecy.* And the implications of that for governing systems that rely on a certain degree of confidentiality.

An Infrastructure for Learning

At the end of our first meeting, one participant summed up the general view:

> This complex of issues is fundamentally important, but it is very difficult for us to address within government because it cuts across all sorts of organizational boundaries, and it requires a time horizon that goes beyond that of most planning we do. We need to invent some way to pursue these questions more systematically, and to incorporate the insights and perspectives of those outside of government.

What we invented came to be called the project on governing in an information society. It was created by practitioners, working with researchers and others, to provide an infrastructure for their own ongoing action-learning process: to support their efforts to develop more effective ways of governing in an information society. The project was supported, in its first phase, by more than a dozen Federal government departments, and was organized as an experiment in participatory action research, in which the subjects of the research (the senior government practitioners in this case) themselves become an active part of the research team.[10]

The project centered on meetings of a roundtable that was composed of senior officials from each of the participating departments, along with members of a small, part-time secretariat, made up of researchers and practitioners, who supported the process, organized the meetings and participated in the discussion. The senior officials participated in their own right, rather than as representatives and, to ensure continuity, no substitutes were allowed. The project proceeded on two parallel tracks:

- roundtable discussions with leading Canadian and international authorities on broad questions related to governance in the information society;
- case studies, undertaken by the senior officials to reconsider (in the context of the project) specific issues within their own areas of departmental responsibility, the results of which also were reported to the roundtable.[11]

Roundtable members received regular summaries of relevant books and articles, which were circulated both by electronic mail (on the government's Senior Executive Network) and in hard copy. During the project, the roundtable defined its own course

10   For a description of the participatory action research approach, see, for example: Maclure and Loevinsohn, *Participatory Research in IDRC* (Ottawa: IDRC, 1988); W.F. Whyte, D.J. Greenwood and P. Lazes, "Participatory Action Research for Science and Society," *American Behavioral Scientist* (1989); D.J. Greenwood, W.F. Whyte and I. Harkavy, "Participatory Action Research as a Process and as a Goal," *Human Relations* (1993), 46:2.

11   In the first phase of the project, the roundtable met 14 times, heard 11 presentations by outside experts and reviewed the results of 12 departmental case studies.

through periodic agenda-setting sessions, at which lessons learned to date were reviewed and used as the basis to define the subject-matter for future roundtables. At those sessions the progress of the departmental case studies also was reviewed, allowing participants mutually to coordinate their studies, and to provide suggestions on the cases being undertaken by others.

After each roundtable (whether outside experts were involved or case studies were reviewed) the secretariat provided participants with a summary record of discussion. The summaries were not transcripts, but rather provided the gist of key ideas and exchanges from those sessions. Participants then were asked to confirm the substantive accuracy and completeness of the summaries. The focused feedback provided by those summaries was an essential aid to the learning process of the roundtable, and provided a valuable chronicle of that process. Throughout this report we shall make frequent use of quotes from the summaries.[12]

The project was not conceived primarily as a problem-solving exercise, but rather as a way to explore how the process of governance is changing in the information society, and to begin to redefine the problems of governance in that context. From the beginning it was clear that we could hope only to begin this process. Our purpose was to explore the territory, to identify promising lines for future development, and to test the extent to which an inquiry of this sort could help to develop more effective ways to understand and to deal with the crisis in governance we now face.

Findings of the Project during Phase I

Initially, the roundtable focused on the disintegrative effects that the information society appears to have on established instruments and practices of governing, and on the crisis in governance that results. But gradually that focus shifted to a search for new ways of governing, new ways of integrating, more appropriate to the realities of the information society.

---

12 Any quotes in this report, which are not otherwise attributed, are taken from those summaries.

Through discussions with international authorities, and case studies undertaken within the participating departments, the roundtable, in its first phase, explored three basic themes:

- developing information-based ways of organizing within government;
- building consensus within the information society;
- making more strategic use of information.

A principal result of that exploration was the realization that, if we are to cope effectively with the complex, rapidly changing environment of the information society, we will need to develop learning-based approaches to how we organize and govern ourselves. Effective leaders of such learning organizations, or learning societies, are those who take the lead in establishing a shared framework of goals, interpretations and values (a shared vision and mission), both within government[13] and across society,[14] and, in that context, give a wide range of players latitude to innovate and learn better ways to achieve that mission.

13 Within government, members of the roundtable emphasized that most issues in the information society now extend beyond the mandate of any one department and beyond the timeframe of most governmental planning. In a sense, the boundaries (both in space and in time) within which we operate correspond less and less with the boundaries of the issues that need to be addressed. That creates institutional impediments to comprehending the very issues on which government most needs to provide leadership. There is a need to enhance our capacity to develop a government-wide perspective (a shared framework) on these issues and, in that context, to learn to organize more flexibly around them. The challenge is to find a way to do that without creating the heavy bureaucratic costs that previous efforts at coordination have engendered.

14 Across society, as more non-governmental players become engaged in the process of governance, it becomes more important, and more difficult, to develop common perceptions, shared agendas and images of the world within which people with different interests and values can work together and innovate. As society and the range of players and perspectives engaged in the process of governance become more diverse, we no longer can take for granted that we share such common perceptions and images of the world. Instead, we continually must construct them. Generating such shared frameworks (shared myths, stories and interpretations) becomes a central part of the process of governance.

Overall, we concluded that what is becoming increasingly clear – as societies become more interconnected, as the boundaries between organizations, economic sectors and states shift and diminish, and as the number of players in the process of governance multiply – is that we need to invest more time and attention in developing a shared understanding of where we want to go, in a more systematic process of agenda-setting. Such a shared framework is the essential context that can allow the multiplying players in the governance process mutually to coordinate their actions.

While the direct role of government in the delivery of services or in traditional forms of regulation may diminish, that will not diminish the responsibility of government to ensure that the public interest is protected and that public goods are provided. To do that will require government to enhance its capacity to play this framework role.[15]

The roundtable only could begin to explore ways to create and renew those shared frameworks, to develop those shared maps. The approaches examined in the first phase of the project included:[16]

- constructing scenarios (shared alternative visions), both within government and beyond;

15   The framework role involves leading the process by which data and information are framed, interpreted, and translated into knowledge. This formulation is based on a distinction suggested to us by Harlan Cleveland at one of our early roundtables. According to Cleveland:
- *data* are unrefined ore, undifferentiated facts without contexts;
- *information* are refined ore, organized data, but data that we have not yet internalized (it is the newspapers we have not yet read, the course we have not yet taken);
- *knowledge* is information that we have internalized, information that we have integrated with our own internal frameworks.
Cleveland's distinctions became important parts of the vocabulary of the project, and helped us to see that the process of translating data and information into knowledge (the process by which data and information are interpreted, given meaning and so made useful as a basis for action) is central to effective governance in an information society.

16   For additional detail on these approaches, see Steven A. Rosell et al., op. cit.

- developing the Public Service as a learning organization, and Public Servants as knowledge workers skilled in the process by which data and information are translated into knowledge, and by which shared frameworks of interpretation are created;
- sharing knowledge as the key to effective leadership (recognizing that, in the information society, it is increasingly self-defeating to try to control the data or information that are released or available, and that the real challenge is to provide leadership to the continuing process by which people interpret and make sense of that information), including:
  - more proactive approaches to the media;
  - using information/communications (interactive) technologies to foster societal learning;
  - developing learning-based alternatives to regulation;
  - alternative dispute resolution;
  - stakeholder summits;
  - a variety of market-based approaches.

The process of governing in an information society came to be seen, by members of the roundtable, as a process of learning both within the government and, more broadly, across society. A continuing reality of the information society will be that the lifespan of particular instruments of governing will be limited. To deal effectively with such a rapidly changing environment, we need to become far more effective at developing new ways of governing appropriate to new circumstances. The project was intended to provide one example (and one beginning) of the sort of ongoing learning process that will be required to underpin governing in an information society.

In publishing the initial findings of phase I,[17] we emphasized the preliminary nature of these conclusions, and suggested that the ultimate success of the project should be judged by the extent to which it was not an end, but a beginning – the beginning of a more systematic search to develop new ways of governing appropriate to the information society.

17 Ibid.

Continuing the Search: The Second Phase of the Project

As the first phase of the project drew to a close, the draft of our report was circulated and discussed widely among deputy ministers and other senior officials in Ottawa. We had been very unsure how other practitioners, who had not been involved directly in the first phase, would respond. Most of us felt that the written text could capture only a small portion of the learning and value we felt we had gained from the process. But the reception of the report was enthusiastic. The Canadian Centre for Management Development was asked to disseminate the results of the first phase across the Public Service, and we were encouraged to publish the report in order to foster wider discussion.

We also were encouraged to develop a second phase of the project, one that would be designed, both in process and in substance, to build on the success of the first, and one that also might be broadened to include non-governmental members. We decided to organize this second phase as an experiment in developing shared frameworks of interpretation, shared mental maps, and to do so by trying to construct a set of scenarios of how the information society may reshape the environment for governance in Canada over the next ten years.[18]

Scenarios were one of the most promising methodologies, identified in the first phase, for assembling a wide range of information into shared frameworks for learning, planning and action. Scenario planning is a process for constructing alternative shared mental maps.[19] It was agreed that the scenarios we produced should be available for wider distribution and use following the

18 While all members of the first phase decided to remain in the project, six new government members were added (for a total of 19) and, in addition, the roundtable was broadened to include three private-sector members.

19 One of the best statements of the development, value and use of scenarios in a corporate setting is contained in a series of articles by Pierre Wack, former head of Group Planning at Royal Dutch/Shell. See P. Wack, "Scenarios: Uncharted Waters Ahead," *Harvard Business Review* (September/October 1985); idem, "Scenarios: Shooting the Rapids," *Harvard Business Review* (November/December 1985).

project. This element of our work also would test the potential for using the scenario methodology more widely in the public sector.

Instead of the departmental case studies, undertaken in the first phase, the roundtable agreed this time to form small groups, to focus on issues that cut across existing sectoral boundaries. The most important issues in the information society generally cannot be contained within existing organizational or sectoral boundaries, and the small-group structure, it was hoped, would help us to address these more effectively. The plan was that the small groups would identify an issue or area of activity, test the emerging scenarios against that issue area, and then use that as a basis to develop more specific recommendations for action. Except for the use of scenarios, and the substitution of small-group work for departmental case studies, the design of the second phase paralleled that of phase I.[20]

Constructing Shared Maps: The Scenario Approach

We began phase II with a roundtable designed to enable us to explore and to better understand the nature of the scenario approach, and how we might best apply it to our work. Our guide was Kees van der Heijden,[21] formerly head of scenario planning at Royal Dutch/Shell, the company which has perhaps most developed the scenario approach in the private sector, and an organization in which scenarios have become central to strategic decision making and internal governance.

Shell is a highly decentralized corporation, and in that respect provides interesting parallels with the organization of the public

20 During the second phase, the roundtable held ten meetings, including a two-day scenario workshop, heard presentations from 14 outside experts and met in smaller groups innumerable times.

21 Kees van der Heijden currently is Professor of Strategic Management in the Graduate Business School of the Strathclyde University in Glasgow. He was for many years a senior executive with Royal/Dutch Shell and served in Shell companies in Manila, Singapore and Curacao before joining Group Planning at Shell headquarters in London. There, as head of the Business Environment Division, he was responsible for Shell's scenario planning process.

sector. It was formed through an agreement between a Dutch and an English company at the turn of the century, and since that time has operated as a multicultural alliance. Most major corporate decisions are taken not by an all-powerful CEO (there isn't one), but by a committee of managing directors. Scenarios have become an important part of the infrastructure for managing this highly decentralized organization in an increasingly turbulent environment.

Kees van der Heijden first took us through the history of the development of the scenario approach at Shell.[22] He told us that scenario planning had begun as a way to avoid forecasting problems. In the 1960s, Shell had developed a planning system similar to that of many corporations of the time. It was a paper-heavy process that tried to forecast prices, demand, and so forth, and use that information to predict a balance sheet two to five years into the future. It didn't take long for Shell executives to recognize that, despite all of their efforts, actual figures bore little resemblance to the projections. They concluded that they should not be trying to predict things that are fundamentally unpredictable, and that led them to explore the approach of scenario planning.

The scenario approach had first been developed by the military, and further refined by Herman Kahn and the Hudson Institute. It involves developing alternative stories about the future, recognizing that there is more than one possible way in which the future may unfold, and then testing proposed decisions against those alternative possibilities. Pierre Wack, then head of Group Planning at Shell, started to develop a scenario process for the company in the early 1970s. One of the early scenarios, developed out of that process, envisioned a world in which those who controlled oil reserves refused to provide access on the same basis as in the past, resulting in a significant increase in prices. In the

22 For a more detailed account of the development of the scenario approach at Shell, see P. Wack, op. cit.; A. de Geus, "Planning as Learning," *Harvard Business Review* (March/April 1988); and the paper by Kees van der Heijden in Part II of this volume.

early 1970s this was an outlandish idea, and it was greeted with considerable skepticism at Shell, but the scenario began to circulate within the corporation. Kees van der Heijden recounted what happened next:

> ... in 1973, ...there was a supply crisis, similar to what had been envisioned in the scenario. Those who were familiar with the scenario, and had been discussing it and thinking about it over the years, were able quickly to recognize that what they were dealing with was the scenario that Pierre Wack had been talking about, and so they had a head start in figuring out what needed to be done to deal with it.... They recognized in that information the elements of the energy crisis scenario they had been discussing, and saw that it was not going to go away, that there was a fundamental driving force behind this, and so they undertook a number of critical strategic decisions. One of the most important, for example, was a change in refining policies, which was worth billions of dollars to the company.

So, in addition to being a useful way to avoid forecasting problems (to avoid having to predict the unpredictable), scenarios came to be understood as a valuable perceptual device, as a means to help people to recognize what was happening in the world. Scenarios extended the mental maps of those who exercised with them, and so provided a different way of interpreting the information they received.

The next step in the development of the scenario approach at Shell occurred in the early 1980s, when it became common practice to approve individual projects and investments against the scenarios. Instead of justifying a project against a single point forecast, proponents now needed to demonstrate how an investment would be expected to fare under each of the company's current set of scenarios. As a result, projects began to be changed so that they would be viable under any of the scenarios, and that led senior management to take a greater direct interest in the scenario process.

Senior management quickly realized that they could use the scenarios to influence decisions being made throughout the corporation. That influence would be exercised not by issuing instructions, but by constructing the context (the scenarios) within which those decisions would be made. So scenarios became a mechanism that enabled top management to set a framework within which to decentralize decision making. Kees van der Heijden emphasized the similarity between this context-setting function of scenarios, and the process of creating shared frameworks that our first report had argued is key to effective leadership in the information society.

He also reiterated that scenarios are not predictions. Indeed, one of the principal benefits of the scenario approach is that it provides a way to talk about the future, without trying to predict what is inherently unpredictable. The separation of the predictable from the unpredictable is a key step in the process of constructing scenarios. The most important predictable elements appear in all scenarios, while the most important unpredictable elements are used to differentiate scenarios (you assume they will turn out one way in one scenario, and a different way in another scenario).

The scenarios that result provide a basis for testing the robustness of particular decisions (will they be workable under all the scenarios, or how can they be modified to be viable no matter which scenario happens). Scenarios also can be used normatively, as a basis for considering what decisions are likely to lead to the realization of a preferred scenario, or to the avoidance of a scenario that is undesirable.

Currently, we were told, the process by which scenarios are developed at Shell includes the following steps:

- interviews with senior managers to determine the issues on which the scenarios should focus;
- development, from those interviews, of a "natural agenda" that details their concerns;
- working with senior managers to narrow that natural agenda to no more than 10 issues (later 5) that will be the focus of the scenarios;

- introducing "new knowledge," through seminars with "remarkable people" to develop new ideas and explore the identified issues – a period of brainstorming (trying, at this stage, to keep an open mind and to avoid premature closure);
- convening an off-site scenario workshop to identify the key predictable and unpredictable elements relevant to those central issues, and using those to develop the scenario structure and logics;
- refining those scenarios and their associated story-lines, in an iterative process with senior managers;
- quantifying the scenarios (if needed for project assessment);
- disseminating the scenarios, and using them to focus the ongoing learning process within the organization and beyond.

Beginning the Process

To begin our own scenario process, Kees van der Heijden suggested that we ask ourselves a question that is used to begin the interviews with senior managers at Shell:

> Let's assume that you have access to a true oracle, somebody who really knows the future. Assume that you are allowed to ask three questions. What would those three questions be? Remember that those questions should be relevant to our subject, which has to do with the implications of the information society for governance over the next decade.

As participants stated what their questions would be, Kees wrote them on magnetic, hexagon-shaped blocks, which then were affixed to a metallic white board. We kept going around the table until all of the questions people wanted to ask were on the board. A few samples of the many dozens of questions suggested follows:

- Will Canada ever attain an unemployment rate of less than ten per cent and, if so, how?
- Will Canada still exist in its current form in ten years?

- What will be the most important skills in the labour market ten years from now?
- What will NAFTA look like in ten years?
- Will we still have a health care system five years from now?
- How many economic trading blocs will there be in the world?
- Is it true that the nation state is a thing of the past?
- Will Canada still be considered a major industrialized country in ten years time?
- What will be the most important technological developments?
- Will technology change the way the public relates to the government?
- What will be the demographic profile of Canada, and, in particular, how many different cultures are we going to have in this country ten years from now?
- Will we be able to ensure that people continue to have the ability to purchase in a world where jobs are disappearing?
- What role will minority special interest groups be playing in the governance process ten years from now?
- Will the economy be able to sustain the level of social safety nets that Canadians expect?
- Will race or ethnic conflict make cities unlivable?
- How will the boundaries between the public and private sector be redefined?
- To what degree will those who hold power change; in other words, will power structures still be largely in the hands of white males?
- How successful will we be in developing learning organizations and a learning society?
- What will be the effects and the progress of the technology of life extension?
- Will demographic changes alter our approach to treatment of the elderly?
- How will the ethics of medicine change?
- More generally, how will moral values change in light of the social, economic and political contexts that are emerging?

Once the process of generating questions had been completed, participants were invited, during a break, to move the magnetic hexagons around on the board, to try to cluster them into groupings that made sense. In the creative, playful atmosphere that resulted, many different configurations were tried, though none, at this stage, received general assent. Following is one example of the different configurations that were proposed:

The roundtable then reconvened and, in the context of the space (the field of issues) we had constructed by our answers to Kees' question, we began to define the issue areas around which the small groups would be organized, and which also would be priority subjects for the next several roundtables. As one round-table member summarized that conversation:

> A fundamental idea, we all have going into this, is that something radically different is happening, it's not business as usual any more. So we have to start to think through an agenda that is quite different.
>
> There's a basic problem with governance, and the relationship between the governed and the governors, there's a fundamental distrust, a fundamental problem about legitimacy, about consensus, about the linkages between the public and private sectors, and that whole cluster of issues must be addressed.
>
> There's also a fundamental question about the economy, what we are dealing with now is not a traditional recession, the recession is overlaying the effects of a major international restructuring, which calls into question the very basis of the Canadian economy.
>
> There's also a series of very fundamental questions about the social contract. How do we organize the kinds of social support mechanisms that are essential to underpin the changes we need to make in the economy?
>
> And, of course, all of these things are interrelated, they are not separate, a major restructuring of the economy depends to a large degree on the nature of the social safety nets, which in turn relates and depends, in large part, on the nature of the deal between the governors and the governed. They are all different facets of a common set of problems. So I think we need to lift our perspective to a higher level to look at these more basic sets of issues.

In the end, the roundtable agreed that we should try to examine four broad issue areas:

- the new information (or knowledge-based) economy;
- the social contract in the information society;
- people, culture and values in the information society;
- the changing relationship between the governors and the governed.

The Shape of the Report

Following this inaugural roundtable, our work proceeded in three stages. In the first stage we examined how the emergence of a global information society is reshaping the environment for governance through changes in three areas: the economy, culture and values, and the social contract. This stage of our work also corresponded to what Kees van der Heijden had described as the process of introducing "new knowledge," which is an essential step leading to the construction of scenarios. It is a process of exploring the key issues that have been identified, using outstanding resource people as guides. That exploration is described in Chapter 2.

The next stage centered on a two-day workshop, during which we constructed an initial set of scenarios. Chapter 3 outlines the process by which we tried to make sense of an overload of information, and presents the set of four scenarios that resulted. Those scenarios describe different ways in which the emergence of a global information society may reshape the environment for governance over the coming decade.

At the end of that workshop, we were struck by the fact that while it was possible for us to construct a relatively desirable scenario even if we did not postulate a booming economy, we were not able to construct a scenario in which any of us would want to live if we did not postulate considerable success in building community and social cohesion. So, in the third stage of the project, we concentrated on exploring ways to build social cohesion in an information society, ways to enhance our capacity to learn together, and the changing role of government in that context. Chapter 4 outlines what we discovered.

All of these chapters describe a learning process that still, very much, is underway. And, in the rapidly changing environment of the information society, it is such a continuing process of learning – rather than the development of any particular policies or products – that becomes most important to our capacity to govern ourselves more effectively. In Chapter 5 we draw together the preliminary conclusions we have reached in this exploration, and suggest ways in which the process of learning (only begun by the project) might be continued and broadened, to contribute to the building of a learning society.

Finally, throughout the project we have had the benefit of the guidance and insights of leading resource people. Their contributions are summarized in the relevant chapters of this report. Six of those resource people subsequently prepared papers, based on their presentations to the roundtable, and these are collected in Part II of this volume.

2 Re-mapping the Territory: Three Perspectives

AT OUR INAUGURAL ROUNDTABLE we had identified several key issues (several dimensions) through which the information society appeared to be reshaping the environment for governance. As each of these dimensions changes in the information society, the environment for governance, in turn, changes. We decided to use our next three roundtables to explore three of these dimensions in greater depth:

- the economy;
- culture and values;
- the social contract.

Our existing mental maps seemed inadequate to make sense of how these dimensions are changing in the information society; so we asked leading experts from Canada and abroad to work with us in these sessions to re-map that territory. This stage of our exploration also corresponded to the process of gathering new knowledge that Kees van der Heijden had described to us as a key step leading to the construction of scenarios. In addition, we had organized small groups around each of these dimensions (or issue areas), and the relevant small group played a role in helping to organize and lead each roundtable.

At each of these knowledge-gathering sessions we sought to examine how the information society is changing the environment for governance, from a different perspective, through a different lens. At our first session that lens was the economy, at our second roundtable it was culture and values, and at the third it was the social contract. Each revealed a different aspect of the transformation underway.[23]

The Economy: A New Techno-economic Paradigm

Christopher Freeman[24] and Richard Lipsey[25] were our guides in exploring how the economy is changing in the information society. They argued persuasively that the effects of the new information and communications technologies (ICT) were so pervasive and fundamental that they constituted a new "techno-economic paradigm." According to Freeman:

> 'Techno-economic paradigm' is an expression coined by the Venezuelan economist Carlotta Perez, to emphasize that what is changing is not just the IT industry or the IT sector, but that every industry has to change its mode of organization, its work organi-

23 These three roundtables were designed to focus on the views presented by an exceptional group of resource persons. While the views of roundtable members were expressed in the course of these sessions, this was done principally through the questions we asked. At this stage of the project, our priority was to understand and to learn from the analysis and perspective provided by these outside resource persons and, in so doing, to open up our own thinking.

24 Christopher Freeman is Professor, and was the founding Director, at the Science Policy Research Unit (SPRU) of the University of Sussex in England. He also works with the Maastricht Economic Research Institute on Innovation and Technology (MERIT) in the Netherlands. He is a leading authority, and the author of numerous books and papers, on economic policy and technical change. Professor Freeman also has participated in major policy research programs of the Organization for Economic Cooperation and Development (OECD), and the Commission of the European Union (CEU).

25 Richard G. Lipsey is professor of economics at Simon Fraser University and Alcan fellow of the Canadian Institute for Advanced Research (CIAR), for whom he is directing a large-scale, international research project on Economic Growth and Policy. He previously held chairs in Economics at the London School of Economics and the University of Essex in England and at Queens University in Canada. He also served as economic advisor to the C.D. Howe Institute. Professor Lipsey is the author of numerous monographs, textbooks and articles on economic policy, and also is an officer of the Order of Canada, a fellow of the Royal Society of Canada and a past-president of the Canadian Economic Society.

zation, and its relationship of design to production and marketing, because of the availability of these very powerful new technologies. This is an extremely pervasive technology and it affects every industry and service.

These technologies do not just affect one sector, but require every industry to change. What we are dealing with is a combination of innovations that is affecting the entire economy, and is changing what designers and managers in all industries regard as "common sense."

Changes of this magnitude are rare, but not unprecedented. Rather, we were told, this is the latest in a long series of technological transformations – waves of change that periodically and fundamentally change economic and social organization. Freeman illustrated that history of past waves of techno-economic change with the following chart:

Table 1

1ST WAVE	(1780s-1840s)	iron*, cotton textiles**, canals
2ND WAVE	(1840s-1890s)	coal*, steam engines**, machine tools, railways (iron)
3RD WAVE	(1890s-1940s)	steel*, electricity**, engineering, chemicals, railways (steel)
4TH WAVE	(1940s-1990s)	oil*, automobiles**, petro-chemicals, aircraft, roads (highways)
5TH WAVE	(1990s-?)	micro-electronics*, computers**, telecommunications, data networks

   * Key factor
  ** Engine of growth

Lipsey added that classical economic analysis largely is blind to this process, in part because it does not see technology as a fundamental (endogenous) part of the economic system, but rather takes technology as a given. Economics does not understand that technology both changes, and is changed by, the economic system: "Technology is one of the fundamental things that is part of the economic system, it changes as the economic system changes, and as it changes it influences our lives."

The new ICT techno-economic paradigm, Freeman told us, differs in very important respects from the Fordist techno-economic paradigm that preceded it:

> The Fordist system, was energy-intensive, based on cheap oil and other cheap sources of energy. The new ICT paradigm, by contrast, finds its key advantages in information-intensive technologies. The old paradigm focused on a rather standardized array of products, but under the new system we see a great deal more customization. For example, in the chemical industry a lot of firms are trying to get out of bulk commodity chemicals and into specialty chemicals....
>
> Whereas under the old paradigm you tended to have a dedicated plant or factory, now we see increasingly flexible types of manufacturing and production systems.... Another way in which the new paradigm differs from the old, is in management structures.... The new paradigm emphasizes people working horizontally rather than vertical control, it is based on the model of distributed intelligence. This is vastly facilitated by the cheapening of computers through the microprocessor, which now means that anyone can have a computer and be connected to the information network.
>
> The new paradigm also depends on a multi-skilled work force, a maintenance worker can't afford to be only a mechanic or only an electrical specialist, usually they need to have knowledge of all of these things. The role of government, too, changes under the new paradigm. Its responsibility increasingly focuses on the development of a broader vision and framework, on long-term coordination, on spreading a shared understanding of the challenges and opportunities we face, rather than on the more directive and interventionist activities of the past. It is just those sorts of frameworks that I think you, in this project, are trying to understand and develop.

Freeman illustrated these differences and more using the following chart:

Table 2
Change of Techno-economic Paradigm

"Fordist" – Old	ICT – New
Energy-intensive	Information-intensive
Standardized	Customized
Rather stable product mix	Rapid changes in product mix
Dedicated plant and equipment	Flexible production systems
Automation	Systemation
Single firm	Networks
Hierarchical structures	Flat horizontal structures
Departmental	Integrated
Product with service	Service with products
Centralization	Distributed intelligence
Specialized skills	Multi-skilling
Government ownership, trol and planning	Government information, con-coordination and regulation "Vision"

Source: Perez (1990).

Yet there is a puzzle in all of this: even as the new technologies are becoming pervasive in all firms and industries, we are seeing a lower rate of growth in labour productivity in OECD countries, and an actual fall in capital productivity.[26] And the overall level of unemployment in almost all industrialized countries in the last 20 years has been much higher than it was in the previous 20 years. Why is this?

While there are many possible explanations, the one that seemed to us most persuasive – and that was stressed by both

26 This argument is made in greater detail in the paper by Christopher Freeman in Part II of this volume.

Freeman and Lipsey – lies in the very pervasiveness, and the fundamental nature, of the changes underway. Making effective use of the new technologies, and operating successfully under the new techno-economic paradigm, requires a huge "social learning process," including developing new skills, new ways of organizing, new system connections, new standards, different ways of generating capital investment and much more. We need to learn social and institutional approaches more appropriate to the new paradigm. It is not surprising that productivity might suffer while that learning process is underway.

What this underlines is that social and institutional factors are key to the relative success that different economies have in adapting to the new techno-economic paradigm. Societies and cultures respond differently to the technologies, and their relative success can tell us much about what social and institutional factors are needed to thrive under the new techno-economic paradigm. For example, in the 1980s, the approaches adopted by East Asian states appeared to be far more successful, and to result in far higher rates of growth, than those of Latin America. What did the East Asians do differently?

Among the differences, emphasized in our discussion, was the greater export orientation of the East Asians. But even more important, Freeman suggested, was the composition of those exports. He pointed out that East Asian countries have a very high and fast-growing share of ICT goods in their export mix. And they are investing in the means needed to increase that performance; for example, by training engineers, developing their national information infrastructures, linking research and development (R&D) and production, and so on.[27] He also suggested that the relatively lower level of social disparities, and the more egalitarian income distribution in East Asian countries (compared to their Latin American counterparts) was an important additional advantage in developing the human capital and social infrastructure needed for a viable knowledge-based economy.

---

27 For a more detailed presentation of this argument, see the paper by Christopher Freeman in Part II of this volume.

One important question that came up, in this context, is the extent to which the success of the East Asians depends on their relatively authoritarian form of government, which in turn permits their single-minded focus on export-led growth. While some contended that this provided an advantage that more democratic societies could not, and should not want to emulate, others pointed out that as the East Asian countries developed, they were becoming more democratic.

As the population becomes more skilled, it was argued, people who are expected to innovate and learn in the workplace will not long be satisfied in a political environment without dissent, and where alternative views are forbidden. Innovation is itself a dissenting, diversity-creating process, and that provides a comparative advantage to countries like Canada and the United States in the information economy.

While no one can predict how a particular society will respond to the challenges posed by the new techno-economic paradigm, Richard Lipsey outlined for us two very different possibilities:

- The first possibility is that we will manage to put in place the institutions, social and other arrangements necessary to make the new techno-economic paradigm work. When that happens we will embark on a new secular economic boom, similar to those that have happened following each previous change of techno-economic paradigm.
- The second possibility is that we will fail to develop the skills, institutions and other arrangements needed to operate under the new techno-economic paradigm, and we will find ourselves in a period of deepening technological unemployment and of low or no economic growth.... Even if this second possibility were not the final outcome, it could well be the predominant circumstance for years while the social learning process is underway.

Lipsey also stressed the inability of conventional economic analysis to make useful predictions about changes in the scale of a new techno-economic paradigm. There are so many variables, and the uncertainties are so large, that conventional economic forecasting cannot be of much help, and can be misleading.

Under such conditions of uncertainty, he noted, scenarios are a very valuable tool. Scenarios enable you to think about different ways in which an uncertain situation might unfold, and to test the viability of possible initiatives against those different scenarios.

Perhaps even more important, scenarios might be used as part of a broader public learning process, to help people to understand that we are in the midst of a fundamental change to a new techno-economic paradigm, and to support the process of developing new social and institutional arrangements, a new social consensus, more appropriate to that paradigm. In the end, success in the information economy will depend, to a considerable degree, on our capacity to learn together, and on related questions of social contract, and of culture and values.

Culture and Values: The Postmodern Challenge

Walter Truett Anderson[28] and Marcel Massé[29] led our exploration of how culture and values are changing in the information society. Anderson began[30] by differentiating the premodern, modern and postmodern belief systems:

- *Premodern* societies did not have to grapple repeatedly with otherness, with fundamental questions about whether what they believed

28 Walter Truett Anderson is a political scientist and the author of numerous books and articles on issues of governance, technology and cultural change. His most recent book is *Reality Isn't What It Used To Be* (San Francisco: Harper/Collins, 1992). Dr. Anderson is a Fellow of the World Academy of Art and Science and is Chairman of the Board of Trustees of the Saybrook Institute.

29 At the time of the roundtable, Marcel Massé was Secretary to the Cabinet for Federal-Provincial Relations. Previously he had served as Undersecretary of State for External Affairs, President of the Canadian International Development Agency (CIDA), Clerk of the Privy Council, and as Executive Director at the International Monetary Fund (IMF). Shortly after the roundtable, M. Massé left the Public Service and was elected to Parliament. He currently serves in the Cabinet as President of the Privy Council, Minister of Intergovernmental Affairs and Minister responsible for Public Service Renewal.

30 Many of these points are elaborated in Walter Truett Anderson's paper in Part II of this volume.

was, or was not, valid. Over time, as populations increased their mobility and there was an increase in trading and contact between civilizations, there was a growing awareness of otherness.

- *Modernism* was a response to that growing awareness of otherness. The great modernizing projects, throughout Western history at least, involved efforts to create some sort of universal value and belief system that might encompass all others. The Greeks, for example, sought to base their view of reality on something deeper and more permanent than their mythic system. They tried to create a methodology through which they could arrive at universal, essential truths. They wanted to establish truths of a validity that could not be assailed by any other civilization. The Enlightenment carried forward that project, developing an increasing reliance on the methodologies of science to find universal truths.
- *Postmodernism* has been defined as being situated in the aftermath of the collapse of the Enlightenment project, in the aftermath of the loss of belief that we can find eternal truths that will be acceptable to all people. Another definition of postmodernism describes it as 'incredulity toward meta-narratives.' Translated into simpler English, what that means is that we are skeptical about any one of the great stories about truth. More and more, in the postmodern world view, those stories are seen as partial and relative.

The information society, Anderson told us, is fundamental to the emergence of the postmodern sensibility. In the information society, the degree of interconnection, the flow of information, vastly exceeds anything experienced in the premodern, or even the modern, context. We all are exposed to an incredible range of different narratives, different lifestyles, different stories, different cultures, different kinds of realities. That proliferation challenges individuals and societies to select from it, to order their realities out of it, and that is the basic postmodern chore. Increasingly, we all are members of many different communities, each with their own values and frameworks of interpretation. Integrating those becomes a personal, as well as a societal, challenge.

At the same time, there are many different ways in which people respond to the postmodern condition. This is not a world in which everyone is self-consciously postmodern, but rather one in which we all have to deal with the postmodern environment, one way or another. While some do adopt the postmodern perspective, others mount the ramparts to defend modernism, while still others try to revert to a romanticized premodern sensibility. Anderson illustrated those dynamics with the following graph

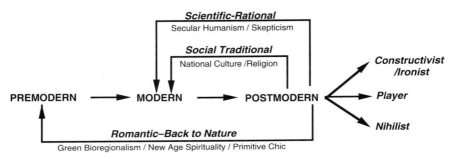

Anderson told us that the diagram begins with the assumption that an evolutionary process has been underway, probably for millennia, that is forcing more and more people out of the traditions of premodern civilization, through a process of modernization (with its efforts to construct universal belief systems), and on into a postmodern era in which there are increasingly articulate questions about whether any of these meta-narratives, any of the great belief systems, is able to prevail and serve as a universal belief system for us all. There are three postmodern types identified in the diagram:

- *Constructivists,* are those who have thought through an approach to reality that is recognizably rooted in postmodern philosophy or epistemology.
- The *players,* are people who (perhaps from reading or merely observing what's possible in the 1990s) have found that all of the various cultural values and systems of symbols from all eras and times are, in some sense, available to them today. So they improvise, play in and out of value systems, and recombine them to make up new cults and new beliefs.

- The *nihilists*, whom Anderson associated with things like the punk rock sub-culture, have been deeply disaffected by what they might call the postmodern tricks. They have come to the more or less rational conclusion that, if there are a lot of different belief systems out there, and they all claim to be true, it's just possible that none of them is true and that everybody is lying. In the words of one song: "if nothing is true, then the only thing that counts is pleasure and pain." Their conclusion is that, in the postmodern context, the only sensible response is to live for the moment. It is the possibility of such a nihilist response that people find most threatening about the postmodern perspective. They dread the prospect that, in a world where skepticism about belief systems is widespread, there will be what Anderson termed "a pell mell jailbreak into hedonism, violence and general disaffection from society."

At the same time, a great number of people, and a great preponderance of our institutions, remain enthusiastically grounded in modernism, and are trying very hard to hold on to it. In Anderson's diagram, two different, essentially modern responses to the postmodern challenge are identified:

- The *scientific-rationalists* who seek to subordinate all other modes of thought to the rational and scientific and for whom the enlightenment project is not dead.
- The *social-traditionalists* who make passionate arguments against relativism in education, and seek to get back to the roots of the Western cultural vision. Advocates of the social-traditional approach often provide lists of things we all need to know to be culturally literate, to be conversant with the language of the Western cultural tradition.

A different response to postmodernism, identified in the diagram, does not try to get back to the certainties of the modern era, but rather seeks the idyllic life of the premodern era. One extreme of that response is the green, bio-regional agenda, which advocates moving back to limited, agricultural communities. Other premodern responses include various strains of primitive chic and new-age religions.

The point that was underlined in this part of our discussion is that postmodernism does not just refer to the relatively small group of people who have adopted the postmodern perspective. Rather, it has to do with all of these various attempts to deal with the fundamental questions being asked about values and belief systems in the postmodern era.[31] People all over the world, in one way or another, are being exposed to a vast range of information that raises fundamental questions about any single culture, any single world view, and they are responding in all of these different ways, and more.[32]

31 To illustrate the differences among the various perspectives identified in the diagram, Anderson outlined how each might respond to the question "what is the true self":

> From a good scientific-rationalist point of view, the true self is to be discovered out there someplace by some experts. To find the answer you need to take a battery of psychological tests and that will tell you what kind of person you are. From the social-traditional point of view the true self is defined by your behaviour in social roles, you find out what you are supposed to be by identifying with your occupation, your place in life, your class, and you live that out with commitment and integrity. In the premodern view the true self is inside you and can be discovered by meditation and spiritual discipline. And from the postmodern perspective, there is no true self. The self continually is redefined in terms of different contexts, in different situations. There's no real you in there that's waiting to be discovered. There's nobody out there that has the final word on what kind of a person you are. There's no particular social role that's going to tell you who you are. From the postmodern point of view, we continually are creating and recreating ourselves, trying on those various perspectives.

32 Anderson also noted that, until a few decades ago, the primary locus of conflict in the world was between different value systems. The emergence of postmodernism has shifted that locus so that now the principal conflicts tend to occur within a given belief system, between those who take a more absolutist stance, and those who have adopted a more relativistic, postmodern stance. Generally the conservatives of any belief system find they have more in common with conservatives of other belief systems than they do with the radicals, the relativists, of their own faith.

Anderson concluded his presentation by sketching three mini-scenarios, three ways in which culture and values might evolve in the information society:

- *Back to basics.* In this scenario people pull back into communities organized around a single belief system and manage to erect barriers that are not penetrated by messages from outside.
- *Tomorrow the world.* Under this scenario a single belief system triumphs and is adopted around the world.
- *A plurality of pluralisms.* In which ways are found for multiple belief systems to coexist and to work together productively.

But what does the emergence of the postmodern view of the world mean for the practice of governance? Marcel Massé drew out some of the implications he perceived. He emphasized, in particular:

- *The necessity of democracy.* If we recognize the relativity of particular belief systems, then the legitimacy for the exercise of power needs to arise from a process in which the widest possible range of belief systems can be included.
- *A crisis of legitimacy.* When we lose the absolute basis for legitimacy that existed in the past, we are faced with a crisis of legitimacy. The legitimacy of decisions in future will rest, not on absolutes, but on the degree to which they arise from an agreed process. That agreement itself will be temporary, contingent and subject to periodic revision.
- *Constructing authority.* In a postmodern world it is much more acceptable to question authority, now authority does not reside just in position, but must be justified by character, abilities, knowledge and the persuasiveness of a leader. It is not permanent, but must be continually constructed.
- *Relativism of lifestyles.* The multiplication of lifestyles in the postmodern world should be seen as a positive development. If we recognize our capacity to construct our lifestyles more consciously, that

may free us to develop the lifestyles that will enable us to live more appropriately in the world we will be facing.

- *Counteracting nihilism.* While some may feel that the loss of absolute systems of belief, in the postmodern era, is a reason to fall back into nihilism, we need to move beyond that. We need to recognize that we live in communities and that, to obtain the benefits of living in that community, there are some norms of behaviour that we need to adopt. Even more important, we need to recognize that the message of postmodernism is not that nothing exists, but rather that nothing can be known in some absolute sense. That does not prevent us from choosing some belief system and treating it, perhaps with some irony, as a reliable guide for action and for making sense of the world. It is unlikely that human beings can operate without some such system of belief.
- *The role of politicians.* While politicians are elected if they can persuade electors that they share their values and beliefs, we now are seeing a multiplication of belief systems, and those systems are changing more rapidly. In this environment, the most successful politicians will not be those who are governed by volatile opinion polls, but rather those who do what they think is right for the long term in accordance with their own system of values and beliefs. These are the politicians that people are more likely to see as governing on the basis of principle and the broader interest, rather than on the basis of their own short-term political interest.

A key question that emerged for us in this discussion, is how it is possible to construct and sustain any sort of consensus in a postmodern society that is characterized by multiplying and fragmenting systems of belief. Underlying this dilemma is the changing basis on which particular decisions can be legitimized. One roundtable member summarized those different bases of legitimacy:

In the premodern era, the legitimacy of such choices rested on the word of God or some other supernatural authority. Then we had the scientific revolution, the enlightenment project, and the birth of modernism. In the modern era, legitimacy increasingly has been based on ideas of research and of scientific method; the notion that if we got the answer by using those scientific methods, if we follow the right procedures (and have the right credentials), we could come up with an answer that, in some sense, was objectively true. That was the new source of legitimacy. It has lasted up to the present day and, as bureaucrats, we are part of that. The legitimacy of the bureaucracy very much is based on its mastery of those rational and scientific methods.

Now we are into a postmodern situation, and the question becomes what is the basis for legitimate choice? If it's not given by God, and if the scientific method cannot yield objective truth, then on what basis can we make legitimate choices? ... one model, which also is championed by a particular school of postmodernists called the deconstructionists, argues that, fundamentally, the basis on which such choices are made, is power. And that also leads to the sorts of nihilism that we've been talking about here today. What I'd like to argue is that there's at least one other possible basis for legitimate decision making in the postmodern era, and that is some version of what we've talked about before in this project, as a learning process. If we see legitimate decisions and legitimate action as being, in effect, a social construction, is there some cumulative way in which we can get better at doing that? Is there some public learning process whereby we can arrive at decisions, which generally we will agree are better than the alternatives, and represent an improvement over what we have now?

As our discussion proceeded, the point was made that the existing political and parliamentary process does not seem to be well adapted to support the development of such a public learning process. Adversarial political discussions lead to telling stories that are very one-sided, and not to public dialogues in which people try to communicate by hearing each other and reaching for a view that encompasses different positions. As a system becomes more confrontational, it becomes less and less possible to find common ground.[33]

The postmodern view also raises fundamental challenges for the legitimacy and role of the Public Service. The legitimacy of the Public Service historically has rested on the modern, rational-scientific world view, which has seen the Public Service as the provider of objective, anonymous, rational, scientific expertise and support to political leaders. Such justification for the role of the Public Service is breaking down in a postmodern world, and that realization is leading to considerable soul-searching:

> Our job has been essentially to assimilate information, increasingly complex information, and to present it to decision makers in a way that helps them to fulfill their role. For a long time we were able to convince ourselves that we did this with objectivity. But one lesson that I take from what Walt Anderson has been telling us today, is that we should stop kidding ourselves, that we are, in fact, a subjectivity. We are a stakeholder and should drop the pretense and be honest.... I think we need to reflect on how our roles are likely to change in this new, complex marketplace of information. Are we going to become obsolete? Are the people going to see through us and insist that we declare our positions rather than sitting anonymously in the shadows? Are we going to want to become more active stakeholder participants, with the risks that involves? Or will we still be able to be valuable and important contributors in the way in which we have been in the past?

Several members of the roundtable suggested that, in this new context, it may be more appropriate to see the Public Service as

33 The parliamentary system, it was argued, institutionalizes and exaggerates conflict, and that undermines its credibility. At the same time, though some saw hope in the pressures for reform of that system, many that arise from Members of Parliament themselves, the challenge is to find ways to preserve what is best about the parliamentary system and, at the same time, to open it to a wider learning process.

providing an essential infrastructure for the ongoing process of public learning that governing in an information society appears to require, and to try to reconstruct its role along those lines.

The media, too, have an important role to play in this process. As the myth of objectivity (an offspring of modernism) breaks down, it was argued, it will be important for the media to recognize that they do play an important role in the social process of constructing reality, and to take that responsibility seriously. One roundtable member went further and suggested that the media can be conceived as providing the institutional base for the postmodern world view, much as science and religion earlier provided the institutional bases for the modern and premodern world views, respectively. But unlike those earlier institutions, which fostered a single system of belief, the media has a vested interest in constantly questioning systems of belief, contributing to the sense of their partiality and relativity.

Some expressed concern that the growth of magazines and newspapers tailored to niche markets, and the coming of a 500-channel television world, would contribute further to the fragmentation of society, to the proliferation of sub-cultures with little in common. Others argued that the emergence of global media institutions like CNN actually contributed to greater degrees of integration, and the development of a common language. But both the fragmentation into sub-cultures within states, and the emergence of global media that cut across national boundaries, raise questions about the extent to which a nation-state, in the information age, can sustain a distinctive national culture, a distinctive system of values and beliefs.

Others emphasized, however, that there are many things that do not have much to do with how we run things, with questions of governance. We need to differentiate those areas where consensus is necessary for effective governance, from those where it does not matter. It may not matter what lifestyles we pursue, or whether we have 500 channels pursuing different themes, so long as we have a sufficient set of shared political assumptions to underpin the operations of the governance system.

If there is sufficient agreement on basic political and economic issues, a sufficiently shared mental map about those matters, then the proliferation of cultural lifestyles does not matter (that realization, too, may be part of the emerging postmodern sensibility). We need to define better those areas where consensus is necessary for effective governance, and to rebuild our social contract in those areas.

The Social Contract: Rebuilding Social Infrastructure

Our exploration of ways of reconstructing the social contract was led by Amitai Etzioni[34] and Charles Taylor.[35] Etzioni began by describing to us the genesis of the communitarian movement in the United States, which arose from the growing sense that there is a need to rebalance the social contract: to balance the current emphasis on individual rights, with a greater sense of social responsibility. He explained the communitarian approach by contrasting it with more traditional whig (liberal) and tory (conservative) positions:[36]

- *Whigs* celebrate the individual. If you push them far enough you arrive at a libertarian perspective, a view, in Etzioni's words, that assumes that history began when a bunch of individuals, roaming the forest, got together, held a committee meeting, and decided to

34 Amitai Etzioni is University Professor at the George Washington University, and also has served as Professor at Harvard and Columbia Universities. He is the editor of *The Responsive Community*, a Communitarian journal, and has written 14 books and numerous articles on issues of social organization and change. His most recent book is *The Spirit of Community: Rights, Responsibilities and the Communitarian Agenda* (Crown Books, 1993).

35 Charles Taylor is Professor of Political Science and of Philosophy at McGill University. He is a fellow of the Royal Society of Canada and of the British Academy. He has written many books and articles on questions of political philosophy. Among the most recent are *Source of the Self: The Making of the Modern Identity* (Cambridge: Harvard University Press, 1989); and *The Malaise of Modernity* (Toronto: Anansi, 1991).

36 For an additional statement of this argument, see the paper by Amitai Etzioni in Part II of this volume.

create a society. Whigs assume that people are inherently good and are corrupted by society. For them, the best form of decision making lies in the aggregation of the individual preferences of voters through the ballot box.

- *Tories*, on the other hand, start not from the individual, but from the nation or church or society. Merit lies in playing a role within that larger entity, and the requirements of the collectivity take precedence. Tories view human nature essentially as evil, and that's why we need strong institutions, in order to make people do good. Decision making for Tories proceeds best when it is undertaken by institutional leaders and the people follow.

- *Communitarians* begin from the assumption that the individual cannot be separated from the social context. The person both creates, and is created by, the culture. There is a necessary and constructive tension between individual rights and social responsibilities. Communitarians believe that human nature has both nobler and more debased aspects, and between these there is a continuing struggle. The challenge is to strengthen the better part of ourselves. Decision making, for Communitarians, is best undertaken through a process of dialogue, by which overarching values are identified that provide a framework within which we can agree to undertake particular actions.

Etzioni emphasized that if we wish to build shared values in the information society, we need to reinforce the social institutions on which those values are based. These value-creating and sustaining institutions, he argued, are the family, the school, the neighbourhood and the community. We need to rebalance our social contract in ways that will strengthen those institutions, that will strengthen that essential social infrastructure. Fundamentally, Etzioni asserted, we are not governed by the state, but by these underlying, value-creating institutions:

> Perhaps one of the best statements ever made on this issue was by Emile Durkheim, one of the great sociologists. He argued that when you have shared values, the law is not that important, but

when you don't have shared values, then the law won't do you much good. You only have to look at Prohibition to see what happens when you have laws without sufficient normative underpinning. Certainly the law sometimes can be ahead of the shared values and, in fact, can encourage their development. But when the law gets too far ahead, that tends to result in deep social problems.

When a community does have shared values, it constitutes what I like to think of as a moral voice, and these shared values can be the most effective way to change behaviour. One good example is the concept of a designated driver, which is being accepted increasingly not because of changes in the law, but because of changes in values, which the laws, subsequently, can embody. But if we had tried to legislate an idea like a designated driver, when more than half of society believed that it was not necessary or appropriate, we would have had great difficulties.

The fundamental importance of these value-creating social institutions argues for application of the principle of subsidiarity. That means that individuals and families should do for themselves whatever they can, and that the community, then, should come in and do only those things that the individuals or families cannot themselves accomplish, and that the state, in turn, should come in and do only those things that the communities cannot accomplish. But this only can work for society as a whole if we have a basis on which those, often very different, communities can work together.

Communitarians argue that there is no need for people to heed the same religion, have the same cuisine, dance the same dances. They can maintain their own sub-cultures (heritages) so long as they buy into an overarching, shared framework. Where that shared framework is missing, a fundamental basis for collective action is lost. We need an overarching set of values, Etzioni argued, from which we can derive and legitimate shared public policies. This echoed the point that had been made in our session with Walter Truett Anderson and Marcel Massé, that we need to differentiate those (relatively limited?) areas where consensus is necessary for effective governance from those where it does not matter.

Charles Taylor underlined the importance of shared values in a society based on the principle of self-rule. In such a society, equal participation in governance becomes fundamental to our understanding of what legitimacy is. A democratic society needs to be based on a strong common understanding that we are engaged in self-rule together, and that we are committed to each other. Earlier authoritarian societies did not require that same high degree of participation, belonging and commitment.

Most liberal theory does not quite grasp this, Taylor said. Liberal theory only goes as far as "the rule of right," acknowledging an individual's need to be able to choose and carry out a life plan, to do so on an even playing field, and to be protected from discrimination. But that is not sufficient as an underpinning of a democratic society. It does not provide any sense that we are engaged in an enterprise together, that we are taking decisions together that are important to our lives. We need something more to provide an adequate basis for a functioning democratic society.

A great value of the communitarian approach, Taylor suggested, is that it tries to construct a basis for what should bind us together from the very requirements of a functioning democratic society.... He proposed, for example, that we do not need a common religious or philosophical view, but we do need to be committed to the view that developing and socializing our children is a fundamental requirement, and to the view that a society in which people actively participate in self-rule is better than one in which people do not take part.

We need to agree on those shared values that are essential for the functioning of a democratic society, and leave the rest for individuals and sub-groups to determine for themselves. This is going to be a perpetually controversial boundary to draw, and we never will get a final definition of that boundary, nor one that is exactly the same from society to society. But drawing that boundary will be an essential part of reconstructing the social contract.

Like Etzioni, Taylor emphasized the importance of strengthening the family to foster the healthy development and socialization of our children:

> Stable relationships with deeply committed persons are fundamental to the development of children. Part of the problem we now face is rooted in the structure of the nuclear family, as it has been developed in our society, with its division of labour between the male head of household and breadwinner, and the female caregiver. Now, as we move away from that division of labour, it is essential that we re-examine the broader structure of work in our society to ensure that the fundamental requirements of raising our children can be met. We currently hear a lot about issues like maternity leave or parental leave and so on, but these seem to me to be very inadequate to deal with the challenge we face. If we agree that the rearing of children, and providing children with a continuous relationship with caregivers, is fundamentally important, then we need to rethink our whole notion of careers, and the related structure of work, to ensure that parents and others are in a position, and are provided with adequate support, to play that vital role.

In this view, we need to place greater value on rebuilding our social infrastructure, to emphasize the importance of investing in our families and our neighbourhoods, rather than simply investing in producing more goods and services. Rebuilding our social infrastructure should be a primary, not a derivative, goal. Etzioni illustrated the need for this change:

> I recently saw a survey, which was taken first in the 1940s and again in the 1990s. School teachers were asked, on each occasion, what are the three problems that troubled them the most in their classrooms? In the 1940s, the top of the list was chewing gum, talking while standing in line, and not putting the chairs back at the end of the day. In 1992, the top three were drugs, rape and murder.

That's what we are talking about. Something fundamental has happened out there.

We have a society that no longer functions, and the challenge is to rebuild the social infrastructure to create a workable, democratic society.

Such fundamental changes are not something that can be legislated, he emphasized, government cannot mandate such changes in values and in social contract, but government can play a facilitating role:

I think the State can do a number of things. First of all, it can help a dialogue to happen. For example, there has been a lot of very good new data, in the last couple of years, on what happens when you put infants into child care. Now we might imagine we could have something we might call a science court, in which you televise a hearing where different camps present evidence on what the implications are of particular kinds of decisions. You could make it look like a real court, and it could foster a nationwide dialogue on whether, for example, it is appropriate to separate a child from its parents before the age of two. I would guess that after three days of such hearings, while there would not be a complete consensus, the quality of both dialogue and agreement would have moved to a new level. And that would help umpteen parents to make decisions about how best to invest their own time, whether in earning additional income, or whether in devoting additional time to child care. That's not something that government can mandate or legislate, but it can foster that sort of public learning process.

The second thing you can do is to ensure that the incentives provided by public policies make sense.... [For example,] we might imagine changing policies that affect fringe benefits, so that someone working part-time will get proportionately the same fringe benefits as someone who is working full time. That would reduce the disincentive to parents to work part-time and to spend the rest of their time in childrearing. And, of course, changing those incentives also affects the public dialogue. So you get double the mileage, you both make certain kinds of behaviours easier, and you encourage the conversation to move in the directions that you believe make sense.

[More fundamentally,] ... if you approach public policy only by looking at each specific issue you face, then you are missing something terribly important. What you are missing is not only shared values, that's the first step, but also the institutions that make them viable in people's lives. Unless you shore up those institutions, your public policy initiatives are not likely to be very successful. It may look like the long way around to focus on fixing the schools and the families and so on, but, in the end, I think we will find that is the best and quickest way of reducing teen pregnancy and alcoholism and of dealing with a whole range of issues and problems we face.... we need to get at the shared underlying institutions and values on which all the rest depend. That's where government can provide the most effective leadership.

In the information society, Taylor added, the role of government in providing that leadership, and in fostering the development of consensus around these issues, has become more difficult. One particular impediment is the growing importance of lobby groups, of single-issue groups who seem to develop a total focus on their particular agenda in a way that further fractures the polity. He underlined the importance of developing mechanisms whereby people can be brought together in a context that is not dominated by these advocacy groups, ways to bring citizens together to focus on the broader public interest:

One extremely interesting proto-example of this occurred during the Constitutional process, in that series of five national citizen fora that were held across the country. The dynamics of those meetings were quite different from those you see, for example, before parliamentary committees, where people tend to defend their particular interests and positions. At the national meetings, by contrast, some very important learning went on, and that learning led to a greater degree of consensus forming around some very controversial questions. It was remarkable to see the extent to which, when Canadians from different regions are brought together in the right context, you do get movement toward consensus, toward being more reasonable, and I find considerable hope in that example. The tragedy of our system, at present, is that we don't do that nearly enough, or nearly well enough.

Can information and communications technologies be used to facilitate that process? Etzioni outlined one possible experiment:

It is conceivable, for example, that you could have the President of the United States make a statement on a Sunday morning at 10:00 o'clock for one hour, to lay key issues before the public. Then you could imagine a structure of dialogue groups across the country that would discuss it for a period of time, and then send a delegate for discussion at the next level (regional, state or whatever), a discussion that could be held by conference call or even teleconference. Mathematically, by that same evening, you could have the vast majority of American voters participating in such groups culminating in a national meeting of delegates to respond to the propositions that had been set forth by the President.

At the same time, he emphasized that these are social and political processes fundamentally, and that it is necessary to give people time to learn. It is almost always unproductive to expect people to reach conclusions on a new idea in a very brief period of time. Instead, it is important to design a process that allows people the time to dialogue and to digest ideas before reaching conclusions. That process, not the technology, is key.

What about the role of the media? Do they not shape the nature of that dialogue and the formation of public opinion? While agreeing that the media can play an important role, Etzioni argued that we should not over estimate their influence. What people watch, and how they interpret what they see, is very much influenced by the community of which they are a part. How you interpret what you see depends on the "internal voice" that comes from your community. So again, the influence of those primary social institutions – the family, school, neighbourhood and community – is key to how we make sense of the world and govern ourselves.

When asked what the Communitarian perspective can contribute to our understanding of the workings of the economy, Etzioni underlined that too much debate has been polarized between the caricature of the free market offered by neo-classical economists, and the competing visions of command and control systems. All societies, he asserted, have deeply mixed economic systems, with an extremely complicated interpenetration of government, business and the voluntary sector. We desperately need a theory of such mixed systems. Another roundtable member added:

> ... there is a growing literature that attacks the frontier myth in the United States; you know, the story that the country was built by individuals who sloshed across the American prairies. What the research shows is the degree of State involvement through land grants, transportation systems and so forth that made that whole enterprise possible. So I agree with you that there is a lot of myth making that needs to be reversed.

One point emphasized, in the course of the roundtable, was that the importance of material incentives, in influencing behaviour, tends to be overrated, and that we need to recognize that the social fabric and shared values play an even more important role. One example that was cited, in this regard, had to do with the differing Canadian and American approaches to liability:

> ... Canadian lawyers were complaining about the limits on liability that exist here, whereas in the United States, people basically can win the lottery if they get hit by the right car. The standard argument, in the U.S., is that those much more generous liability awards are a mechanism for enforcing safety, because the compa-

nies who know they would be liable for large settlements will make extra efforts to ensure safety. But, according to statistics, the U.S. is not a safer society than Canada, quite the contrary. That appears to contradict the standard, market-based argument that material incentives are key.... In the U.S., the material penalties are larger, and there still is more abuse, while in Canada the material penalties are lower, and there is less abuse.

This discussion reinforced for us the understanding that society needs to have most people, most of the time, do what is right without having to be policed or coerced. And that emphasizes, in turn, the importance of investing in strengthening the social fabric, and in rebuilding the social contract.[37]

Conclusions

The three perspectives we explored at these roundtables provided a rich, often overlapping, and sometimes confusing, picture of how the environment for governance is being reshaped in the

37 At a subsequent roundtable several participants noted that, unlike previous resource persons, Amitai Etzioni and Charles Taylor had not explicitly framed their presentation in the context of the changes being engendered by the emergence of a global information society. Such a framework, they suggested, provides valuable additional insight:

I think there are some very important links that could be made between the information society and the problematique that Etzioni and Taylor described. The key would be to focus on the challenge of sustaining a social fabric in the kind of rapidly changing and fragmenting world we have been inventing in the information age....

One of the things I think we could say, in that context, is that the information society accelerates the trend toward rapid commercialization of a lot of previously non-traded activities. That, in turn, reinforces individualism and atomization, and accelerates the kind of moral decline that is the starting point of the analysis presented to us by Etzioni and Taylor. That then leads to the conclusion about the importance of rediscovering the threads of social collaboration in this new world. Whether one finds those threads in the family and in communitarianism, at the micro level, or in grander structures of international collaboration, the direction is the same.

information society. Just as combining three lenses (red, blue and green) can be used to produce a full colour portrait, we used these three perspectives to construct a richer portrait of the changing environment for governance. It provided a three-dimensional, though still very rough, map of the territory. In that process, a number of points emerged on which there appeared to be wide agreement:

- the deep and pervasive nature of the changes engendered by the information society, both in the economy and in society, which have rendered obsolete many of our existing mental maps;
- the importance of social and institutional adaptations, and of values, in addressing those changes;
- that the primary communities, formed by institutions such as the family, the school, the neighbourhood, religious organizations, the workplace, voluntary associations, and so on, are the principal loci for the construction of shared values; and that we need both to recognize their role as basic units of governance (through the principle of subsidiarity), and to find ways to construct overarching values, institutions and shared mental maps that can knit together those various communities into a viable society;
- the need, in that context, to develop a new consensus, not about everything, but about those elements that are central to effective governance; a task that is made all the more difficult, in the postmodern environment of the information society, by a proliferation both in the number of those primary communities, and in the range of perspectives and behaviours they embody;
- that government cannot mandate such a consensus, nor such changes in social values and institutions, across these increasingly varied communities, but it can lead and facilitate a process of public learning and dialogue (a role for government in the information society that parallels the one suggested in our first report);
- the possibility that scenarios can be used to facilitate such a learning process, a process of developing and updating our mental maps, both within government and, more broadly, across society.

We next turned to the process of actually constructing a set of scenarios. We wanted to try to translate this overload of information into useful knowledge, to construct a shared framework, a shared mental map, that might help us (and others) better to understand the challenges of governing in this changing environment, and the different ways in which these challenges might evolve.

3 Constructing Scenarios

The Scenario Workshop

DURING OUR INITIAL ROUNDTABLE, Kees van der Heijden had commented that it was helpful, even desirable, to develop a serious case of information overload during the process of gathering "new knowledge" that leads up to scenario construction. As the roundtable convened for a two-day scenario workshop, one member commented ruefully that we certainly had achieved that objective.

The workshop was facilitated by Adam Kahane,[38] who began by showing a videotape of an earlier scenario process he had facilitated in South Africa. That workshop had involved representatives of the African National Congress, business, labour unions and academics and had produced, what have come to be called, the Mont Fleur scenarios.[39] He then drew on that experience to remind us of some of the key characteristics of good scenarios:

38 Adam Kahane is a Canadian who currently is Director of the Programme in Participative Strategic Planning at the University of the Western Cape in South Africa. Prior to that, Mr. Kahane was responsible for scenario planning at the headquarters of Royal Dutch/Shell in London, and earlier was an executive at Pacific Gas and Electric in California. He has conducted scenario work in more than 25 countries.

39 The Mont Fleur scenarios have been distributed widely in South Africa, and have helped many of the players to develop the kinds of new, shared mental maps needed to facilitate the transition to democracy. Copies of the Mont Fleur scenarios can be obtained from the Institute for Social Development, University of the Western Cape, Private Bag X17, Bellville 7535, South Africa.

Scenarios help in developing a common language, a common model of how things work, and a common vision....

To do that, scenarios need to be logically consistent, clear and simple. If you want them to be used as a language for discussion, then people have to be able to understand them and grasp them quickly. We need to resist our usual temptation to make them very subtle and complicated....

Good scenarios also need to be plausible. If they are completely ridiculous they won't be useful in generating strategic discussion. You should be able to open the *Globe and Mail* on any day and find stories that correspond to each of the scenarios....

[In addition,] scenarios have a role as "transitional objects,"[40] as something people can play with, and use to learn about particularly sensitive subjects.... At Shell, for example, if the "Sustainable World" scenario we developed in 1989 had been presented as a forecast, or as recommendations, people would have rejected it out of hand. But because it was presented as a story of something that could happen, it was able to be discussed very widely and very deeply....

[Generally, a good] scenario is an internally consistent hypothesis, a story, about how the future might unfold. It is not a prediction. One of the important differences between scenarios and a forecast is that rather than assuming away the uncertainties, scenarios highlight the uncertainties and the risks. By definition the scenarios are differentiated, one from the other, along the lines of the uncertainties. That is why it is important that you have spent as much time as you have in the roundtables leading up to this workshop thinking about the uncertainties.

40 For a more detailed discussion of scenarios as transitional objects, see de Geus, op. cit. The term transitional object is taken from the psychoanalytic work of D.W. Winnicott. See, for example, D.W. Winnicot, *Playing and Reality* (London: Tavistock Publications, 1971). The leader in translating Winnicott's work to the realm of social organization has been Harold Bridger. See, for example, H. Bridger, "Courses and Working Conferences as Transitional Learning Institutions" in W.B. Reddy and C.C. Henderson, *Training, Theory and Practice* (Washington D.C.: NTL Institute/University Associates, 1987).

Adam Kahane then led us through essentially an inductive process to develop a set of scenarios for how the information society might shape the environment for governance over the coming decade. Prior to the workshop, we had worked in smaller groups to identify some of the major certainties and uncertainties in how the environment for governance might evolve in the information society. Early in the workshop we reviewed the reports of those small groups and synthesized them into a preliminary, agreed list of key certainties and uncertainties.[41]

Then, working individually, we were asked to write short causal sequences (which Adam Kahane dubbed "snippettes") describing how various of those key elements might develop. Snippettes are bits of stories that causally connect two or three events that might happen. For example, one snippette might read:

> education focuses on information technology skills –> surge of young people entering information industries –> Canada becomes key player in software.

We were encouraged to write the snippettes in a telegraphic style. The next step was to break into three, small syndicate

41 The key certainties we identified included:
- fiscal pressure;
- increasingly pervasive information technology;
- accelerating change;
- demographics;
- the growing capacity of politicians and others to address the public directly;
- the provision of entertainment and information increasingly merge;
- the changing role of governments.

Among the key uncertainties were:
- the effects of footloose capital markets;
- the capability of government to cope;
- whether we will continue to see jobless economic growth;
- the role of the public in decision making;
- whether the Canadian educational system can adjust;
- the degree of polarization in the distribution of wealth and income;
- the impact of information technology.

groups, which worked to combine the snippettes that their members had produced into several longer "mega-snippettes." Those, in turn, were presented to a plenary session. As they were presented, each mega-snippette was given a name:

SYNDICATE GROUP I

- *Wired World* told the story of a very successful, high-technology society, where the economy, education and culture flourish through intelligent use of information technology.
- *Brave New World* was premised on a continuing maldistribution of wealth and income in the information society. In its positive version, it envisioned measures being taken to reconstruct the social contract, to develop a more sustainable society and economy. In its negative version, we fail to adapt and polarization increases.
- *Dark Ages* told a nightmarish story of economic and social disintegration.

SYNDICATE GROUP II

- *Changing Role of Government* envisioned a world in which government is more of a facilitator, and in which there is increasing public involvement in governance, and a degree of direct democracy.
- *World Institutions* postulated the development of stronger world institutions for the environment, peacekeeping, trade and international standards.
- *Lifelong Learning* was based on increased job sharing, resulting in greater leisure time and increased demand for educational services, so that "increasingly we become involved in educating each other."
- *Social Unrest* was a story that involved chaos and warfare in the streets, and possibly the emergence of new, extreme political movements.
- *Educational Standards* began with a recognition that the quality of our educational system has deteriorated unacceptably and envisioned that, in response to growing demands for change, federal and provincial governments would cooperate to strengthen the educational system.

SYNDICATE GROUP III

- *New Economy* was a story in which jobs that were lost in the industrial economy are more than replaced by jobs in the information economy.
- *Clockwork Orange* told the opposite story, of continuing structural unemployment leading to growing social unrest, an unsustainable federal debt and, ultimately, to a breakdown of fiscal federalism resulting in the fragmentation of the federation.
- *Shared Transfer* also began with continuing structural unemployment, but in this story we find a way to share the hardship, and help those who are unemployed to continue to be part of the economy;
- *Global Teenager* told the story of the emerging global youth culture, with its similar music, dress and consumption patterns.
- *Social Fragmentation* was a postmodern story about the lack of shared myths and national identity, and the decreasing legitimacy of leaders in all sectors.

We then worked together, in plenary, to organize these mega-snippettes into an initial set of scenarios. Each of the snippettes was written on a yellow, adhesive post-it note. The mega-snippettes were constructed by stringing together sequences of these notes. As the mega-snippettes were presented in plenary, and then developed into first-cut scenarios, the walls of the meeting room soon became covered with large, and lengthening, yellow paper streamers: snippettes, becoming mega-snippettes, becoming preliminary scenarios.

In that plenary discussion a generally positive scenario, built around the "Wired World," "New Economy" and "Global Teenager" mega-snippettes, began to be developed, along with a largely negative scenario built around the "Clockwork Orange," "Social Unrest" and "Dark Ages" mega-snippettes. There also was a generally positive, mid-range scenario that started to emerge around a combination of "Brave New World" (the positive version), "Shared Transfer," "Lifelong Learning" and "World Institutions;" while a more negative, mid-range story started to emerge around "Brave New World" (the negative version) and

"Social Fragmentation."[42] At a number of points in this discussion, participants suggested a possible structure to order the stories that were emerging, but none, at this stage, received general assent.

The process of combining and recombining the mega-snippettes and arguing which story lines made the most sense, and which structures should be used to differentiate the scenarios, was complex, fractious, generally good humoured, frustrating, stimulating and often chaotic. The pivotal moment came when one member of the roundtable suddenly saw a new way in which we might structure the scenarios we had been developing:

> It seems to me that the starting point of all of these stories is that the information society changes the world. Then there are two dimensions that basically define the scenarios. The first is whether we have economic growth or not, and the second is whether we have structural change or not. So, in the first scenario, information technology changes the world, we do have economic growth and we do make structural adjustments. The result is the positive scenario built on "Wired World" and "New Economy." In the second scenario, information technology changes the world, but there is no economic growth and there is no structural change, and the result is the "Dark Age" scenario. In the third scenario, information technology changes the world, we do get economic growth but we don't get structural change, and the result is the "Social Fragmentation" scenario; disparity increases – the rich get richer and the poor get poorer. And in the fourth scenario, information technology changes the world, there is no economic growth, but we do make structural changes, and the result is a very Canadian form of muddling through; it is related to the "Shared Transfer" story and the positive version of "Brave New World."

42   The "Changing World of Government" and "Educational Standards" mega-snippettes were linked both to the positive ("Wired World," etc.), and to the positive mid-range ("Shared Transfer," etc.) scenarios.

Amidst the general agreement that greeted this insight, there was a sudden spark of recognition among members of the secretariat. Some weeks earlier three members of the secretariat had been reviewing the findings of our first several roundtables and trying to determine, through essentially a deductive process, what scenarios it might be possible to derive from that complexity of information.

That deductive process had begun by noting that, in our discussion of the information economy, Christopher Freeman and Richard Lipsey had outlined two polar possibilities for the development of the economy over the next decade. Either:

- we learn how to use the new technologies to their potential and embark on a new secular boom, of the sort described by Kondratieff; or
- the structural changes in the economy produced by the information age give rise to persisting unemployment and low or no growth (as conventionally measured).

Similarly, our discussions of the social and cultural dimensions, with Walter Truett Anderson, Marcel Massé, Amitai Etzioni and Charles Taylor had defined two polar possibilities. Either:

- we manage to find ways to construct a new social consensus, appropriate to the information society, that rebuilds social cohesion and renews the social contract; or
- we face continuing and accelerating social fragmentation and disparities, as the realities of the information age undermine our ability to construct a shared perspective (postmodernism) and overwhelm basic social institutions.

These two sets of possibilities, while necessarily oversimplified, had illustrated different ways in which the information society could shape the environment for governance over the next decade, through the changes it might produce in our society and economy. The next step, in our deductive process, was to try to interrelate these two dimensions. We constructed the following matrix to illustrate the possible environments for governance that might result from an interplay of such social and economic changes:

New Social Consensus		
Social Fragmentation		
	Low/No Growth	*New Secular Boom*

SOCIETY (left axis)

ECONOMY
(as conventionally measured)

But once we, in the secretariat, had constructed this matrix, we were not sure what to do with it, and whether there were viable scenarios that could be devised to fill the various cells. So we had put the matrix aside and did not circulate it. Now, as a member of the secretariat presented this structure to the workshop, we all were struck by the degree to which the scenarios, which we had constructed through the inductive process of the last day, seemed to fit within the matrix that had been developed deductively, based on the results of the earlier roundtables. This, despite the fact that only three of the workshop participants had seen the matrix beforehand. Somehow, the inductive and deductive routes had led us essentially to the same destination.

With this striking realization, and with the basic structure for differentiating the scenarios now agreed, we broke into four syndicate groups to develop each scenario further. The groups worked well into the night, thinking through the sequence of events that might lead to their scenario, and trying to make the most compelling case for it that they could. By the following morning, each group had convinced itself that their scenario was the most likely (or only possible) way in which the environment for governance would develop over the coming decade.

There was a good deal of humour (and some heckling) as each group presented their version of "the real future" to a plenary session. Much of that humour arose from a recognition that each syndicate group, in its claimed certainty about its own scenario, was parodying more standard planning approaches, which are based on a single forecast or projection. Scenarios illuminate the inadequacy of such single forecasts. As Pierre Wack, the father of the scenario approach at Shell, phrased it: "By presenting other ways of seeing the world, decision scenarios allow managers to break out of a one-eyed view."[43]

Following these presentations, the plenary refined the scenarios further, began the process of naming them,[44] and considered, in a preliminary way, the implications of each for governance.

The first scenario, which we named *Starship,* envisioned a world characterized by a secular economic boom, coupled with the development of new social consensus. The second scenario, which we named *Titanic,* was the other extreme, with low or no economic growth coupled with growing social fragmentation. The third scenario, christened *HMS Bounty,* combined a booming economy with continued social fragmentation and polarization; while the fourth scenario, named *Windjammer,* envisioned

43   Pierre Wack, op. cit.
44   In the end we adopted ship names for the scenarios, which seemed particularly appropriate, given that "governance" has its etymological roots in the Greek "kybernetes" which means "pilot or helmsman."

SOCIETY	*New Social Consensus*	Windjammer	Starship
	Social Fragmentation	Titanic	HMS Bounty
		Low/No Growth	*New Secular Boom*

ECONOMY
(as conventionally measured)

new social consensus emerging around a low or no-growth economy (at least as conventionally measured).[45]

The following pages outline each of these four scenarios, which provide alternative visions (an alternative map) of how the realities of the information society may reshape the environment for governance over the next decade.[46]

---

45 In terms of the initial scenarios that we had developed inductively, *Starship* corresponded to the positive scenario built around "Wired World" and "New Economy," *Titanic* corresponded to the negative scenario built around "Clockwork Orange" and "Dark Ages," *HMS Bounty* corresponded to the negative mid-range scenario built around "Social Fragmentation," and *Windjammer* corresponded to the positive mid-range scenario built around "Shared Transfer."

46 Our purpose had been to develop a set of scenarios for how the emergence of a global information society might reshape the environment for governance in Canada. As we examined the results, however, it seemed to us that, with very few modifications, these scenarios also could be helpful in thinking about how the environment for governance might evolve in other countries, especially those in the developed world.

Starship *Scenario*

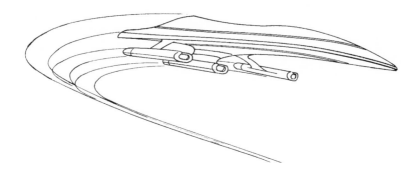

This scenario envisions a booming economy coupled with the development of new social consensus. In this scenario, the difficulties of the early 1990s turn out to be transitional and, as institutions learn to adapt to the requirements of the information economy, a new, global, secular economic boom develops, in which Canada plays a leading role. Institutions and individuals have reached the point, in their learning curve, where they can begin to realize the full potential of the new information technologies (IT).

Global information flows, connectivity and international trade are liberalized and increase; IT is an important new production tool that drives change, and produces new jobs in both information and other industries. IT also increases the productivity of Canadian workers to the extent that many manufacturing jobs can be repatriated from lower-wage economies.

Governments establish national and international standards to facilitate interconnection. Canada is at the forefront of this initiative, and gives priority to ensuring that its own information infrastructure is second to none.

Labour and skills shortages, along with the favourable quality of life in Canada, lead to increased immigration. At the same time the public and private sectors cooperate to strengthen the education and training system, recognizing it as an essential contributor to Canadian competitiveness in the global information economy. Increasing the technical literacy of the workforce becomes a key priority. As the work ethic is reinforced, measures also are developed to facilitate labour mobility. Canada's stability, quality of life and superior education system provide it with unique advantages in the knowledge-based global economy.

Enormous adaptation in all public and private institutions is required in order to keep up with these changes; institutions either reform, are forced to reform, or die; funds are diverted from old to new activities. There is ongoing restructuring and change, as Canadian individuals and organizations continually must adapt and learn in order to succeed in this turbulent environment.

Capital mobility and volatility also keep Canada on its toes. Canada meets these challenges and is globally competitive. Canadian companies are active in global markets, and expect the Canadian government to facilitate this.

Prosperity builds consensus (a rising tide lifts all boats), and it is a liberal, free-market consensus. That consensus is not limited to Canada, but increasingly is shared globally. Individuals and corporations are the leading actors in this world, governments provide support. This is a market-driven world, dominated by the priorities of competing in the global marketplace. At the same time, this global consensus (and the associated harmonization processes) makes the maintenance of a distinctive Canadian identity increasingly problematic and, for some, increasingly irrelevant.

As the fiscal deficit becomes a surplus amidst rapid economic growth, the social safety net, regional transfers and equalization are sustained, but reformed in ways designed to strengthen the work ethic and to encourage labour mobility. Measures are taken to ensure there is a more equitable distribution of income both to avoid destructive social polarization and to provide a broader consumer base. Information technologies also enable a simpler, more client-centered administration of social programs. The government increasingly leads the construction of a shared framework and vision, and then enables a wide range of players (especially the private sector) to innovate better ways to achieve those objectives. Political stability and government legitimacy rebound, but stability takes on a different meaning in this world of continuing turbulence and change.

Titanic *Scenario*

This scenario envisions a world with low or no economic growth, coupled with growing social fragmentation. In this scenario, the information economy does not produce nearly enough high-paying jobs to replace those being lost, and there is persistent high structural unemployment, and low or no growth.

Institutions, both public and private, respond defensively and inadequately. Governments keep waiting for "a recovery" that never comes, and pay disproportionate attention to conventional economic indicators, which occasionally show spurts of growth.

There is a lack of understanding that the economy has fundamentally changed – from a labour-intensive, industrial economy to a capital- and technology-intensive, information economy (where not only new sectors, but also traditional manufacturing and resource industries, need to become more technology-intensive to be competitive).

Industry under-invests in innovation and fails to go global, concentrating instead on the North American market. The education system does not adapt to produce the highly skilled individuals the information economy requires. Young people lose interest in education, since it is not preparing them for anything that is useful (it is socializing them for jobs and industries that no longer exist), and become more alienated, rootless and violent.

As tax revenues decline, and demands for income support increase, the deficit becomes unsustainable. The value of the dollar continues to fall and capital flight grows.

The wealthy and the highly skilled also begin to flee in large numbers to those countries that have been more successful in adapting to the challenges of the information age. Some countries have been successful in recognizing and adapting to the new realities, but Canada is not among them. Canadians become increasingly inward-looking and cling to visions of the past, as our situation deteriorates. Canada falls behind.

As the economic pie continues to shrink and social distress grows, alienation, unrest and violence increase. As the social fabric continues to fray, there is an increase in racial and regional 'scapegoating', and extremist groups gain adherents. Families, neighbourhoods and communities either fragment or attempt somehow to withdraw behind walls and insulate themselves from outsiders.

Canada begins to seem more and more like a sinking ship, and different interests and regions scramble to save themselves. Those with incomes resist contributing to help others. There is a growing tax revolt. As the tax base continues to shrink, holes in the social safety net increase and an underclass grows. Regionalism becomes rampant as fiscal federalism breaks down. The breakup of the federation becomes a real and present possibility.

Government responds to persisting economic distress by reinforcing traditional approaches, by trying to maintain existing transfer programs and by seeking to defend industries that are less and less competitive. Government continues to wait for the recovery. The credibility of leaders and institutions is undermined as their responses to the growing crisis are seen to be less and less relevant and effective. Demagogues emerge preaching simplistic solutions. Government is forced to ever more draconian measures to preserve order.

HMS Bounty *Scenario*

In this scenario, a booming economy is combined with continued (and growing) social fragmentation and polarization. One image is Los Angeles: high tech and dynamic, with many people doing very well, but with society very polarized and very difficult to govern.

As in the *Starship* scenario, the information economy ushers in a new global secular economic boom, IT transforms the economy and work, and Canada is well placed to take advantage of this, and is a success story. There are lots of high-tech jobs and high-tech exports, with high inward investment. The private sector sets the agenda and leads the way.

Liberal, free-market economics prevail, with continued liberalization (including an Americas Free Trade Agreement (AFTA)), deregulation and privatization.

But unlike *Starship,* efforts are not made to ensure that all Canadians can participate in the boom. Education and training is inadequate and many emerge unequipped for high-tech jobs. Private education, as well as training provided by companies, is world class, but the public education system continues to deteriorate.

There is growing polarization between those who can participate in the global information economy and those who cannot. There are high returns to capital (including human capital), but low returns to labour. Government policies are designed to serve the interests of the knowledge elite and the companies (and regions) in which they work. Otherwise, given the immense mobility of capital and highly qualified individuals in the information economy, it is feared that those companies and people will leave Canada. As policies increasingly turn to "building on strength," regional disparities grow.

In pursuit of the priority of maintaining Canadian competitiveness, and of reducing the "overhead" that such programs represent to society, social safety nets are reduced. The "harmonizing" pressures of AFTA, and pressures from global financial markets, reinforce this trend. Government continues to deregulate, privatize and downsize. Economic growth and government cutbacks brings the deficit under control, at least for the moment.

While the elite share, with their global counterparts, the liberal, free-market consensus described in the *Starship* scenario, the growing underclass see and experience quite a different world. The elites can withdraw behind the walls of their communities, neighbourhoods and families, and try to insulate themselves from the increasing poverty around them. For the rest, the world in which they live is marked by shrinking opportunity, growing insecurity and fragmenting families and communities. The information society benefits mostly the (increasingly, globally homogenized) elite, for the masses it means only "infotainment" and palliatives. Crime and youth gangs proliferate. Social and regional cleavages grow.

By the end of the scenario period, in 2005, social and regional disparities, and growing conflict between haves and have-nots, no longer can be covered over. The decline in consumer purchasing power among the multiplying have-nots also is threatening to smother further economic growth. As social and regional tensions continue to increase, there is growing rebellion and pressure to realign the economic and political system. Storm clouds gather....

Windjammer *Scenario*

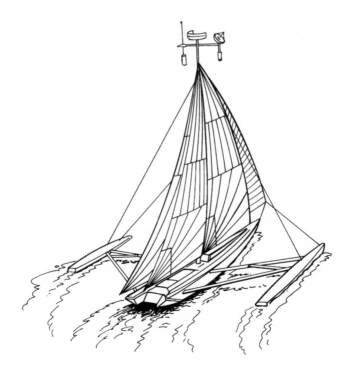

This scenario envisions a new social consensus emerging around a low or no-growth economy, at least as conventionally measured.[47] As in the *Titanic* scenario, the information economy does not produce enough high-paying jobs to replace those being lost, and there is low or no economic growth. But, unlike *Titanic,* a series of events triggers growing public awareness and concern, and action is taken in time to change course.

The events that trigger that public awareness, that act like the canary in the mineshaft, highlight the negative "externalities" of current growth patterns. Possibilities might include the loss of major regional industries (the Cod fishery many times over), major environmental horror stories, increasing stories of people falling through the fraying social safety net, and incidents that dramatize a loss of Canadian independence in the continental and global marketplace.

These events generate growing insecurity and demands for action. There is a reassertion of nationalism, a cry that Canada will not survive if current patterns, driven solely by the demands of the marketplace, continue. Economic institutions, some leaders argue, must not impoverish their society and environment. Canada always has been an act of collective and political will, the will to maintain a distinctive community north of the 49th parallel. Canada's survival now depends on a reassertion of that will. These arguments are made widespread by the media, and demands for change grow throughout Canada. Organizations and groups across the country mobilize public debate.

Almost too late, Government recognizes this major shift in the concerns and priorities of the public. It leads a national process, involving the public, private and voluntary sectors, to develop and implement a new national strategy to take Canada into the 21st century. Such a strategy is defined as one that would enable Canada to be internationally competitive while sustaining

---

47 Roundtable members emphasized that, as this scenario developed, there, in fact, might be a high degree of growth going on (including personal and non-material growth), which would not be captured by conventional economic measures.

Canadian communities, social fabric and environment. Some advocate such a strategy as a response to immediate economic constraint, arguing that we need to hang together and make the best of a bad situation. Others are convinced that older patterns of economic growth are destructive and unsustainable in any case, and that the new strategy offers a better, longer-term quality of life for ourselves and (especially) for our children.

The consensus that results is quite different from that described in the *Starship* scenario, with greater emphasis being placed on values of fairness and sustainability. There also is greater emphasis on ensuring that decisions can be made as close as possible to those affected (subsidiarity), and on fostering mutual respect and harmonious relations among diverse communities. The new consensus is driven by the realization that the growth patterns of the industrial past cannot be sustained, and that if we cannot pull together, and more equitably share both the burdens and the opportunities of the information age, Canada is unlikely to survive.

The strategy that emerges emphasizes the importance of developing Canada as a leader in the new, knowledge-based industries, and in the application of less resource- and energy-intensive technologies to existing industries. That strategy depends on a major investment in research and development and in the continuous learning of the population. Canada's capacity to learn increasingly becomes seen as a critical competitive advantage. The strategy includes policies to foster a more equitable distribution of income, and the use, by government, of information technology to provide more cost-effective social services. The strategy also includes an emphasis on community-based economic development, and on telework, recognizing the priority Canadians attach to being able to remain, and to earn an income, where they now live. In addition, it provides measures to strengthen the social fabric of our neighbourhoods, families and schools, premised, in part, on an increasing role for the voluntary sector.

By the end of the scenario period, in 2005, the terms of public debate in Canada have shifted. The need for a sustainable development strategy is taken for granted, and debate revolves around the details of the best mix of actions to achieve it. That strategy includes effective ways to manage the deficit. While there has been some flight of companies unable, or unwilling, to participate in the new economy, it has been far less than opponents had forecast, in part because the adoption of similar sustainability strategies around the world means there are very few places to which to fly. Canada, acting in its own interest, has played, and continues to play, a leadership role in fostering the adoption of such sustainable strategies around the world, and in strengthening international institutions dealing in areas such as trade, the environment, peacekeeping and standards.

Conclusions

At the beginning of the scenario workshop, Adam Kahane had emphasized that scenarios are a mechanism for organizing a huge amount of complex information in a comprehensible way. Scenarios translate that information into a set of stories or images that can provide a shared language and mental models for those concerned about the issues in question. To perform that function effectively, scenarios need to be relatively clear and concise and, at the same time, plausible and internally consistent. Good scenarios offer different ways of interpreting information, and so help people to perceive things not included in their current mental maps, and to expand or redraw those maps. As stories, rather than forecasts, they also can serve as a "transitional object," as something people can play with and use to explore and to learn about sensitive questions and "unthinkable" dangers.[48]

As the workshop drew to a close, it seemed to us that the scenarios we had produced met the criteria that both Kees van der Heijden and Adam Kahane had described to us. The scenarios were not comprehensive – scenarios never are – but were designed

48   For a more complete presentation of the concept of the "transitional object," see, for example, Bridger, op. cit. and Winnicott, op. cit.

to address our principal concern; namely, how the information society might reshape the environment for governance over the next decade. We had identified two key uncertainties that we had used to differentiate those scenarios: whether or not there would be a new secular economic boom, and whether or not we would find ways to build social cohesion in the information society. The resulting set of four scenarios seemed to us to provide a promising framework for further exploration, for agenda-setting, and for developing and testing policy options.

One striking realization that emerged for us, as we reviewed the scenarios, was that we could design a relatively desirable scenario even if we did not postulate a new economic boom. But we could not come up with a scenario in which any of us would want to live, if we did not postulate success in building social cohesion. We decided, therefore, that the next stage of our work should focus on the process of building social cohesion in the information society.

4 Changing Course: Toward Social Cohesion

IN CONSTRUCTING THE SCENARIOS, we had developed a new mental map of the different ways in which the information society might reshape the environment for governance in the coming decade. We now tried to use that map to guide our exploration.

As we began that exploration, it seemed to us that only two of the scenarios pointed toward a future that appeared to be desirable (though we disagreed about their relative desirability); namely, *Starship* and *Windjammer*. What those two scenarios had in common was a strong degree of social cohesion. It was no surprise that none of us wanted to live in the *Titanic* scenario, with its weak economy and fragmenting society. Equally, none of us thought the *HMS Bounty* scenario was desirable, and most of us questioned whether it was sustainable (either socially or economically) over the longer term. This despite the fact that *HMS Bounty* postulated a booming economy (though coupled with a highly polarized society).

As a result, we decided to focus our next two roundtables on ways of constructing social cohesion in the information society. This focus also reflected the realization, emphasized to us by Christopher Freeman and Richard Lipsey, that success in the new information- or knowledge-based economy depends fundamentally on social and cultural factors. It echoed, as well, the need to find better ways to construct social consensus amidst the multiplying, fragmenting belief systems of a postmodern society, that had emerged as a central issue in our session with Walter Truett Anderson and Marcel Massé. And, it responded to the urging of Amitai Etzioni and Charles Taylor that we need to pay more attention to social questions, and not to regard social issues as secondary to economic concerns.

This represented a turning point in the work of the roundtable. Up to this point we had focused on constructing scenarios. Now, we turned to explore a path illuminated for us by those scenarios. While we (or certainly other groups) might well have chosen to explore other paths, we concluded that in this direction lay some of the most critical issues for governing effectively in the information age:

> There were a lot of paths that we might have followed, but we didn't. ... there were obviously a myriad of directions we might have taken. But we chose to focus on ways to build social cohesion in a context of continuing and rapid change. I don't think we give enough attention to this notion of continuing change.... There are no longer any fixed points around which one can organize so, instead, we need to be in a process of continual learning and invention, of rediscovering the art of management.
>
> In one sense that is a very exciting world, but in another sense it is quite exhausting.... What became clear to us, out of the scenarios, is that sustaining social cohesion is going to be a dominant concern in a world of rapid change. Otherwise that world will fragment and fall apart. Not only will Canada become the Titanic, the world will become the Titanic.

Social cohesion involves building shared values and communities of interpretation, reducing disparities in wealth and income, and generally enabling people to have a sense that they are engaged in a common enterprise, facing shared challenges, and that they are members of the same community. In the rapidly changing environment of the information society, roundtable members emphasized, social cohesion needs continually to be constructed. It depends, fundamentally, on the capacity of individuals and social institutions continually to learn and to adapt together. In this world of rapid change, social cohesion depends, fundamentally, on our capacity to construct a learning society.

But "learning" and "learning society," in this sense, mean much more than the narrower uses of those terms that now are becoming commonplace:

> I think one thing we need to emphasize is that learning can be used in at least two senses. One is the more traditional sense of human investment and training: that all we need to do is to re-tool workers to bring them technologically up to speed and Canadian competitiveness would be restored. It is that sense of learning that underpins a lot of the "learning society" discussion that is current today. But there is another sense of learning, that goes much more to what we are talking about, that is more radical. That sense of learning accepts the notion that there is a deep techno-socio-economic revolution going on, and that we can manage it only by continuing to re-learn in a much more fundamental sense....

To better understand this more fundamental sense of learning, and of a learning society, we decided to explore two basic questions:

- what are some essential requirements for building such a learning society;
- how can we develop a better, ongoing process for constructing social consensus within that society?

Some Essential Requirements for Creating a Learning Society

Our guides in trying to understand, and to explore, some of the essential requirements for creating a learning society were Daniel Keating,[49] Judith Maxwell[50] and Steven Klees.[51]

Daniel Keating began by providing a striking historical context for our discussion.[52] He noted that if we could compress the 100,000 years since the emergence of modern humans into a single year, we would see that our species moved into small urban centers, supported by agriculture, at about the end of November, started an industrial revolution on the afternoon of New Year's Eve, and launched experiments in instantaneous global communication, information technology, and multicultural metropolitanism only in the last few minutes.

The historic process of development has been based on an interplay of social and technological dynamics, Keating noted. In reconstructing our species' history, we have tended to focus on the technological aspects (for example, making tools, cultivating crops, harnessing energy from non-animal sources and so on). What is less obvious, but equally true, is that each of these major technological revolutions depended, in turn, on new forms of social organization (for example, inter-tribal trade, the congregation of people in urban settings, sharing risk through capital investment and so on). Our history more accurately is seen as a mutual causal process, in which changes in technology generate demands and opportunities for societal change, and changes in society generate demands for technological innovation.

The emergence of a global information society is only the latest revolution in this ongoing process, and one that still very much is underway. But in the course of our history, the time available for

49 Daniel P. Keating is a Royal Bank Fellow at the Canadian Institute for Advanced Research, and Director of the CIAR Program in Human Development. He also is Professor in the Department of Applied Psychology at the Ontario Institute for Studies in Education and a member of the Graduate Faculty at the University of Toronto. Dr. Keating has written and edited six books and more than fifty articles on issues of human development and education.

50 Judith Maxwell is Executive Director of the Queen's/University of Ottawa Economic Projects, and Associate Director of the School of Policy Studies at Queen's University. There she is responsible for guiding research projects on government and competitiveness, human resource management policies and the cost effectiveness of the health care system. Prior to that, Mrs. Maxwell served as Chair of the Economic Council of Canada.

51 Steven J. Klees is an economist and Professor of Educational Policy at Florida State University. Prior to that he served on the faculties of Stanford and Cornell Universities. He also has worked extensively in the developing world. Professor Klees is the author of three books and numerous articles on educational policy, economics and technology.

52 Many of the points made in Daniel Keating's presentation to the roundtable are elaborated in his paper in Part II of this volume.

society to learn (and to adapt) to such transformations has shrunk from eras, to generations, to the span of a single life. Seen in this historical context, the magnitude of the learning challenge we now face is striking.

Successful societies, in the information age, Keating told us, are likely to be those who have the greatest capacity to learn from universally available information, and who can adapt quickly and productively to rapidly changing conditions. To do that, they will need to develop the learning capacity both of individuals and of social institutions.

Developing the Learning Capacity of Individuals

Keating emphasized that the quality of the social environment, especially in the early period of life, is a key factor in determining the health and well-being of individuals, and their ability to cope and to learn:

> In the first five years of life we lay down the essential neural net-works that govern the way we perceive other people and the ways we interact in the world. If we so damage our social environment that our children do not receive the nurturing they require in their first five years of life, then we will find that some of the goals we desire, as a society, are impossible to attain because we will not have the individuals available who will have the capacity to get us there.... Moreover, if we socialize kids in ways that are destructive of the social fabric, that's not something we easily can overcome at some later point. It's relatively easy, in a complex, self-organizing system, to create a downward spiral toward greater fraying of the social fabric, greater polarization, greater hostility and greater violence.

At present, we can see that we are not providing the sort of social environment that is conducive to the healthy development and socialization of our children. In that regard, Judith Maxwell pointed to a recent press report that 40 per cent of high school students in Ottawa have been described as dysfunctional. They are "physically and emotionally unhealthy children, neglected children, children whose parents lack the time and energy to be with them, substance-abusing children, children with minimal social skills, children with a vast range and variety of abuse, stress and fragile families." This is not simply a problem of the schools, she noted, but something that can be traced back to troubles in the development of our children from an early age.

A number of roundtable members added that it is unrealistic to equate learning (and developing the learning capacity of individuals) with what happens in schools. While schools play an important role, they are only part of the infrastructure (and culture) that is needed, in a rapidly changing society, to support individual learning throughout a lifetime. For example, schools cannot be expected to compensate for failures of families to provide for early childhood development,[53] or for failures of the labour market to offer opportunities for people to develop further their skills and learning capacity.[54]

53 Like Etzioni and Taylor, Keating noted that the family is having increasing difficulty in carrying out its primary responsibility to provide a quality social environment for the developing generation. Given labour market forces and changes in family structure, many families simply do not have the time or resources necessary to carry out this function fully. He emphasized that we need to find ways to provide for the developmental needs of our children, given the realities of our society. Several roundtable members added that we have not yet begun to address these issues very well, and now have a set of social policies that were designed for a different era.

54 Steven Klees noted another factor that can truncate the development and learning capacity of individuals; namely, the absence of good quality work opportunities that make use of their talents. At present, our policies tend to focus on the supply side, on the improvement of the quality of human resources. A too-exclusive focus on the supply side, Klees suggested, is both irresponsible and unworkable. It is irresponsible because there is no reason to believe that supply will create its own demand. It is unworkable because people respond to incentives and, if they see there is no demand, that there are no good jobs where the skills they are acquiring can be used, they will not invest themselves in education. Klees argued that we also need to focus on the demand side, on the creation of jobs and opportunities that make use of the talents of our people, and so develop their learning capacity and that of our society.

Learning Organizations and a Learning Society

At the same time, Keating emphasized, two societies that are equally successful in developing individuals, may be extraordinarily different in how well they function, depending on how well they organize those individuals. In that regard, one of the most promising models is that of the learning organization:[55]

> A learning organization is capable of adapting over time to changing conditions in a way that is productive for the organization and its members. Learning organizations have "distributed intelligence," it is not the case that there are a few people at the top who do the thinking, and everyone else implements their decisions. Rather, the thinking function is distributed throughout the organization, as is the implementing function.[56] Learning organizations tend to have more horizontal information flow and less vertical decision making. They command a diversity of expertise, and they are united by a shared sense of the overall goals of the organization.

As the conversation proceeded, it seemed to us that these characteristics of a learning organization also could be applied to defining what is required to create a broader learning society.

---

55 Keating's presentation on the learning organization echoed many of the points we had made on that subject in our first report (Rosell et al., op. cit.). The work of Donald Michael, who was a resource person to the project during its first phase, also is especially valuable on questions having to do with the nature, limitations and requirements of organizational and societal learning. See, for example, Donald N. Michael, "Governing by Learning in an Information Society" (in Rosell et al., op. cit., 121–33); and idem, *On Learning to Plan and Planning to Learn* (San Francisco: Jossey Bass, 1973).

56 Keating noted that this quality of "distributed intelligence" also is analogous to how the brain appears to be organized (into distributed neural networks). Others added that creating such learning organizations will involve learning how to reduce hierarchy and to create a more democratically structured workplace.

DISTRIBUTIONAL ISSUES ARE FUNDAMENTAL TO THE CREATION OF SUCH LEARNING ORGANIZATIONS AND LEARNING SOCIETIES

There is no incentive to contribute your creativity and energy to a group effort, Keating noted, if you don't believe that you will benefit fairly from that group effort. The proceeds of a successful learning organization (or learning society) need to be shared more equally among its members, if they are to continue to participate and to contribute fully.

At the societal level, especially given fiscal constraints, a number of roundtable members suggested that a better approach to these distributional questions might be to find ways of redistributing work, rather than income. The shorter work week, and different forms of worksharing, are being tried in Canada, and in other jurisdictions, as one means of redistributing work.

Several participants also suggested that such efforts to redistribute work could be designed to provide more creative ways to address some of the pressing human developmental concerns we had been discussing, including the need to provide better support for raising children. On the one hand we have a supply of skilled people who are un- or under-employed, and on the other hand we have a range of serious social problems that need to be addressed. It should be possible to devise innovative ways to bring together that supply and that demand:

> For example, the voluntary sector of the economy deals with many of the fundamental social issues, including providing services for children and families. We need to learn how to take money that now is being pumped into treating symptoms, and focus that on supporting activities that will deal with some of the underlying causes we have been discussing. We also need to think about mechanisms that would provide parents with adequate income if they decide to stay at home to do the job of raising children. The challenge is how do we foster a social debate that will allow us to move in that direction? We need to think more creatively about these questions, if we want to enhance the learning capacity of our society.

At the same time, it was emphasized, no one has the answers on how best to construct a learning society:

> One unfortunate aspect of political discourse, in my view, is that it so often presumes that somebody out there has the final answer to these things, someone has the secret key or the plan that will take care of all of this. And it just isn't so. We don't know what the future is going to be and we don't know how to deal with these kinds of issues. So we need to feel free to experiment and not assume that there is some sort of turnkey project to create a learning society, because that just doesn't exist. We are going to have to build it step by step.

In other words, building that learning society itself will involve a process of public learning of a high order.[57]

FUNDAMENTALLY, THIS LEARNING PROCESS NEEDS TO PROCEED AT THE LEVEL OF VALUES

If we want to build a new social consensus, and an effective learning society, Keating emphasized, we need to be able to have a much more open discussion of values. "Government needs to lead the construction of a shared understanding of the public agenda, and of an effective context for public discourse about our common values and goals." His words echoed the emphasis in our

---

57 One important contribution that government can make to such a process, Keating suggested, is to call attention to a whole host of indicators that tell us how well we are doing:

> That kind of feedback is basic to a learning process. We monitor financial markets and the economy on a day-to-day, minute-to-minute basis using a wide range of indicators. We don't have indicators nearly so sophisticated or timely with respect to human development, or with respect to things like education. We don't have anything like a systematic monitoring system or a systematic devotion of public attention to these issues. At the same time, we know from public opinion polls that people are deeply concerned about these questions. So we need to provide people with indicators and with other means to think about these issues and to develop new solutions.

first report about the importance of constructing shared frameworks of goals, interpretation and values, in the context of which a wide range of players mutually can coordinate their actions.[58]

Much of this process needs to occur at local levels, Klees suggested. In the information society, increasingly we do not have a place where we can develop shared values. We need to rethink this, and that means rethinking community. We need to develop places in which we can come together to talk about values and to talk about what we want out of our institutions. For that to work, these need to be places where people have the power to do something. Others added that such initiatives need to be relatively local, relatively community-based, because in many of these areas we are not going to come up with solutions that are going to work across very diverse types of communities. People need to participate actively in constructing these sorts of initiatives within their own communities.[59]

58 Keating also noted that the construction of common values and goals is even more important in the information society, in the face of eroding boundaries, and the resulting questioning of systems of belief that those boundaries had protected (the postmodern condition we had explored in our session with Anderson and Massé):

> The decline of organized religion around the world, as well as the growth of multicultural communities, means that we are once again faced with the challenge of finding ways to define fundamental meaning in the world in a manner that we all can accept as legitimate.
>
> We can listen to a lot of current political debates and realize that what is in fact being said has less to do with the supposed surface issues, the ostensible subject of the discourse, but rather is really reflecting a much deeper set of psychological issues about who I am as a person in the world and what is the meaning of it all? How do we get at those kinds of issues? I don't know the answer to that question, but increasingly our political debates will be driven, and perhaps distorted, by that subliminal search. So it is essential that those questions are brought to the surface so that we can address them more directly.

59 This also recalled our earlier discussion with Amitai Etzioni and Charles Taylor about the importance of value-creating institutions like the family and the community, and the need to reinforce their role by applying a principle of subsidiarity.

Building on Diversity

But, if we concentrate on building shared values within our local communities, does not our very diversity become a barrier to building social cohesion and an effective learning society at the national level? Keating disagreed, and argued that such diversity actually is an advantage in building a learning society:

> ...a multicultural society can have a real advantage because it has a much greater storehouse of cultural information. Our different cultures give us different ways of seeing, and the ability to call on such diversity can be an important asset in becoming a learning organization.

Klees added that the often conflicting perspectives of our diverse communities should be seen as an asset. Working through these conflicts should be seen as an essential stage in developing both a better understanding of the issues and a more viable consensus:

> Playing down conflicts can blind us to important perspectives and be self-defeating. We talk with like-minded people too much, and tend to underplay the extent to which knowledge is contested. Instead, we need to bring the conflict in our perspectives to the fore, and use that as a basis for learning.
>
> We need to stop pretending that the other side does not exist, is wrong, or does not matter. We need to stop viewing debates and conflict from a technical perspective, to stop regarding them as error, the error of others who disagree with us.... To develop effective learning organizations, and learning societies, we need to focus on conflict, not tiptoe around it. We need to set up mechanisms for dialogue and negotiation that use conflict as an essential stage in the building of that consensus.

Many roundtable members agreed that we need to see consensus and conflict as two sides of the same coin, but noted that we have not yet developed a style of discourse that allows us to undertake consensus-building in a manner that incorporates conflict very productively. Instead, we have developed a more adversarial style of discourse, a "zero-sum" game in which conflict is resolved either in your favour or in mine. Another approach is that of negotiation and compromise, in which everybody gets the minimum that they need, so that no one walks away from the process feeling they are a total loser. But in a learning society, Keating suggested, we need to develop a third possibility, which makes more productive use of conflicting perspectives:

> Even more intriguing is a third possibility; namely, developing a process that builds consensus in a way that enables us to recognize that we have a great deal more in common than we originally had believed. It is that sort of consensus-building that shows the most promise and that increasingly is being developed in learning organizations. The challenge, in that approach, is to find some transformative new way of seeing and dealing with these issues.

A number of roundtable members emphasized the inability of many current political institutions to foster that third approach to consensus-building:

> We, in Canada, have pushed the parliamentary form of government in a direction that has exaggerated conflict in a very unproductive way. The result frustrates many of the people who work within the system, both politicians and public servants.... Another institutionalized problem for our political system is the extent to which debate occurs in secret, either in caucus or in Cabinet. It's hidden from the people, and that limits the extent to which people can see and understand how the various interests represented in Parliament are being articulated, and how conflicts are being resolved. In the information society that sort of covert process may no longer be sufficient.

We need to find better ways, many suggested, in which the operation of our political system can be developed to foster more of a public learning process.[60]

Usually, political and policy discourse is framed as an exercise in problem solving, as an effort to find lasting solutions to problems that often are posed in technical terms. In the rapidly changing environment of the information society, however, the lifetime of those particular "solutions" is likely to be short. In that environment, we need to focus more on strengthening the ongoing learning process, by which we construct shared mental maps, shared values, objectives and frameworks of interpretation, in the context of which a wide range of players then can devise a continuing succession of more particular solutions:

> It seems to me that one of the real failures of our political system, in the current context, is that everything seems to be solution-driven. This contrasts with the situation in some Asian countries, for example, where they know that they are dealing with constant change, and that there's no such thing as a once-and-for-all solution.... The learning society really needs to be based on the assumption of continuing change, one that recognizes that the only sustainable, competitive advantage in that changing environment is the capacity to learn.
>
> ∗ ∗ ∗ [61]
>
> I agree, we tend to focus too much on the solution and not enough on the ongoing learning process. The focus on solutions, and the underlying assumption that solutions last, devalues the learning process.

60 Some suggested that relatively small Parliamentary reforms could have significant effects. A number of examples were cited, many of which already are underway. These included, referring Bills to Committee after first reading (that is before there is a vote approving the Bill in principle), and enabling Parliament to conduct hearings and consultations prior to the presentation of a Budget.

61 The row of asterisks indicates the division between one speaker and the next.

How to strengthen that process of public learning and consensus-building, as a key infrastructure for a learning society and for constructing social cohesion across our diverse communities in the information age, became the focus of our next roundtable.

Building Consensus:
The Art of Coming to Public Judgement

We invited Daniel Yankelovich,[62] Elly Alboim[63] and David Cameron[64] to lead our exploration of the process of building social consensus in the information age.

As the number of players and the range of perspectives that need to be taken into account multiply in the information society, we no longer can take social consensus and shared values for granted, but need continually to construct them. That construction requires a much greater degree of public participation in the

---

62 Daniel Yankelovich, a leader in the development of public opinion research, is the founder of Yankelovich, Skelly and White, the Chairman both of DYG, Inc. and of WSY, Inc., and the founder and President of the Public Agenda Foundation. Previously he was a Professor at New York University and was on the Graduate Faculty of the New School for Social Research. Mr. Yankelovich is the author of numerous books and articles on issues of governance and public opinion, the most recent of which is *Coming to Public Judgement: Making Democracy Work in a Complex World* (Syracuse: Syracuse University Press, 1991).

63 Elly Alboim is a principal of the Earncliffe Strategy Group. Prior to that he was, for many years, National Political Editor and Parliamentary Bureau Chief for CBC Television News. Mr. Alboim also is a founding member and Director of the Canadian Journalism Foundation, and teaches in the School of Journalism at Carleton University.

64 David Cameron is Professor of Political Science at the University of Toronto, and Special Constitutional Advisor to the Premier of Ontario. He also served, in the Ontario Government, as Deputy Minister of Intergovernmental Affairs, and as the Ontario Representative to the Government of Québec. Prior to that Dr. Cameron served as Director of Research for the Pépin-Robarts Task Force on Canadian Unity and, in the Government of Canada, as Assistant Secretary to the Cabinet for Strategic and Constitutional Planning, and as Assistant Undersecretary of State for Education Support.

governance process, a more extensive ongoing process of public learning. But our current institutions, our leaders, our political culture and our conceptual models, Daniel Yankelovich told us, are not very well equipped for that task:[65]

> Our governance system mainly is one of representative democracy, which implies that the electorate holds those who govern accountable for results after the fact. In this model, the people do not have to be involved in formulating the decision, they just have to be ready to throw the rascals out if they don't like the results. Our institutions, and our conceptual models of communications with the public, reflect this limited involvement of the people, which is a premise of representative democracy.

Yankelovich identified two more traditional models of communicating with the public, in which most of us are trained and to which we tend to resort automatically:

- the PR-persuasion model, where policy makers arrive at decisions and then devote time and effort to figuring out how best to sell it to the public;
- the public-education model, where policy makers and experts realize the public isn't sufficiently aware of a threat or an opportunity, and spend time and effort bringing the public up to speed.

These more traditional models, he said, pre-suppose that the public has nothing positive to contribute to the formulation of policy or the framing of problems. The resulting communication essentially is one-way – the leader is persuading the followers, or the expert is educating the public. The communicator is active and the audience is passive. Yankelovich argued that while, for the majority of issues, the more traditional models of persuasion and education still are applicable, for the most important issues they

---

65 For a more detailed treatment of many of the points raised by Daniel Yankelovich, see his paper in Part II of this volume.

no longer will suffice.[66] For those issues Yankelovich proposed a "public judgement model," in which:

> ... communication is two-way. The emphasis is on resolving conflicting values rather than on imparting information. In the public judgement model, the public is assumed to have something positive to contribute to formulating policy choices and to framing the issues. So the model doesn't imply that policy makers define the issue, define the options, propose the policies and the public simply says yea or nay. Instead, the public voice is constitutive of the process itself, it is central to formulating policies. In the public judgement model, communication is not achieved in real time, but with immense lags to allow time to work through, and to deal with the kinds of issues that are raised by conflicting values.

The Public-judgement Model

Yankelovich stressed two characteristics of the public judgement model. First, the model is grounded in the empirical finding that there are gradations of public opinion, ranging from raw opinion at one extreme to public judgement at the other. "Raw opinion is composed of first reactions, spontaneous, impulsive,

---

66 Yankelovich noted that the traditional models continue to be valid in circumstances, for example, when:
  • public interest is low and people don't have a direct stake in an issue;
  • policy decisions are made within a framework of set principles and where risks appear to be low;
  • there are no serious conflicts of values involved.
These traditional models are not adequate, he suggested, when:
  • citizens feel they have a right to a say and insist upon it (for example, when citizens are being asked to make a sacrifice);
  • consensus hinges on resolving conflicts of values;
  • public mistrust, and the stakes, are very high.
These circumstances are becoming more common in the information society, where shared values seldom can be taken for granted, and where the number of players demanding a voice in the governance process continue to multiply.

unconsidered, top-of-the mind, incoherent views. Public judgement, on the other hand, is thoughtful, considerate, considered and firm."[67]

Second, the public-judgement model is rooted in the empirical finding that public opinion evolves in stages:

- the first is people becoming aware of an issue;
- the second is developing a sense of urgency about it, and framing it in a way that leads to a sense of urgency;
- the third is a search for solutions and the first reactions to possible solutions;
- the fourth, which is the most interesting and the one that is least understood, is dealing with people's resistances to the solutions that come to the fore, and the ways of confronting these resistances;
- the fifth is what Yankelovich calls "choice work," that is where people have choices to deal with and do the hard work of wrestling with those choices;

67 Yankelovich noted that it is difficult to differentiate the two by simple inspection, because people tend to insist on having an opinion on any subject, whether or not they have thought about it, or whether or not they know anything about it. But there are three tests that can be applied to determine whether expressed views are closer to the raw opinion or the public judgement ends of the spectrum:
- Determine volatility. With raw opinion, people's views tend to differ every time you ask a question. If you change the wording slightly you get a different answer.
- Search for contradictions and compartmentalized thinking. With raw opinion people often have two views in different compartments of their mind. If you are talking about protectionism, for example, when they think about preserving jobs people will be for it, but when they think about costs to them as consumers, they will be against it. And they won't perceive the compartmentalization and the contradiction unless it is pointed out.
- Determine the extent to which people are conscious of the consequences of their own views and accept responsibility for them. If you point out those consequences to people and they say "oh, I didn't realize that" and change their view, then you are dealing with the raw opinion end of the spectrum. On the other hand, if they say "yes, I understand that and accept it," you are dealing with something much closer to public judgement.

- the sixth is where people make up their minds intellectually;
- the seventh is final acceptance of that resolution in emotional and moral terms.

For democracy to work successfully, Yankelovich argued, there must be a critical mass of public judgement on key issues. About 70 per cent of the electorate need to have thought through a position and endorsed it. Not many issues have made it to the stage of public judgement, and there are a great many issues where the public is stuck somewhere between raw opinion and public judgement. A principal reason for that is that we lack important institutions necessary for the process of coming to public judgement:

> I think that our current institutions are well geared to the beginning and the end of the seven-stage process, but not to the middle. I think the press and other institutions do a superb job of raising consciousness and of creating awareness. But what they do is get the public agitated and aroused, and then move on to another issue just when people are ready to engage an issue. They move on because they see their role as creating awareness.
>
> There also is a tendency, in our current institutions, to leap from the awareness stage to the stage of legislation and resolution, skipping all of the steps in between. We need to build institutions that help people to work through these choices, these intermediate stages.

The development of such institutions and practices to enable people to "work through" issues came to be seen, by members of the roundtable, as one of the important social adaptations we need to make if we are to build a learning society, and to govern ourselves effectively in the information age.

The Importance of "Working Through"

The public-judgement model, Yankelovich emphasized, is not about elite accommodation and the brokering of agreements among interest groups. The public-judgement model is about engaging the broader public in a search for common ground, for consensus.[68]

Fundamentally, coming to public judgement is about dialogue: Martin Buber defined dialogue as "a process where both participants' lives were changed through the dialogue. If you have a dialogue between I and Thou, both lives are changed," in a way that is unlikely to happen in a process of bargaining about interests. Ideology and interests play a more reduced role in that process than they do in more traditional, political exercises of elite accommodation. We need to develop institutions that are designed to help people to engage in such dialogue, to "work through" key issues, and to form public judgement.

One example mentioned by Yankelovich had to do with affirmative-action programs in the U.S.:

> If you look at an issue like affirmative action, on the surface it looks irreconcilable, and political leaders have assumed that it is an untouchable issue. But, if you dig beneath the surface, you find that the reason Blacks are so pro-affirmative action is because they are convinced that, without it, an unqualified white could get the job. And Whites are against affirmative action because they believe that it will lead to an unqualified Black getting the job. What is interesting is that there is a shared belief that the best qualified person should get the job, and that core belief is something we can work with. It's a common ground on which there is a possibility of building a shared judgement....
>
> It's an extraordinary fact that Blacks and Whites do not talk to each other. But if you bring Blacks and Whites together, in a focus group, while they begin by being very mistrustful and dancing around each other, if you stay with it long enough, they gradually begin to talk to one another. And, as they talk to one another, you

68 The few institutions we do have that are intended to permit people to "work through" issues, Yankelovich told us, are designed to serve elites. The public simply are not effectively engaged in that process, and so do not get a chance to work through the issues and to reach the necessary level of public judgement.

get a change that is palpable, and they leave that brief encounter with a different point of view.

A roundtable member recalled a comparable experience during the series of weekend fora on the Constitution, which were organized among a wide range of Canadians leading up to the Charlottetown Accord, but noted that experience also raised a fundamental question of scale:

> You wouldn't believe the electricity in the air in that Conference. But in a few days it all dissipated, and it wasn't effectively transmitted into the broader process or to the rest of the country. So there's a real question of how we scale-up from small meetings, or focus groups, to the broader kind of consensus building we are discussing.

Yankelovich agreed that we need to learn more about ways of moving from the scale of smaller groups, to the scale of broader public judgement. He cited one example of a Congressional debate that apparently had succeeded in fostering such a wider process of public judgement. This example also seemed to speak to the concern we had raised at our previous roundtable about how the operations of political institutions might be modified to foster public learning:

> Before the U.S. entered the war in the Gulf, there was a very different kind of Congressional debate. Instead of Congresspeople using their background as lawyers to present an adversarial case, they agonized in public, airing their concerns and enunciating the shades of gray that led them to their conclusions. The public was able to identify with that process in a way they never could have identified had there been a "lawyerly" debate. That sort of Congressional process enabled people to participate in what amounted to a surrogate experience, and it is well worth studying what works, and what doesn't work, in creating that sort of proxy experience. What kind of symbolic interaction, presented in a

television debate or some other format, can help people to work through the issues?

Another way in which the process of coming to public judgement, and especially working through the intermediate stages, can be facilitated is through skillful political leadership. The challenge for those leaders is to recognize the stage of development of a particular issue and to respond appropriately. Problems arise when issues get stuck at a particular stage, and that is when the intervention of political leaders can be most helpful.[69]

Some roundtable members questioned the degree to which the public really is interested in being involved in such an effort. People have busy lives, they noted, and simply don't have the time, or often the interest, to be so fully engaged. Yankelovich agreed that the process of coming to public judgement is not

---

69 Yankelovich mentioned three such points at which the time delays tend to be the longest:

> The first hang-up occurs when people are aware of a problem, but don't feel a sense of urgency about it. The reason for that usually is that they don't connect the issue to something important in their lives. That can go on for years, but you can move it to the next stage in a matter of weeks by making the connection. That's what Ross Perot managed to do on the deficit issue.
>
> The second hang-up is when people resist confronting the hard choices that need to be made, when they deny that those choices are necessary. That's the "waste, fraud and abuse" syndrome. You know, we can have all the spending we want without raising taxes so long as we just eliminate waste, fraud and abuse. This can hang up issues for years, and what is needed is to confront people with the issue in a way that sobers them up, shows them that the easy choices are not available. Then they are ready to move on.
>
> The third point that can hang up the process is when the choices with which people are confronted are either too narrow or inadequate or not really formulated as choices. By intervening intelligently at these three points of the process, it is possible to take an issue, that otherwise might hang around for decades, and deal with it in a period of perhaps six months to two years. To do that, we need to establish urgency, confront the wishful thinking resistance, and formulate the choices well.

needed, or appropriate, for some issues. At the same time, he cautioned, when it comes to the most important issues, public interest is real, and public involvement is essential to a legitimate and effective outcome:

> I think it is the case that [people] don't want to be involved in technical issues. They don't understand them, they get impatient with them, and their feeling is that this is something that we pay other people to take care of for us. But on issues like the budget deficit and the like, I think we are dealing with a different kind of resistance that needs a different kind of response. Very often we have the experience, in conducting focus groups and bringing up a complex subject like the deficit, that there is a bit of squirming in the room and finally someone says 'well, you know, this may be a case of mistaken identity, we're not the experts.' Once you reassure people that we know they are not the experts, that it isn't a case of mistaken identity, and that we really want to hear their views, there is such an outpouring that you cannot get away from it.
>
> So I would not be put off by early manifestations of wishful thinking, of unrealism, of feeling 'who me, why are you asking me these questions?' The desire to be involved, to be part of the decision-making process that affects our own destiny, is so powerful, it's one of the most powerful human feelings. And, most often, the detachment, mistrust, aloofness, cynicism, and so on that we are seeing on the part of the public is an angry reaction to not being involved, to not being consulted with genuine sincerity.

Navigating Some Obstacles to Public Judgement

Elly Alboim suggested that there are a number of deeper obstacles to the process of consensus building. Principal among these is the role played currently by the media, which Alboim described as becoming progressively more destructive as we move to the later phases of the process of coming to public judgement:

That is because journalists have begun to arrogate to themselves a function that was never contemplated for them, they've begun to take on the job of representing the electorate in the process of decision making and of establishing choices. They are doing this because they find that it sells, and that reflects the increasingly commercial priorities that drive journalism. To further increase their sales, the press seek to pose as the representatives of the people. They do that in a system where cynicism and distrust of central institutions is rampant and, to cater to that, they articulate that distrust and cynicism, they expand on it. They seek to portray themselves as adversarial agents against those central institutions. Their reward is that it builds circulation and yields viewership and builds financial returns.

That role played by the media, he suggested, and the ways in which the media tend to frame issues and to tell stories, devalue and obscure the learning process on which the formation of public judgement depends:

The news media in this country also have great difficulty finding an appropriate framework in which to present the views of ordinary people.... Journalists continue to seek to frame issues in terms of the narrative, dramatic model, so that if it doesn't have a personality base, a conflict, and a clear conclusion, it does not count as a news story worthy of mention. Most stories are selected on the basis of how they fit the narrative model, not on the basis of their intrinsic importance for national discussion.

So news people take what appear to be genuine attempts to have these kinds of debates, to form public judgement and consensus, and redefine them into their narrative framework. The result is that they begin to intrude on Dan's stage six, because they transform the available choices into a much narrower set, those that involve winners and losers on a personality basis. In addition, in their search for clear conclusion, they militate against the kind of thoughtful slow process that often is required.

Yankelovich acknowledged the destructive potential of the media, when they operate in the fashion that Alboim had described, but suggested that the media also can be a powerful ally in the process of building public judgement:

> I think it would be the worst mistake in the world to accept the pretensions of the media to represent the public. Journalists, as a group, are very remote from the public, they live in their own culture and talk mostly to each other, reinforcing each other's craziness. The media is a powerful institution that flows into any available vacuum. I think it is the responsibility of other leadership groups not to provide vacuums into which the media can flow in ways that would distort the political process. At the same time, I have found that, if you can get the idea of forming public judgement across to the media, and help them to understand how they can contribute to that, they will be very responsive. We need to find ways of engaging the media more constructively in that process.

Alboim underlined a number of other basic obstacles to the formation of public judgement in Canada. He noted that we seem to have developed an antipathy to conciliation on a variety of fronts, and speculated that Canadians interested in consensus building and reconciliation now comprise considerably less than a majority of the population. Moreover, in a country as geographically scattered as Canada, and with a tendency for different cultural groups to live in separate communities, there are great impediments to the sort of face-to-face interaction that can build shared perspectives and mutual understanding. The media reinforce those geographic and cultural cleavages, he argued, because no news organization believes it has a mandate to define news items as important beyond what its readership or viewers want to see. So the media panders to its local audience and, in so doing, creates idiosyncratic news and information agendas from region to region. As a result, we lack the shared awareness that is a basic pre-condition for building national public judgement. At an even more basic level, Alboim added:

A very important impediment to the kind of dialogue that would be needed to form public judgement is that it would require us to face (to unmask) a number of feelings and emotions that we have denied having. Canada has prided itself on not having feelings of racism, feelings of threat by immigration and multiculturalism, an unwillingness to accept the century-old compact on equalization, or an unwillingness to subsidize Canadians to remain where they are in outposts in Newfoundland or wherever. Now, we all intuitively sense that we no longer are willing to bear those costs, but we're not sure we are prepared for open discussions that would unmask those social cleavages and make us reassess our own sense of identity as Canadians, and whether, in fact, that identity exists after all.

Several roundtable members challenged the bleak picture painted by Alboim, and Yankelovich suggested an alternative interpretation:

[Elly Alboim] describes a culture that may not have core common values and, lacking such core common values, may not have the basis for compromise or conciliation. That is one hypothesis, but there's another hypothesis that would account for the same phenomena. The second hypothesis is that there is a core of shared values, but there's an overlay of cynicism, of mistrust, of disillusionment that is reinforced on an almost daily basis by the media (fanning the flames, presenting false choices too early, or in the wrong way, or in an oversimplified way, or in an adversarial way).

David Cameron added that there is considerable evidence that Canadians do have a set of shared core values, and suggested that the best way to build public judgement, on that shared-value base, would be by focusing on more concrete issues:

... most of the studies with which I'm familiar suggest that, with respect to many of the ways of being (and existing) in the contemporary world, Canadians share most basic values. There is a common denominator of shared conviction and values that is quite evident across the country.

While, on the one hand, we do have those shared values, on the other hand we have very deep social cleavages, and the one that is perhaps most important, and most dangerous to our existence, is the cleavage defined by language.... Perhaps the best way to address a profound social cleavage, whether French/English or Black/White, is to try to address it concretely, to tie it to specifics, to the practical and to the immediate. One of the ways in which the leadership of this country (not just the politicians, but the broader elites) may not have served us well, is by permitting discussion relating to the French/English cleavage to ascend to heights where it has become almost purely symbolic. That symbolic conflict, and the way it has been played out in this country recently, has become a zero-sum game, and that's the trap into which we've allowed ourselves to fall.

The reason I feel some optimism is that I think a free society is based ultimately on will, the will that is expressed through countless daily acts. I think there is real potential for this country to assert itself in ways that do not involve the joining of issues at a level, and in a format, where they cannot be resolved.... If we join those issues at a symbolic level in a moment of high heat and passion, the probability of failure is high. But if we avoid that, and find some way of managing our way through and dealing with issues at a more concrete level, I think there may be real hope for the future.

Yankelovich agreed that when an issue takes on a kind of symbolic absolutism, it is important to find ways to de-escalate it:

In the words of diplomacy, when you have that kind of cleavage grow up, you can't deal with the basic issues all at once, so you need to begin by introducing confidence-building measures that rebuild the foundation for discussion.... So, I think that there might be value in thinking about modest confidence-building steps, searching for where there might be common ground, and building possibilities for individuals, on each side, to talk to each other, perhaps around more concrete questions.

Do we want those dialogues to develop into a genuine process of forming public judgement? If so, Yankelovich emphasized, we need to pay careful attention to how they are designed:

> ... there are at least 19 wrong ways of conducting a town meeting for every right way. And I think we've been working our way systematically through all the wrong ways. So we have forms of consultation that are pro forma, forms of consultation that give people an opportunity to sound off their grievances, to express their opinions in a thoughtless way.
>
> The best dialogues are when you have good choices, and you can force people to focus on those choices. When you can do that, the discipline and responsibility of dealing with the choices has an almost magical effect. People get much more constructive as they wrestle with the issues, they listen and they are thoughtful. One typical result of those kinds of dialogues, that surprised me initially, is that support for all of the choices may diminish. What I think that indicates is that people are becoming more sober about the downsides of all of the alternatives, they are seeing the negatives, they don't see it as all black or all white, and so they move to a more realistic appreciation and a resolution.

Yankelovich went on to propose that the scenarios we had been constructing in the project could provide a very valuable basis for such a public judgement process, and urged us to think about using them in that way:

> I think your scenarios contain those kinds of real choices; for example, whether the people will accept a society that is a little bit fairer as opposed to a society where they may be richer in the aggregate, but where there are huge disparities. This is a proper subject for engaging people, and I think it would fascinate the average citizen to be engaged in that kind of discussion. It's not

above people, it's not over their heads. You may have to find a language for discussing it that is a bit different from the set of abstractions that would be appropriate among professional intellectuals, but these are exactly the sorts of questions about which people are very thoughtful, and about which they have views. I hope that you will think of ways of presenting those scenarios in a language that people can engage.

Conclusions

The scenarios had provided us with a new mental map of how the information society might reshape the environment for governance in the coming decade. That map indicated to us that the only routes to a future that seemed desirable (the worlds described in the *Starship* and *Windjammer* scenarios) depended on there being a high degree of social cohesion.

Amid the rapidly changing environment of the information society, social cohesion needs continually to be constructed. That construction requires individuals and institutions continually to learn together, in order to build shared values and frameworks of interpretation, reduce disparities and other impediments to the creation of a more cohesive society, and generally build the sense that we are engaged in a common enterprise, facing shared challenges, and that we are members of the same community.[70] In short, constructing social cohesion, in this turbulent environment, involves constructing a learning society. But a learning society, in this sense, means something more fundamental than the narrower uses of that term that now are becoming commonplace.

We explored, in a preliminary way, a number of essential requirements for creating such a learning society. In that process

70 Nor should social cohesion be confused with social uniformity or "groupthink." Instead, cohesion builds on diversity, and involves constructing a sufficiently shared framework within which those from very different backgrounds, and often with very different interests, can debate, resolve disputes and innovate.

we came to realize that no one has "the answer," there are no blue-prints. Building that society itself will involve a process of public learning of a high order. It will involve enhancing the learning capacity both of individuals and of social institutions. That will include finding better ways to support the healthy development of children, and to encourage lifelong learning. Perhaps even more important, it will involve basic changes in how we organize and govern ourselves, moving away from vertical, bureaucratic structures, and toward more horizontal, network structures, in which:

- the authority to make decisions, and to innovate, is widely distributed;
- the network can reorganize itself flexibly to deal with a rapidly changing environment;
- the proceeds of the work of the organization or society are distributed more equitably among its members so that they continue to participate and to contribute fully;
- the whole is held together by rich communication and a shared framework of overall goals and values.

But how can we construct such shared frameworks of overall goals and values, such shared mental maps, from among the increasingly numerous, diverse and often conflicting perspectives of the communities that make up our society in the information age? In our first report we had concluded that government has a key role to play in leading the process by which those shared frameworks are constructed. Now, we examined, in some detail, one promising approach for doing that: the "public-judgement" model of consensus building.

The public-judgement model is not about elite accommodation and the brokering of agreements, it is about engaging the wider public in defining issues and options, dialoguing, deliberating, and searching for common ground, for consensus. It focuses on the process whereby people "work through" issues, moving from a stage of raw opinion to one of considered public judgement. Currently we have few institutions or practices designed to enable people to work through issues in that way. We came to see the development of such institutions and practices as one of the important social adaptations we need to make if we are to build a learning society, and to govern ourselves effectively in the information age.

5 Continuing the Process: Building a Learning Society

TOO OFTEN, AS WE NOTED EARLIER, political and policy discourses are framed as exercises in problem solving, as an effort to
find lasting solutions to problems that frequently are posed in
technical terms. In the rapidly changing environment of the
information society, however, the lifetime of those particular
solutions is likely to be short. In that environment, we need to
focus more on strengthening the ongoing learning process by
which we construct shared mental maps, shared values, objectives
and frameworks of interpretation, in the context of which a wide
range of players then can devise a continuing succession of more
particular solutions. Building such a process, based on the work
begun by the project, is the subject of this concluding chapter.

We begin by summarizing briefly the course we have followed
so far and, in that context, outline a body of path-breaking
research, encountered late in the project, which added an important dimension to our own learning. Then, we sketch a preliminary agenda of policy and institutional initiatives that we hope
can provide a focus, together with the scenarios, for a broader
dialogue, designed to widen and deepen the learning process
begun by the project. Finally, we offer some reflections on the
value and limitations of the process we have undertaken, and suggest some next steps to encourage that broader dialogue.

Summary: Reviewing the Course We Have Followed So Far

We concluded our first report by noting that the challenges, and
the implications for governance, of the transition to a global
information society, are even more basic and far-reaching than

we had at first imagined. As society becomes more interconnected, splintered, complex and turbulent, more traditional ways of organizing and governing are being overwhelmed. In a more interconnected, information-rich environment, governing systems predicated on a limited flow of information, including both bureaucracy and representative democracy itself, lose their credibility and authority. Unless those systems can adjust themselves to the realities of the information society, that process of overload and fragmentation, which we are witnessing in Canada and around the world, will continue and will accelerate:

> ... the nature of the system has changed so much that government, as it has operated in the past, simply cannot cope with the complexity of the information society, and so its role needs to be rethought....

* * *

In some areas the role of government may be becoming irrelevant, while in others that role is changing dramatically. For example, look at the billions of dollars that are traded everyday on computers. There is a massive capital movement going on between countries all around the world. What Department of Finance can hang on to that?

To deal with that more rapidly changing environment will require fundamental innovation, and the development of more learning-based approaches to how we organize and govern ourselves:

> What is becoming increasingly clear, as societies become more interconnected, as the boundaries between organizations, economic sectors and states shift and diminish, and as the number of players in the process of governance multiply, is that we need to invest more time and attention in developing a shared understanding of where we want to go, in a more systematic process of agenda setting. Such a shared framework is the essential context that can allow the multiplying players in the governance process

mutually to coordinate their actions. The development and continual evolution of that strategic framework, of that learning environment, is central to effective governance and leadership in the information society.[71]

The second phase of this project has been organized as an experiment in constructing shared frameworks, shared mental models, using a scenario approach. One of the realities of the information society is that our existing mental models seem to map less and less adequately the world of our experience.

In a time when the world changed relatively slowly, when we had little contact with those from very different cultures, we were able to take our mental maps for granted, to assume they were the only way in which the world could be perceived. That no longer is tenable in a world of instantaneous communication, widespread and rapid travel, globalized markets, more educated and demanding populations, proliferating information, social fragmentation, and rapidly changing products, organizations and societies.

Now, we are confronted by individuals who look at the same data through the lens of their own framework of interpretation (developed in a different culture or sub-culture) and see a different reality. And we are confronted by accelerating change that can make any single perspective (any single mental map) obsolete, and an impediment to perception and to learning.

We use our mental maps (our frameworks) to construct the reality that we perceive. Those maps tell us what to pay attention to and what to ignore, what is information and what is noise. We use them to screen out information that does not fit our world view, and we use them to fill in the blanks when we have only fragmentary data. Rohrsach tests are based on this insight, we see patterns in the ink blots, patterns that we construct using our frameworks of interpretation and, in so doing, we reveal often telling aspects about the frameworks that we use. It takes very little data (very little sensory input) for us to be able to spin out quite detailed stories, to construct quite detailed realities.

71 Rosell, op. cit., 94.

That reality-constructing process bears the seeds both of a tremendous capacity to learn and of irreconcilable conflict. When we converse with others, particularly those from quite different world views, the challenge is to find ways to construct a shared reality within which we can communicate and learn from each other. The risk, if we fail, is that we will end up in escalating misunderstanding as we seek to defend our separately created worlds.

To thrive in the more diverse, rapidly changing environment of the information society, we need to be able to see more patterns, to have access to more mental maps, to more lenses through which we can see. We need to learn how to communicate better with those coming from very different perspectives and cultures, who see different patterns in the same flow, and learn how to use those differences to enhance our understanding, to create a stereoscopic view.

Scenario construction can help in that effort. It is a methodology for creating alternative mental maps that we can use to broaden our perception, to try out different perspectives, and to provide a shared context and language for decision making.

Drawing on the perspectives provided by the resource persons at our first several roundtables, as well as on our own views and experience, we constructed a different map, four scenarios, of how the realities of the information society might reshape the environment for governance over the next decade. Throughout the project, and in constructing these scenarios, our intent was not to describe all of the various factors that might affect the process of governance, but rather to focus specifically on the fundamental challenges, for how we govern ourselves, created by the emergence of a global information society:

> In all of this it is important to be clear that we are not constructing scenarios...that are intended to deal with all aspects of governance in Canada or anywhere else. Our focus, from the outset, has been on the implications of the information society for governance.... Fundamentally, in the information society, what we are seeing is a change in the ways in which work can be organized, and in the

ways in which ideas can be organized, which probably is as dramatic as what occurred with the industrial revolution. The scenarios are an attempt to anticipate the alternative possible directions in which a society might evolve as a consequence of that fundamental set of changes. Seeing the governance challenge from this new direction, and working through some of its implications more systematically, is a principal value of this project in my view.

We used two key uncertainties to differentiate those scenarios: whether or not there would be a new secular economic boom, and whether or not we would be able to find ways to construct social cohesion in the information society. The first scenario, which we named *Starship,* envisioned a world characterized by a secular economic boom, coupled with the development of new social consensus. The second scenario, named *Titanic,* was the other extreme, with low or no economic growth coupled with growing social fragmentation. The third scenario, christened *HMS Bounty,* combined a booming economy with continued social fragmentation and polarization, while the fourth scenario, named *Windjammer,* envisioned new social consensus emerging around a low or no-growth economy (at least as conventionally measured):

		Windjammer	Starship
SOCIETY	*New Social Consensus*	Windjammer	Starship
	Social Fragmentation	Titanic	HMS Bounty
		Low/No Growth	*New Secular Boom*

ECONOMY
(as conventionally measured)

We then began to use those scenarios as a shared map to guide our exploration. One thing that this map helped to bring into sharper focus was the importance of social cohesion. It was possible for us to design a relatively desirable scenario even if we did not postulate a new economic boom, but we were not able to come up with a scenario in which any of us would want to live if we did not postulate success in building social cohesion. So we decided to concentrate the next stage of our work on the requirements for building social cohesion in the information society.

In this rapidly changing environment, we concluded, social cohesion needs continually to be constructed. We need continually to learn together, as we build shared values and frameworks of interpretation, reduce disparities and other impediments to the creation of a more cohesive society, and generally build the sense that we are engaged in a common enterprise, are facing shared challenges, and that we are members of the same community. In other words, constructing social cohesion, in this turbulent environment, requires that we enhance our learning capacity and build a learning society.

Building a Learning Society: Re-balancing Economic and Social Concerns

Constructing a learning society, in this sense, itself will involve a process of public learning of a high order. There are no blueprints. It will include learning how to support the healthy development of children and how to encourage lifelong learning. Equally important, it will involve learning how to organize and govern ourselves in a manner that moves away from vertical, bureaucratic structures and toward more horizontal, network structures in which:

- the authority to make decisions, and to innovate, is widely distributed;
- the network(s) can reorganize itself flexibly to deal with a rapidly changing environment;
- the proceeds of the work of the organization or society are distributed more equitably among its members so that they continue to participate and to contribute fully;

- the whole is held together by rich communication and a shared framework of overall goals and values.

At its most basic, though, the construction of a learning society will need to be based on a different understanding of the relationship between the social and the economic. Late in the project, we encountered a body of path-breaking research that helped us to see this.[72] Most influential, perhaps, was the work of Robert Putnam.[73]

Putnam and his colleagues have spent more than 20 years on an in-depth study of political and economic development in Italy. Their work, although published only recently, already has been hailed widely as a classic, and has been compared favourably, for its insight and importance, with that of de Tocqueville. A principal conclusion of their study is that there is one reliable predictor of both political and economic success. That critical factor is the existence of norms of reciprocity and networks of civic engagement, a dense interlocking web of horizontal associations that they term "social capital." Putnam cites the work of James Coleman in defining social capital:

> Like other forms of capital, social capital is productive, making possible the achievement of certain ends that would not be attainable in its absence.... For example, a group whose members manifest trustworthiness and place extensive trust in one another will be able to accomplish much more than a comparable group lacking that trustworthiness and trust.... In a farming community... where one farmer got his hay baled by another and where farm

---

72 See, for example, D.C. North, *Institutions, Institutional Change and Economic Performance* (New York: Cambridge University Press, 1990); E. Ostrom, *Governing the Commons: The Evolution of Institutions for Collective Action* (New York, Cambridge University Press, 1990); J. Parr, "Civic Infrastructure," *National Civic Review* (Spring 1993); and R.D. Putnam, *Making Democracy Work* (Princeton: Princeton University Press, 1993a). A good, earlier statement of many of these points can be found in F. Hirsch, *The Social Limits to Growth* (Cambridge: Harvard University Press, 1976).

73 Putnam, 1993a, op. cit.

tools are extensively borrowed and lent, the social capital allows each farmer to get his work done with less physical capital in the form of tools and equipment.[74]

After studying a wide range of possible explanations for why some regional governments in Italy were working, while others failed, Putnam concludes that the only variable that appears to explain that variance to any significant degree is the presence or absence of social capital:

What best predicted good government in the Italian regions was choral societies, soccer clubs and cooperatives. In other words, some regions...of Italy have a rich network of community associations. Their citizens are engaged by public issues and take an active role in politics. They trust one another to act fairly and obey the law. Social and political networks here are organized horizontally, not hierarchically. In these "civic" communities democracy works. At the other pole are the "uncivic" regions, where the very concept of citizenship is stunted. Engagement in social and cultural associations is meager, and the social structure is hierarchical. Public affairs is someone else's business, not mine. Laws are made to be broken, and people live in fear. Trapped by these vicious circles, nearly everyone feels exploited and unhappy – and democracy fails.[75]

Even more striking, Putnam and his colleagues also found that social capital was the only reliable predictor of economic success:

... if we draw a map of Italy in 1993 according to wealth, we will find that communities with many choral societies are also more advanced economically. I originally thought that these fortunate communities had more choral societies because they were

---

74 J.S. Coleman, *Foundations of Social Theory* (Cambridge: Harvard University Press, 1990), 302, 304, 307.

75 R.D. Putnam, "What Makes Democracy Work?" *National Civic Review* (Spring, 1993b), 101–2.

wealthy. After all, I thought, poor peasants don't have time or energy to spend singing. But if we look closely at the historical record, it becomes clear that I had it exactly backwards. Communities don't have choral societies because they are wealthy; they are wealthy because they have choral societies – or more precisely, the traditions of engagement, trust and reciprocity that choral societies symbolize.

Of two equally poor Italian regions a century ago, both very backward, but one with more civic engagement and the other with a hierarchical structure, the one with more choral societies and soccer clubs has grown steadily wealthier. The more civic region has prospered because trust and reciprocity were woven into its social fabric.... Wealth is the consequence, not the cause of a healthy civics.[76]

Putnam summarizes the basic thesis in this way:

... social capital, as embodied in horizontal networks of civic engagement, bolsters the performance of the polity and the economy, rather than the reverse: Strong society, strong economy; strong society, strong state.[77]

Putnam also emphasizes that social capital is created primarily at the local level, "... in our communities by renewing our civic connections."[78] And the construction, or destruction, of such

---

76 Ibid, 105–6.
77 Putnam, 1993a, 176.
78 Putnam, 1993b, 107. To illustrate that, Putnam tells the story of a poor neighbourhood in Costa Rica which, while no wealthier than its neighbours, is both safer and more pleasant, and has taken effective measures to reduce the level of crime endemic to the area. It managed to do this by establishing a strong sense of neighbourhood solidarity (a form of social capital) through the use of a practice called "the law of the greeting." This was an agreement, among members of the community, that everyone would leave for work five minutes early to have the time to say "hello" to each of his neighbours. This informal norm, Putnam says, soon built ties of friendship and mutual solidarity, which made it relatively easy to agree on practical crime-fighting steps. Putnam concludes that "the law of the greeting" represents investment in social capital in its very simplest form.

social capital is a self-reinforcing and cumulative process, forming virtuous or vicious circles:

> Virtuous circles result in social equilibria with high levels of coop-
> eration, trust, reciprocity, civic engagement and collective well-
> being. These traits define the civic community. Conversely, the
> absence of these traits in the *uncivic* community is also self-rein-
> forcing. Defection, distrust, shirking, exploitation, isolation, dis-
> order, and stagnation intensify one another in a suffocating
> miasma of vicious circles.[79]

We came to see this process, this virtuous circle of creating
social capital and a civic community, as being parallel to what we
meant by building social cohesion and a learning society. And, as
Putnam argued so persuasively, it is on that social process that
both economic prosperity and good governance depend.

The work of Putnam and others demonstrate that giving primary importance to building social capital, or social cohesion, is
in no way unique to the information age. What does seem to be
new in the information society, however, is the number, the diversity and (especially) the growing degree of interaction of those
primary communities within which such social capital, such
shared values, perspectives, sense of solidarity and trust, are constructed.

Now, more than ever before, as boundaries shift and blur,
people from different communities, often with very different and
even conflicting views of the world, need to find ways to live and to
work together. Building a civic community, and a learning society,
in the information age, will involve not only reinforcing the primary role of local communities, but also finding ways to develop
social capital and social cohesion across those communities.

One approach to doing that, which we examined in the course
of the project, was the public-judgement model of consensus
building. It provides a framework for understanding the process

---

79　Putnam, 1993a, 177.

by which a wider public, drawn from many different communities, can dialogue, deliberate, and work through issues to construct shared mental maps and to reach a considered public judgement. Today, we have too few institutions and practices designed to enable people from diverse communities to work through issues in that way. We came to see the development of such institutions and practices as one of the important social adaptations we need to make if we are to build a learning society, and to govern ourselves effectively in the information age.

Scenario building is one such practice, designed to enable diverse groups to construct shared mental maps. More generally, the project itself has been an example, in microcosm, of the process of working through. As the second phase of the project drew to a close, we concluded that we should try to continue and to broaden that process, to find ways to include a wider range of participants in an effort to work through these issues, focused around the scenarios.

As one step in that direction, we tried to define a very preliminary agenda of policy and institutional initiatives that might be considered to build social cohesion and a learning society (in other words, initiatives that might move us toward the worlds described in the *Starship* or *Windjammer* scenarios, and away from the worlds described in *Titanic* or *HMS Bounty*). Our hope was that this preliminary agenda, together with the scenarios, could be used to encourage a wider dialogue around these questions.

Continuing the Process: A Preliminary Agenda

To construct that preliminary agenda, we worked in the smaller groups we had established at the outset of the project. The small groups reported their progress periodically to the full roundtable. The intent of their work was not to develop comprehensive or final recommendations, but rather to suggest items that should be on the agenda for a wider dialogue.

In the project we have had a chance only to begin to define

these questions, and to begin to understand the terms in which they might be addressed. There are, in addition, a wide range of issues, that have come up in the course of our discussions, which we have not had the time, or resources, to address even in a cursory way. And, given the limitations of our own mental maps, there are many important questions that we do not yet have the understanding even to ask. We hope that many of these, too, will be defined and addressed in the wider dialogue we would like to encourage.

After reviewing the ideas and initiatives generated by the smaller groups, we agreed to recommend that the following questions especially should be on the agenda for further consideration in such a dialogue.

RENEWING THE SOCIAL CONTRACT

A first major agenda item might be to consider what revisions in our social contract are needed to deal with the changed world of the information age, and to build a learning society in that context. Learning inherently is a social process, and occurs in multiple and overlapping communities of interpretation or communities of practice:

> Learning ... essentially involves becoming an 'insider.' Learners do not receive or even construct abstract, 'objective,' individual knowledge; rather, they learn to function in a community – be it a community of nuclear physicists, cabinet makers, high school classmates, street-corner society.... They acquire that particular community's subjective viewpoint and learn to speak its language. In short, they are 'enculturated.' Learners are acquiring not explicit, formal 'expert knowledge,' but the embodied ability to behave as community members. For example, learners learn to tell and appreciate community-appropriate stories.... The central issue in learning is becoming a practitioner, not learning about practice.[80]

Central to constructing a learning society will be enabling people to participate in such learning communities. That theme of participation also is central to some recent work of the Organization for Economic Cooperation and Development which calls for the development of an "active society." Christopher Freeman outlined that OECD work to us:

> One of the new ways of thinking about these questions, that I find particularly appealing is in a recent report of the OECD which advocated the development of an 'active society.' That's a society that redefines full employment to take into account issues like women seeking work at different stages of their careers, or part-time employment, or the wish of many fathers of families to spend more time with young children, or the need for education and retraining throughout a lifetime, and so on. These are concerns that really are not well considered within our older concepts of unemployment. The idea of the active society is that while we can't guarantee the old concept of full employment, we should be able to guarantee the possibility of training or education, or employment or otherwise useful work for, and participation in, society; and that we ought to be able to ensure that people receive an adequate income in return. That seems to me to be a promising beginning to rethinking the social contract, which, for all the reasons we've been discussing, is so important.[81]

Such an active society (or learning society) implies a different social security system, one designed to ensure opportunities for lifetime learning, employment and service, and to provide a rea-

---

80 J.S. Brown and P. Duguid, "Organizational Learning and Communities-of-Practice" *Organization Science* (Vol. 2, 44–57, 1991). See also, for example, J.S. Brown, A. Collins and P. Duguid, "Situated Cognition and the Culture of Learning" *Education Researcher* (Vol. 18, 32–42, 1989); S.D.N. Cook and D. Yanow, "Culture and Organizational Learning" *Journal of Management Inquiry* (Vol. 2, 373–90, 1993); M. Douglas, *How Institutions Think* (Syracuse: University of Syracuse Press, 1986); J. Lave and E. Wenger, *Situated Learning* (New York: Cambridge University Press, 1990); J. Orr, "Sharing Knowledge," in D.S. Middleton and D. Edwards (eds), *Collective Remembering, Memory in Society* (Beverley Hills: Sage, 1990).

81 See, for example, *Labour Market Policies for the 1990s* (Paris: OECD, 1990).

sonable income for those individuals who make the effort to participate. There are many issues that such a system would need to address. For example, how can we strengthen the capacity of the family and of the schools to foster the healthy development (to strengthen the ability to learn) of the next generation? How can we encourage the development of a culture that values continuous learning, and provide opportunities for learning throughout life?[82] How can we remove barriers to participation, and provide people with the information and support they need to make choices about how best to participate?

More basically, such a system will need to be founded on a different understanding of the nature of employment and careers in the information society:

> ... traditional notions of jobs and careers are being replaced by the understanding that, in the new economy and society, periods of work and training and leisure alternate. We all will have to change jobs frequently and that will involve a capacity to learn of a very high order. It also will require changes in our institutions, and in our assumptions, so that we see periods out of the labour force, and in training or in cultural renewal or whatever, as part of a normal way of living. We are talking about a more fundamental process of social learning, and a more fundamental rebuilding of our social contract....

Such a social contract also raises important distributional issues. Building social cohesion and a learning society requires that we find ways to provide a reasonable distribution of the proceeds of that society to its members. Otherwise, people will not participate fully, and we shall end up drifting toward the world of increasing social polarization described in the *HMS Bounty* scenario (or worse). At the same time, we are reaching the limits of the tax/transfer system to address issues of redistribution. As a

---

82 One idea that roundtable members thought might be worth pursuing, in that regard, was the development of a "smart card," which would provide every citizen with credits that could be applied toward a wide variety of learning and retraining opportunities ("a ticket to relearn").

result, a variety of alternative approaches have been suggested to deal with the question of distribution. These include different ways to redistribute work,[83] different ways to encourage wider participation in capital ownership,[84] and more. How best can we address these distributional issues in the information society?

More broadly, this process of renewing the social contract will require that we provide at least a partial answer to a question that underlay many of our discussions; namely, to what extent must we be driven by the imperatives of the globalized marketplace, and to what extent can we make choices about the sort of society we wish to construct and sustain:

> One of the things this conversation underlines for me is the extent to which a lot of current discussion about competitiveness and the like assumes that globalization and economic imperatives are given. And obviously it's clear that globalization is a reality and one that constrains the degrees of freedom of any given nation-state. At the same time, though, we need to think more creatively about what we can do within those degrees of freedom we do have.
>
> One of the things we need to do, and have not done enough of, is to try to define some of the values, some of the things we want to do together, which go beyond some kind of global lowest common denominator. We need to recognize that how we do things together, in the information society, also is changing. The old "Fordist" idea of government, as a great big institution that does

83 Examples of proposals for the redistribution of work include a four-day work week, and policies to promote a variety of flexible work options, or at least to remove disincentives for those options (for example by providing benefits for part time workers).

84 As one roundtable member phrased this idea: "we need to become not only a learning society, but also a society of investors." One of the most articulate proponents of this is Louis Kelso, the originator of the Employee Stock Ownership Plan (ESOP), who contends that all citizens should be able to earn wages from capital, as well as from labour, in this increasingly capital-intensive economy. Kelso has suggested a range of specific proposals to that end, but we did not have a chance to examine them in the course of the project. See, for example, L.O. Kelso and P.H. Kelso, *Democracy and Economic Power* (Cambridge: Ballinger, 1986).

all sorts of things for people, is passé. What we're saying now is not that government is supposed to do everything and provide everything, but rather that it has a responsibility to provide people with the knowledge, with the skills, and with the support systems to make their own decisions, and to do so in a way that fosters the public interest. I think that's at the heart of the new social contract we're trying to develop.

FOCUSING ON VALUES

A second major item for the agenda might be to consider how we can foster a more effective public dialogue, focused at the level of values, about the governance issues we face. Any social contract (and any public policy) needs to reflect, and to be supported by, the values of that society, values that are shared across the communities of which that society is composed. The legitimacy and effectiveness of those policies depends on that value base.

The importance of shared values in the process of governance was underlined most effectively in a recent article by Charles Schultze.[85] Schultze argued that the major economic and social institutions of society cannot be made to work effectively simply through the laws, regulations, social policies and monetary incentives that govern them. Rather, to work, they require that the citizens of a society hold, and transmit from generation to generation, an appropriate set of supportive values and attitudes. Schultze cited a wide range of examples to illustrate his thesis:

- *The free enterprise system.* A web of implicit contracts, informal understandings, and ideas of fairness underpins the modern free enterprise system, a set of relationships which cannot practically be governed by explicit legal contracts.... A firm that violates those

85 What follows is drawn from an unpublished paper by Charles Schultze, prepared in 1991, which was circulated to members of the roundtable about midway through phase II. That paper had been prepared for a meeting of experts, convened by the OECD Directorate for Education, Employment, Labour and Social Affairs, on the subject of developing more coherent approaches to policy making. Charles Schultze currently is writing a book on many of these same themes, which is due to be published in 1996.

implicit contracts with its workers, suppliers, or customers will suffer a loss of reputation which causes it, in turn, to suffer a long-run
loss of profits, difficulty in retaining skilled and energetic workers, as
well as difficulty in retaining customers on a long-term basis.

- *Tax collection.* Revenue collection from an income tax system cannot
  be enforced by audits and penalties alone. Were taxpayers' decisions
  about whether or not to cheat to be based solely on a calculation of
  the likelihood of being caught, the system would not work, except
  perhaps with a huge enforcement mechanism that would violate
  other important social standards.

- *Income support systems.* If the only deterrent to keep people from
  claiming government support payments is their inability to get
  through the regulatory screen, and if there is little "self-policing"
  through individual values relating to the desirability of independence and self-support, the resulting budgetary drain will force a set
  of excessively rigid regulations and eligibility requirements that are
  both unfair, and potentially damaging to other aspects of social life....
  It is impossible to design a welfare system, within any reasonable budgetary constraints, if the only motivation for leaving welfare is the
  immediate after-tax monetary return.... The existence of individual
  values that give a significant weight to the virtues of self-support and
  to the long-term future is probably necessary to underpin a technically well-designed welfare or unemployment insurance system.

- *The criminal justice system.* The criminal justice system cannot work
  effectively and fairly if the fear of punishment is the only deterrent to
  illegal acts. Neither hard-line law-and-order methods nor rehabili-
  tation measures will be sufficient to deter crime if supporting individual values are significantly weakened.... Where impulsiveness and
  aggression are the norm, and when individuals place very low values
  on future benefits and costs, then no system of criminal penalties
  and law enforcement that is consistent with a civilized society can
  successfully deter a large volume of criminal activity.

The more fundamental the changes in social contract and policies being contemplated are, the more essential it is that the result
reflects and will be supported by, values that are widely shared
within the society. But as the number of players and perspectives

engaged in the process of governance multiply in the information society, we no longer can take for granted the existence of such shared values. Instead, we need continually to construct them.

Such a dialogue is central to building social cohesion and a learning society. In the words of one roundtable member, a learning society is: "... not just about learning to do keystrokes. We need to focus on learning about values much more than learning about technique." Such values help to structure the mental maps we use to translate data and information into knowledge, and so to make sense of the world.[86] Those shared mental maps, in turn, provide the context within which a wide variety of players can communicate, work together and mutually coordinate their actions.[87]

Government needs to find ways to provide leadership to that process, and to embody those values in its own operations.[88] Indeed, as the environment becomes more turbulent in the information society (and as the number of players proliferate) more

86 One group of roundtable members noted that a good illustration of this can be found in the very mixed history of efforts at "technology transfer," of trying to transfer technology between societies. They noted that if a very similar cultural and value base is not present in the recipient society, then the information about the technology is not properly encoded (into usable knowledge) and cannot be applied by that society. You cannot simply "transfer" the technique and hope that will be enough. A much more fundamental process of learning is required, which translates a particular technological approach into the value and cultural context of the recipient society.

87 Such shared mental maps (in the form of shared myths) are an essential underpinning for legitimate and effective public action. William McNeill stated this eloquently:

> Myth lies at the basis of human society. That is because myths are general statements about the world and its parts, and in particular about nations and other in-groups, that are believed to be true and then acted upon whenever circumstances suggest or require common response. This is mankind's substitute for instinct. It is the unique and characteristic way of acting together. A people without a full quiver of relevant agreed upon statements, accepted in advance through education or less formalized acculturation, soon finds itself in deep trouble, for, in the absence of believable myths, coherent public action becomes very difficult to improvise and sustain.

(McNeill, W., "The Care and Repair of Public Myth," *Foreign Affairs* Vol. 61, No. 1, 1982.)

traditional, hierarchical approaches to organizing and governing break down. In that environment, the appropriate form of leadership becomes one that operates at the level of values, of leading the construction of a shared vision and framework of interpretation in the context of which a wide range of players can learn, innovate and adapt more flexibly.[89]

BUILDING AN INFRASTRUCTURE FOR PUBLIC LEARNING

A third major agenda item might be to consider what new kinds of infrastructure will be needed to support that ongoing process of learning throughout society. In particular, what institutions, practices and tools might we construct to facilitate what Daniel Yankelovich referred to as the process of working through (a process of trying to develop a consonance between our judgements on particular issues and our more basic values)?

Such institutions and tools could include a variety of fora where people can come together to learn about and actively engage real choices, and to work through to some sort of resolution. In some respects a number of the experimental public fora developed during the constitutional process provide interesting prototypes that might be developed further. There is much (both positive and negative) that we can learn from those experiments.[90]

88 Roundtable members also stressed the importance of consistency between espoused values and actions. One of the effects of the information society is to make more visible any lack of correspondence between professed values and actual behaviour. In a sense, hypocrisy is less feasible in an information society! Such inconsistency has a serious corrosive effect on society, resulting in rising cynicism and eroding legitimacy.

89 A seminal statement of this argument at the level of organizations can be found in F.E. Emery and E.L. Trist, "The Causal Texture of Organizational Environments," *Human Relations* (Vol. 18, 1965), 21–32. See also Rosell et al., op. cit., 26–7.

90 Examples include the weekend citizen fora during the period leading up to the Charlottetown Accord, and the variety of initiatives taken by the Spicer Royal Commission to foster dialogue at local levels and to use those to build a wider public learning process. Some roundtable members suggested that one of the principal deficiencies of both those experiments was that most people did not perceive enough of a linkage between those efforts and the final constitutional proposals that emerged.

Another possibility might be to develop what one group of roundtable members called "public policy juries:"

> The idea would be that citizens would be selected to do a week of public policy jury duty, and that different levels of government could present policy issues to those juries, who then could work them through Yankelovich's seven steps of public judgement, and do so in a manner that might help the broader community to do the same.

How can we build better institutions and tools to facilitate that process of working through?[91] Participants noted that no one seems to have the answer to that question, and so we need to try a range of experiments to develop approaches and institutions that might work. Those experiments would need to be premised on the understanding that such a process of learning, and of reconciling particular issues and deeper values, takes time. Providing that time, in the process leading up to decisions, will be essential to the legitimacy and effectiveness of the result.

A related sort of infrastructure for public learning is the provision of useful information and feedback. The indicators we use and the feedback we receive, are central both to the process of learning and to the process of governing. In both cases we are, in a sense, flying on instruments, reading those gauges. A number of participants (including Richard Lipsey and Daniel Keating) emphasized the inadequacy of many of the current measures and indicators we use. How can we construct better indicators; for example, of human development, of the quality of life, of social

91 Parliamentary institutions also can play a more central role in this public learning process. A number of steps have been taken, or are being considered, to that end, and more can be devised. Examples of such steps include:
- referring Bills to committee after first reading for more open consideration and hearings (before the Bill has been approved in principle);
- experimenting with public workshops and other alternatives to the usual hearing format;
- Parliamentary and public examination of different budget scenarios prior to the presentation of a budget.

capital, or measures more appropriate to the new economy? More generally, what sort of measures or indicators should we develop to guide the process of public learning and of governing, and what institutions should be responsible for undertaking those measures and for providing that feedback?[92]

The media provide another important part of the infrastructure for public learning and also could be encouraged to undertake experiments to create more effective formats to facilitate the process of working through. For example, in Yankelovich's words: "What kind of symbolic interaction, presented in a television debate or some other format, can help people to work through the issues?" In addition, as the influence of the media grows, in the information society, questions of accountability for the use of that influence will become more important. How might the media strengthen their internal accountability processes in order to encourage high standards, and to provide better mechanisms through which public complaints could be aired and mistakes corrected?

In our initial report we also proposed a number of changes the government might initiate, in its own operations, which could help to support a broader process of public learning. We suggested, for example, that we consider how to develop public servants as knowledge workers (skilled in the process by which data and information is translated into knowledge, and by which shared frameworks of interpretation are created), and the implications of that for questions such as recruitment, training, promotion, methods of management and so on. More broadly, how can the

---

92 Another example we might explore is Christopher Freeman's suggestion of creating an office of technology assessment, along the lines of the Dutch model, which: "... not only produces expert reports on particular issues, but also sponsors a continuous debate among the various groups affected by technical change and seeks to develop constructive solutions to the dilemmas posed by those changes."

Some roundtable members also suggested (though others disagreed) that we might consider developing a public agency to undertake, assess and disseminate results of public opinion polls. Clearly there are many possible areas for new indicators, measures and related institutions, and we need to determine which are the most important, where to begin.

Public Service be developed as a learning organization, and as a key infrastructure for a learning society:

> If government is to provide the sort of leadership needed in the information society, it will require the support of a different sort of Public Service, one that is more attuned to change, more able to learn and adapt flexibly to a turbulent environment, more able to address longer-term issues that cut across departmental boundaries. This means strengthening the learning capacity of the Public Service, and finding better ways to engage other sectors of society in that learning process.[93]

We also suggested that government needs to become much better at sharing knowledge, including framing issues and providing information in ways that will assist in the formation of public judgement. In the information society, it becomes self-defeating (and fruitless) to try to control what data or information is released or available. Instead, in this new context, the challenge is to lead the continuing learning process by which people interpret and make sense of that information. We need to find ways for government to be more open, to get out more information, and (especially) to communicate the frameworks it uses to make sense of that information.[94]

INFORMATION TECHNOLOGY: NEW TOOLS FOR A
LEARNING SOCIETY
A fourth major agenda item might be to ask how we can use information and communication technologies, and the new informa-

---

93 Rosell et al., op. cit., 98.
94 More generally, we might consider ways in which the concept and requirements of building a learning society could be used, as an overarching theme, to guide a range of governmental activities. In the words of Judith Maxwell:
>   What I would like to suggest is that there is a tremendous potential in the language of the learning society. I would like to suggest that it can become a vision that could be used to drive a lot of policy, and a filter that could be used to test a variety of initiatives of government in the social and economic spheres.

tion infrastructure,[95] to assist our efforts to build social cohesion and a learning society. So far, those potential applications of the new technologies have received relatively little attention:

> As I listen to this conversation, I can't help but think that, as a country, we are under-investing in this technology. It seems to me, more and more, that this is a technological revolution made in heaven for Canada, and yet we are allowing private players to control this game and there appears to be no sense of public urgency about it. If we're concerned about reversing tendencies toward social fragmentation, and about knitting together a country that is spread over an immense territory, it seems to me that this technology offers us an immense opportunity. We need to ask ourselves what role government can play to ensure that the technology is developed in ways that serve public purposes as well as private interests.

For example, that information infrastructure can provide a more cost-effective and responsive mechanism for the delivery of public services.[96] In addition, information technology can be used to integrate service delivery not only across departments, but also across levels of government. Such an initiative would raise important questions of accountability, and of Ministerial responsibility, but those questions will need to be addressed in any case if we want to develop a more client-driven model of providing public services.[97]

95 Roundtable members were of the view that the currently popular metaphor, "the information superhighway," creates a misleading (and too narrow) image of what it is about. As an alternative, we decided to use the term "new information infrastructure."

96 Some interesting steps in this direction already are being taken within the Government of Canada. See, for example, *Blueprint for Renewing Government Services Using Information Technology* (Ottawa: Treasury Board Secretariat, 1994). More broadly, both in its internal operations and in its dealings with citizens, government ought to be a leader in using the new information infrastructure to encourage dialogue, improve decision making, provide information and deliver services.

97 This issue also is explored in our first report. See Rosell et al., op. cit., 41–5.

The new information infrastructure also can create new opportunities for people to work at home, or in less developed regions of the country, and telecommute to work. This can be used to help parents spend more time raising their children, while maintaining their careers. It also can help to reduce regional disparities and enable people to earn a living without having to leave their communities. How might these uses of the information infrastructure be developed further?[98]

Even more important is the potential to use the new information infrastructure as a medium to foster public dialogue and learning across the country. A wide range of interactive electronic fora could be established for that purpose. These might include:

- varieties of "electronic town meetings;"
- ongoing discussion groups around particular issues (similar to Internet newsgroups);
- interactive interviews with political and other leaders, perhaps including the development of a parliamentary computer conferencing (or bulletin board) system in which a wide range of Canadians might participate;
- enabling citizens to "broadcast" their own programming, contributing their perceptions to the broader learning process, and perhaps helping us to articulate those values and perceptions that we hold in common;
- using a common database, and simulation models of important issues, to construct a "shared spread sheet" and so to help to form public judgement;[99] and so on.

We need to develop better ways to use the potential of the information infrastructure to support such public dialogue:

I think one important theme that will come out of all of this is the importance of how individuals relate to each other and of conver-

---

98   To respond to such questions more effectively, roundtable members suggested that the government also needs to establish a stronger focal point to address the development of the new information infrastructure, and the broader policy ramifications of the information economy.

sation and dialogue. One of the most popular developments, in this new world of information and communication, is people communicating with each other. In the midst of all of the passive technology we pump out, what people respond to most positively is the interactive aspects. When we offer people even very crude interactive capabilities, the response is phenomenal. Ted Turner is right, he said that it is not video on demand that people want, it's people on demand that they want. People are trying to find ways to use these tools to communicate with each other, and the process of constructing shared maps and developing a learning society is fundamental to that.[100]

On the Importance of the Process

Constructing a learning society is itself a process of learning. No one knows fully how to do it, there is no blueprint. The agenda of policy and institutional initiatives we have outlined represent preliminary ideas only about some of the steps we need to take to construct such a society, ideas which we hope can be considered and developed further in a wider dialogue.

99 Essentially, the idea would be to provide members of the public (as well as deci-sion makers from government and from other sectors of society) with access to a shared database and simulation models that could be used to explore the implications of different policy options. The players could use the models to ask "what-if" questions and to develop a shared understanding of the issues, and of the options that were available, in effect to be involved in a shared learn-ing process. To the degree that a shared interpretation of the issues and of the implications of the various policy options could be achieved, there would be a greater possibility of moving toward a workable consensus.

100 For the new information infrastructure to fulfill its potential to promote pub-lic dialogue, it will need to be developed in a manner that ensures universal access at a reasonable cost. Access to public dialogue channels, as well as to those delivering public services, for example, will need to be part of the basic service to which all have access. Issues of diversity also will be important:

> A more diverse society generally is a better society; having people with multiple skills and different perspectives enables you to be more flexible and to do different things. In the information economy that becomes a critical advantage. We need to develop our information infrastructure in a way that encourages that.

A basic conclusion of our work has been that to govern our-selves more effectively amidst the rapidly changing environment of the information society (in which the lifetime of particular political or policy "solutions" is likely to be short), we need to enhance our capacity to learn together. This will involve developing learning organizations, and learning societies that are skilled in the ongoing process by which we construct and update shared mental maps, shared values, frameworks of interpretation and policy, or institutional agendas. Those shared mental maps, in turn, provide the context within which a wide range of players can devise a continuing succession of more particular policy solutions. The work of the project has been a microcosm of that process.

The project has provided members of the roundtable with an opportunity to step outside of day-to-day concerns, and to examine issues that cut across organizational boundaries and whose time horizon exceeds that of most planning. It has provided a forum in which we can consider more systematically the fundamental, tectonic changes that are reshaping the environment for governance in Canada and around the world. It has encouraged a dialogue between public and private-sector participants, and with leading international authorities, through which we have been able to engage other views, test ideas, debate and learn. It has enabled us, through the scenario process, to interrelate our various perspectives, and those of the outside experts, and to construct a shared map, a shared framework for understanding how the information society might reshape the environment for governance over the next decade, and what we might do about it.

As the second phase of the project drew to a close, members of the roundtable reflected on the value of the process we had been through in general, and of the scenario process in particular. Participants emphasized that a principal benefit of the project had been the process itself:

> ... the process of getting there is at least as important, and perhaps even more important, than the final product. The learning

process fundamentally is what this project is about, and any particular products really are byproducts of that process. There is a danger that any one of those products may seem a bit obvious but, in a sense, all real insights seem simple and straightforward in retrospect. As we know now, the process of getting there is not all that easy, and is very important.

* * *

The broader process of the project has helped us to recognize the shift in paradigm that we are living through, and to start to work out some of the implications of that for how we do our jobs. The concept of a learning society, and of the Public Service as a microcosm of such a society, is one with which we have begun to grapple. Speaking personally, I walked away from every one of our sessions saying that this has been the best few hours I have spent for a long time. The discussions have been both challenging and helpful, and of great value.

Roundtable members also concluded that the scenario process had proven its value:

We need to emphasize the power of the scenario approach, and that it has demonstrated its utility to people who usually are very skeptical about such things.

* * *

... As I think back on our experience at the scenario workshop, where we were trying to deal with a wide range of topics and a diverse universe of thought, although we were very confused at the outset, I found scenarios to be a very valuable, disciplined way of taking that broad subject matter and coming to grips with it in a way that was useful and productive.

* * *

... it also is important to underline that what really is important about the scenario process is not so much the scenarios that result, but rather the ways in which the process changes our understanding, our mental models, the different alternatives we can perceive.

* * *

Yes, what the scenario process does is to force us to think about these issues in different contexts, and to suspend some of our doubts and enthusiasms for a moment as we try to see where those different perspectives might lead, what new possibilities they might open up.

Several participants added that they had begun to use the scenario approach within their own organizations. Others indicated that they already had presented the set of scenarios we had constructed to groups, both within and outside Canada, and that in each case there had been a very positive reaction and a lively discussion: "I have had that experience with a number of groups now, so I think the scenarios really do work, and that people are very interested in the issues they raise."

Some roundtable members expressed concern that the scenarios we had constructed were too general and not specific enough to Canada: "For example, there is no federal-provincial issue or no discussion of trade barriers. We have all sorts of problems that are Canadian that aren't reflected here specifically." Others countered that this broader perspective was an essential strength, rather than a weakness, of the approach:

The value of the scenarios, for me, is that they enable us to get above all of the more specific problems that we continually run up against. The scenario process gives us a broader view and lets us see connections that otherwise might get lost in the day-to-day rush. If we start to throw in all of those very particular Canadian problems, we risk getting lost in the trees. The most dramatic thing about the scenarios, for me, was that we could look at them and say: "my god, that's where we are going and if we don't do something, we are going to end up where we don't want to be."

One shortcoming of the scenario approach, identified by participants, was moving from scenarios to policy: "There were times, at least in my experience, when the scenarios became frustrating.... There seems to be some real difficulty in moving from scenario analysis to the investigation of more specific policy options." One way to make that link, as Kees van der Heijden and Adam Kahane had suggested, would be to use scenarios to test policy options (to ensure they would be robust under all scenarios). We would like to see decision makers, in a variety of fields, try to apply the scenarios in this way.[101] Another way to provide a better link between scenarios and policy making, it was suggested, would be to try to design policies that would lead us toward the scenarios that we regard as more desirable:

> ... one way to remedy that is to think about the differences between those scenarios that we regard as desirable, and those scenarios that seem to paint a picture of where we currently are going. Where

101 We had hoped to begin this process within the project, to have the small groups apply the scenarios to particular policy issues, and use that to generate more specific recommendations. At about the time of the scenario workshop, however, there was a major government reorganization that directly affected most of the Public Service members of the roundtable. As a result, the time and energy that participants were able to devote to this aspect of the work of the small groups was much reduced. We now hope that this essential task can be carried forward in the follow-up to the project. As one roundtable member expressed the general view at our concluding session:

> My sense is that we have gone through a process that we really haven't finished, and I think most of us probably have a sense of incompleteness or frustration about that. We have talked about the reasons why the small groups weren't able to carry out the job originally planned for them, but the fact remains that there is unfinished business here. It seems to me, therefore, that we need to focus on ways in which that can be completed, ways in which the scenarios and other ideas can be applied to important issues that we are facing, and be used to generate more specific recommendations. I also like the idea that we should find a way in which there could be some kind of continuing cross-departmental forum of ADMs to pursue these questions, including bringing together the results of the work that would be done on the more specific issues.

we want to be is different from where we appear to be going. We then could focus on developing policy and institutional initiatives that could move us away from our current path, and onto a path that could lead toward the more desirable scenarios.

In fact, toward the end of the project we had adopted a similar approach. We had developed a preliminary agenda of policy and institutional initiatives which were intended (by fostering social cohesion and a learning society) to lead us toward the worlds described in the *Starship* or *Windjammer* scenarios, and away from the worlds of *HMS Bounty* or *Titanic.*

But again, more fundamentally, in the rapidly changing environment of the information society, what is most important is not any particular policy or institutional initiative, nor even any particular scenario or mental map. The lifetime of those initiatives, and even of those mental maps, is likely to be short. What is most important is the continuing learning process by which we construct those shared mental maps, and so provide the framework within which a wide range of players can innovate a succession of policy (and other) initiatives to deal with rapid change.

Next Steps

We hope that the scenarios, and the preliminary agenda of initiatives we have developed in that context, can be used to stimulate, and to focus, a continuing process of dialogue and learning. We would like to see that learning process, only begun by the roundtable, carried forward in a manner that can engage a wider range of participants within the government, among the interested public in Canada, and within the global community of governance practitioners.[102]

102 The OECD recently convened a meeting of senior officials, from its member governments, organized around the basic issues and themes raised in our first report. We hope this can be one step toward a wider dialogue about these issues among the global community of practitioners.

One step in that direction would be to seek wide dissemination of our findings. In addition to the more usual approaches of book distribution, conferences and briefings of interested groups, we agreed to explore ways in which the new information and communications technologies might be used to aid that process of dissemination. More fundamentally, however, we concluded that, to widen the dialogue, we need to find ways for different groups to engage in a learning process similar to the one we had experienced.

For example, we might envision a series of workshops with different groups, in which participants are presented with the scenarios and the preliminary agenda of initiatives, and then are facilitated in a process of working through some of the opportunities and threats raised by each scenario ("what would we do if..."). In addition, they might be asked to consider:

- toward which scenario (or variation) are we now moving (i.e., what is likely to happen if present trends continue);
- which scenario (or variation) would they prefer (i.e., which is their desired future);
- (if the first two are not the same) what initiatives could they take, or could others take, to close the gap between where we seem to be headed and where we would like to go?

In addition, in the context of the scenarios, participants might be asked to examine an important policy issue they are facing. The question for the workshop would be: is that particular policy decision likely to be viable under all of the scenarios and, if not, how might that decision be modified in order to be more robust?

Such workshops could be undertaken within government departments, in interdepartmental fora, and with a wide range of other groups. In such an effort we would be widening the learning process begun by the project, and incorporating a broader range of perspectives. At the same time we hope we can find ways to deepen that process. That would involve drawing together those wider dialogues, perhaps through additional work by the roundtable, into more specific recommendations of measures to build a learning society, and to govern ourselves more effectively in the information age.[103] That work also could be used to produce a further iteration of the scenarios, one that would incorporate the insights derived from the wider dialogues.

Indeed, one of the principal potentials of the project (and of the scenario process) lies in the extent to which it can help to foster a broader, strategic dialogue around the critical issues we face as a society. In the words of one roundtable member:

> ... one of the real values of the scenarios, in my view, is that they can contribute to, and encourage, a more strategic conversation about these questions, both within government and among a wider range of groups. Currently, we tend to get lost in the trees on too many issues. A principal value of the scenarios is that they can help us to lift our perspective, to focus on some of the value-based tradeoffs involved, and perhaps to encourage others to do that.

Such a strategic conversation is central to the process of constructing shared agendas, shared frameworks, which our first report concluded is so essential to effective governance in an information society. Now, in the context of the work undertaken in the second phase of the project, the importance of that process of constructing shared frameworks and agendas was underlined:

> I work in the private sector, and we spend an awful lot of time on that agenda-setting function, both within companies and between companies. Developing a shared understanding of the environ-

---

103   One way to do this, for example, might be for smaller groups of roundtable members to organize a number of workshops within or outside government. The results of those workshops would be reported to the full roundtable, which would draw both on the results of those dialogues and on continuing sessions with leading international resource persons, to develop more specific recommendations and a new iteration of the scenarios.

ment in which we are operating, and what we are going to do about it, is an essential task. It seems to me that government does that a lot less right now, and it is very important that government invest far more in that sort of effort....

* * *

Just picking up on that point, I think that one of the important inventions that has come out of this project is a new instrument of governance. The traditional instruments of governance are taxation, regulation, spending and that sort of thing. I think what this project has added to that list is the notion of a framework, of the value and importance of generating a shared framework, on the basis of which the multiplying players in the governance process mutually can coordinate their actions.

It seems to me that one of the implications of the Putnam argument also is to emphasize the importance of creating such shared frameworks. Putnam indicates that social capital and social cohesion lead to wealth, and not the other way around. If we accept that, then the construction of shared frameworks, which is central to social cohesion and to a learning society, becomes all the more important.

The need to construct learning organizations and a learning society is discussed more and more, but usually in an economic framework, as being essential for competitiveness and success in the information economy. In the course of the project we have come to recognize that enhancing our capacity to learn together also is essential to human development and to social cohesion, and that these objectives are at least as important. Indeed, success in building social cohesion seems to be central to constructing any sort of society in which we would like our children to live. Moreover, as we have seen in the work of Putnam and others, some degree of social cohesion also appears to be a prerequisite for economic success.

The link between social cohesion and our capacity to learn together seems to be two-way: to be a mutual-causal process. Our capacity to learn together, to construct shared mental maps and communities of interpretation, depends, in turn, on some degree of social cohesion. A high level of social fragmentation and social polarization can constitute a significant learning disability, and can undermine our efforts to construct a society that can be successful either economically or socially.[104] If we are to construct a learning society, then, we need to re-balance our perspective, to give at least equal attention to questions of social cohesion, and to the building of social capital.[105]

Building social cohesion in the information society involves an ongoing process of public learning. The dialogue begun in the roundtable, and which we hope now can be continued and expanded to a wider range of groups, is one example of (and one contribution to) the sort of learning process we require. It is a process by which we construct shared values and perceptions, by which we imagine the sort of society we wish to build, and how each can contribute to that effort. It is a process by which we construct shared frameworks, shared mental maps, in the context of which we mutually can coordinate our actions. And it is a process by which we use the results of those actions to test and further to develop or change those mental maps, thereby providing the starting point for the next cycle of a continuing-action learning process. Fundamentally, it is the process by which we construct and sustain a learning society. We need to learn better how to do that, and how we can provide the leadership, infrastructure and support that such an effort requires.

In the information society, as the environment for governance changes more rapidly, and as the number of players multiply and

104 This conclusion also was reached in the work of Putnam and others. Equally, of course, too high a degree of social uniformity (groupthink) can constitute a learning disability, depriving society of the different perspectives and unconventional viewpoints on which learning so much depends. While amid the growing diversity, blurring boundaries and multiplying voices of the information society this does not appear to be an immediate danger, it will be important to ensure that efforts to build social cohesion do not overshoot into efforts to enforce social uniformity.

become more diverse, that process of constructing shared mental maps becomes more continuous and more difficult. It also becomes, more than ever, the basis on which we govern ourselves.

105   Another way to state this would be to note that, in the information society, market-based approaches are being applied more widely. Markets can be seen as a particular type of learning organization, and one that is extremely efficient at allocating resources and creating wealth. At the same time, the success of markets depends on the existence of appropriate social institutions, a social contract, and an adequate level of social capital and cohesion. (On the importance of such social and institutional factors for the effective development and operation of markets see, for example, D. North, op. cit.) The totally unfettered operation of markets can undermine the very social capital on which their effectiveness depends. (The long history of this idea in economic thought is well presented, and extended, in R. Heilbroner, *Twenty-First Century Capitalism* (Toronto: Anansi, 1992). See also F. Hirsch, op. cit.) It becomes all the more important, then, as our reliance on market-based solutions increases, that we also focus our attention on measures required to build and to sustain social capital and cohesion. One roundtable member summarized this point of view at our concluding session:

> In the information society things are continually changing, and many of our institutions no longer are adequate to deal with that. It is for this reason that we need to develop ways of organizing and governing based on a model of continuing learning. A lot of our discussion of the information society has focused on its fragmenting effects, on the breakdown of belief systems, on the erosion of institutions, on the multiplication of interest groups, and so on. But the learning society notion points us in a direction of re-integration. Not integration on a permanent, once-and-for-all basis, because that no longer is possible, but integration through a process of continual learning, construction, adaptation and change.
>
> In this context, one of the insights that has emerged from our consideration of the scenarios is that the information society cannot be a world merely of individuals, of markets and of fragmentation. We also need to find new ways to build social cohesion amid that rapid change, to develop the shared norms and institutions that provide the essential infrastructure that enable markets to work.

Moreover, as markets become more globalized, in the information age, we shall need to address these issues of social institutions, contract and cohesion not only at local and national levels, but increasingly at the global level.

Part II

Selected Papers Presented to the Roundtable

Introduction

THROUGHOUT THE PROJECT, the work of the roundtable has been stimulated and focused by presentations made by a wide range of international authorities. A number of those authorities agreed to develop their presentations into formal papers, which are presented here.

The discussions those presentations sparked are outlined in the report of the roundtable in Part I of this volume. The discussion of Kees van der Heijden's presentation is in Chapter 1. The presentations by Christopher Freeman, Walter Truett Anderson and Amitai Etzioni provide the focus for Chapter 2. And the papers by Daniel Keating and Daniel Yankelovich helped to shape the discussions described in Chapter 4.

In some cases, those discussions closely tracked the issues raised in the presentations, while in others the presentations triggered more wide-ranging examinations, and elicited from the resource people insights not contained in their papers. Generally, I think it is fair to say that the resource people also learned from their involvement in the discussions of the roundtable. Certainly, developing that sort of mutual learning process was something we tried to foster throughout the project.

Of course, much more was presented to the project than is included in Part II. A number of the outside authorities who made valuable presentations to the roundtable were not in a position to prepare a more formal paper. There also were a wide range of previously published books and articles that were very influential in the work of the roundtable, which are not reproduced here. In sum, the papers presented in Part II represent a small but important sample of the presentations made to the roundtable, and provide valuable additional insight into many of the issues that the project was designed to address.

6 Scenario Thinking About the Future

Kees van der Heijden[*]

Problems

PROBLEMS ARE NOT OBJECTIVE PHENOMENA (out there) in the world. They are created in our minds; we define problems; they are entirely subjective. We spend a lot of time on the process of problem solving but, in actual fact, few problems are ever solved. It would be more appropriate to talk about finishing with problems (Eden 1987). We define when something is a problem and when it is no longer a problem.

We define a situation as being problematic when we feel we do not have enough control over matters that affect us strongly. Solving a problem is done by gaining control. It may involve nothing more than understanding a situation that previously was not understood – nothing has changed out in the world, what has changed is our newly gained understanding.

The power of "scenario analysis" lies in the potential to help us develop an understanding of situations that appear to be unstructured and threatening. Scenario analysis forces us to consider the horizon, to extend our mental models, to consider cause and effect, and to identify levers that we can use to establish a degree of control over a situation. Even if scenarios do not give us answers, they can be real problem-finishing tools, which will enable us to feel more on top of our situation.

[*] Kees van der Heijden is Professor of Strategic Management in the Graduate Business School of Strathclyde University in Glasgow. He was for many years a senior executive with Royal/Dutch Shell and served in Shell companies in Manila, Singapore and Curacao before joining Group Planning at Shell headquarters in London. There, as head of the Business Environment Division, he was responsible for Shell's scenario planning process.

Traditional Approach to Dealing With the Future

We will take it as axiomatic that we are in a time of rapid change (Mensch 1979, Hirschhorn 1984). Bureaucratic institutions are particularly at risk in such times because they are frozen in a particular logic. Bureaucratic organizations may be appropriate in stable circumstances, but during periods of rapid change their lack of flexibility becomes a major liability (Normann 1993). As well, more traditional problem-solving techniques, based on the "predict-and-control" paradigm, equally become inadequate at such times.

In the less turbulent 1950s and '60s, planning for the future was based on the predict-and-control principle (Mintzberg 1985). It is an approach that works well when questions for the future are well defined; when there are relatively stable relationships between sectors of society; and when there are clear, shared objectives and values. When the nature of what needs to be done is clear, the problem becomes one of designing and optimizing a detailed blueprint to get there. That is when predict-and-control planning works well. But in times of rapid change, when new factors are introduced (often aided by new technology), when relationships between sectors shift, and when the environment becomes more uncertain, predict-and-control planning fails.

Often, this inadequacy is first perceived in the field of forecasting. Our forecasts seem to become less and less accurate as change accelerates. Forecasts are based on the assumption that the past can be extended into the future. At the simplest level, forecasting is a statistical extrapolation of past data, and it is the first mode to fail in periods of rapid change.

A more sophisticated mode of forecasting involves the development of a simulation model that allows more complex and dynamic inter-relationships among variables to be taken into account. Examples of this approach range from macroeconomic models to war games. However, simulation models also are based on projecting the past into the future. They are based on the assumption that there is a stable underlying structure of relation-ships. In times of structural change, that assumption cannot hold.

The predict-and-control approach cannot deal effectively with structural change. It simply does not ask the right questions. To remedy this, we need to move from a forecasting model to a more flexible way of looking at the future. Scenario analysis is one approach that can enable us to deal more flexibly with the uncer-tainties of structural change.

Discoveries in the Use of Scenario Analysis

Scenario planning has a long history, beginning with its use by the military in war games. It was adapted to civilian use by the RAND Corporation during and after World War II and, subsequently, was developed further by the Hudson Institute, which was set up by Herman Kahn after he resigned from RAND. Kahn's most quoted scenario was his book *The Year 2000* published in 1967 (Kahn 1967).

Beginning in the late 1960s, scenario planning became popular in the corporate world. It was used as an extension of the predict-and-control approach to planning. A single-line forecast was replaced by an assessment of the probabilities of the future, which, in turn, was used to define a "most likely" projection. This type of scenario planning was based on simulation models and did not offer a fundamental improvement over other forecasting approaches. It has largely been abandoned.

The late 1960s also saw the start of a different, more flexible and conceptual use of scenario analysis in the work of Pierre Wack, then head of Group Planning at Royal Dutch/Shell (Wack 1985). This type of scenario analysis relies more on qualitative, causal thinking. It is designed to help decision-makers in their search for enhanced understanding of the changing structures in society.

Shell has been using scenario analysis since the late 1960s. The use of the methodology has evolved considerably since then and, perhaps, a short history of its evolution will help to make clearer the basic principles involved.

A BETTER ALTERNATIVE TO FORECASTING

At Shell, analyzing scenarios began as a way to deal with some of the limits of forecasting. Interest in scenarios arose in the mid-1960s as it became more evident that forecast-based approaches to planning were failing. Scenarios were introduced as a way to plan without having to predict things that everyone knew were unpredictable. These early attempts were based on the approaches developed by Herman Kahn, who emphasized that planning must be based on the assumption that something is predictable. If the future is 100 per cent uncertain, then planning obviously is a waste of time. The problem, therefore, is to separate what is predictable from what is fundamentally uncertain. The predictable elements became known as the "predetermineds." The predetermineds are reflected in all scenarios. Key uncertainties, on the other hand, appear in various scenarios in different ways.

The alternative futures described in the scenarios, then, can serve as a "test-bed" for policies and plans. At Shell, as in most engineering-dominated companies, big decisions tend to be project-related. Each project is evaluated against a set of, perhaps, three scenarios, so three outcomes are generated, one for each scenario. A decision on whether to go ahead with a particular project is made on the basis of the three possible outcomes. The objective is to have projects that are likely to have positive returns under any of the three scenarios. The scenarios themselves are not the decision criteria, indicating whether or not to go ahead with a project, but rather serve as a mechanism for producing information that is relevant to the decision. Decisions are never based on one scenario being more likely than another. Project developers optimize simultaneously against three alternative futures. In this way, both the value and the risk of the project is assessed.

Similarly, if a particular strategy or plan needs to be evaluated, the evaluation is done against each scenario. This produces three outcomes, which are presented to the decision-makers. Instead of one picture, they are given three. After more than 25 years of scenario analysis, senior management would not accept anything less. They know that assessing a strategic decision against a single forecast, rather than against several different possibilities, involves filtering out important knowledge about the fundamental risks involved.

STRETCHING MENTAL MODELS

One of the early findings of the scenario planners at Shell was that the search for predetermined elements required them to consider in some depth the driving forces of the business environment. Separating the predetermined from the uncertain cannot be done without a considerable degree of basic analysis of causal relationships.

The earliest scenarios at Shell are good examples of this. The main item on the scenario agenda in the late 1960s was the price of oil. Planners had to consider what was predictable and what was uncertain in the price of oil; what drove supply, and what drove demand.

In those days world-wide demand was taken for granted. It was regarded as being predictable, with growth around six per cent every year. This had been a consistent pattern since 1945 and was not questioned. So attention turned to supply. To what extent was this predetermined and to what extent was it uncertain? That, in turn, depended on where the supply was coming from. Of course, the Middle East loomed large in the equation.

Shell's technical people had concluded that supply was predetermined, the resources in the ground were plentiful, and the necessary number of wells could be drilled. But Pierre Wack wasn't satisfied with that answer. He looked behind it, at the people who controlled the reserves, and at those who would make the production decisions. In the late 1960s these people were still the major oil companies, but the producing governments had already begun to establish their authority. It was one of Pierre Wack's great contributions to the scenario process that he insisted on looking at the people behind decisions, not just at the technical phenomena.

The planners started to wonder whether it would make sense, from the point of view of the producing governments, to continue to supply the increasing quantities of the resource required. They concluded that this was sufficiently uncertain, that it was worth developing a scenario around that uncertainty. This became known as the crisis scenario, in which producing countries would refuse to continue to increase production beyond what made sense from their perspective.

When the oil crisis actually occurred, in 1973, it became clear within Shell that scenario analysis had put the company on a "thinking" track that traditional forecasting never could have attained. Mental models had been stretched well beyond that which forecasting could have achieved. Forecasting may produce answers, but scenario planning had made people ask the interesting questions. Scenarios had allowed the company to override the paramountcy of the credible, but very wrong, "business-as-usual" scenario. As Shell's managing director, Andre Benard, commented, "Experience has taught us that the scenario technique is much more conducive to forcing people to think about the future than the forecasting techniques we formerly used" (Benard 1980). This was the second important accomplishment of scenario planning at Shell.

ENHANCING CORPORATE PERCEPTION
Shortly thereafter, a third powerful effect (and benefit) of using scenario techniques was observed. People who worked with the scenarios found that they were interpreting information differently than they otherwise might have done (compare Ingvar 1985). For example, people in manufacturing at Shell recognized, in the 1973 developments in the Middle East, elements of the energy-crisis scenario they had been discussing. They interpreted those persistent signals to be indications that we were moving toward the crisis scenario, and took a number of critical, strategic decisions. The most important decision was a change in refining

policies. This change was later shown to have been essential in enabling Shell to come through that turbulent period very successfully overall.

Other parts of the company, such as the marine transport sector, which had not worked with the scenarios, did not appreciate the depth of the changes underway, and so did not adjust to them very effectively. They continued putting money into tanker investments. That part of the business never has recovered fully from the losses it incurred as a consequence.

The scenarios enabled the manufacturing people to be more perceptive, and to recognize a different pattern in the events. As a result, they were able to respond quickly to events, as they unfolded, in a way that would not have been possible without the mental preparation provided by the scenario process.

AN IMPORTANT MANAGEMENT TOOL

A fourth aspect of scenario planning emerged later when senior management began to use scenarios as a way to influence decision making throughout the organization. In all organizations there are "rules of the game" about how to obtain the approval of senior management for important decisions. At Shell, a simple but important change was made in those rules. Previously, a major project for which approval was sought was justified using only a single forecast of how the environment for that project would develop. This rule was changed at Shell to require that any such project, henceforth, would need to be justified against the current, full set of corporate scenarios. The result of this change was significant. Since the scenarios now provided the context for making key strategic decisions, project developers had to pay attention to them.

For example, when project developers, matching a project against scenario A, find an attractive pay-out, but against scenario B find a dismal return, they now will be reluctant to submit the project because it likely will be rejected for its poor performance under scenario B. Instead, they will try to modify the project so that its performance under scenario B is improved, even if that means a slight reduction in its performance under scenario A. What this means is that project development now is being influenced by the scenarios even before the project is submitted to senior management. The scenarios set the context within which subsequent decisions are made.

A further consequence of this is that the interest of senior management in the scenario process is much increased. They become more involved in the generation of scenarios because they recognize that they are a powerful tool for influencing the development of projects, and decision making, throughout the organization.

At Shell, senior management use scenarios to provide leadership for the organization. For example, in 1989 (Kahane 1992), senior management became concerned that Shell, as a whole, was not addressing the issue of the environment as well as it should. They thought that the general attitude of the company toward this issue had become too defensive. To encourage change, one of the 1989 scenarios described a world in which environmental factors developed in such a way that only companies responding positively to environmental factors could survive. That possibility, then, needed to be factored in whenever a project with significant environmental impact was considered.

Important in all of this is the institutional aspect. Decisions of the type described are not made by an individual, they require a considerable degree of institutional consensus. That consensus, in turn, depends on there being enough people who jointly have acquired, or have constructed, the mental model on which the consensus is based. Institutionalizing the scenario process can greatly facilitate the formation of those shared mental models and that consensus. Scenarios, then, quickly become part of the shared institutional language, and so can help to shape decision making throughout the company.

THE SCENARIO CULTURE

Scenario thinking now underpins decision-making at Shell. It has become part of the culture, so that people throughout the company, when they deal with significant decisions, normally think in terms of multiple futures. This is known as focused scenario thinking. Focused scenarios tend to be ad hoc, and to focus on an immediate decision that needs to be taken. They are unrelated to the global scenarios used by senior management to establish the strategic framework for the next couple of years. The company is satisfied to have scenario analysis take place in this way at different levels, without trying to connect them up formally. What matters, in this culture, is the thinking process rather than bureaucratic planning.

Shell can claim that strategic thinking and strategic tools (scenario analysis) have co-evolved in the company. Better tools have created more effective thinking, and enhanced conceptualization has created room and demand for superior tools, such as scenario analysis.

Issues in Scenario Analysis

The previous section gave an overview of the experience with, and evolution of, scenario techniques at Shell. In this section we shall summarize the major steps involved in developing scenarios, and also indicate some important lessons that we have learned from our experience with scenario planning.

IDENTIFYING THE "CLIENT"

The world is very large and very complex, a sea in which a scenario planner easily can drown. To avoid that, a scenario project needs to have defined boundaries. To that end, the first thing a scenario planner needs to do, in every scenario exercise, is to identify the client. The needs of the client, and the specific context, narrow the world to a manageable set of variables within which scenarios can be constructed.

In Shell, senior management is the client for global scenarios, but scenario planning also is undertaken at lower levels within the company for particular purposes. In these cases the clients need to be clearly defined, and the scenarios focused accordingly.

INTERVIEWING

Having identified the client, the next step is to map out, in detailed open-ended interviews, the client's key visions and concerns for the future. The scenario planner needs to find out what about the business the client's concerns are. In this process, an agenda for the scenario exercise emerges. Experience has shown that not listening to the client, and following the scenario planner's own agenda instead, is a guaranteed recipe for failure.

The scenario planner starts the process by engaging the client group in a series of open-ended interviews. An open-ended interview is one in which the interviewee sets the agenda, reacting to questions posed by the interviewer, which function only as triggers for the conversation.

Open-ended interviews with senior executives typically last two to three hours each. The interviewer collects observations as interviewees talk freely about the business and what is of concern to them. Typically, some 60 observations can be extracted from each interview, so that in interviewing a dozen senior managers, some 700 important observations about the future can be collected. These, then, are grouped into broader issues. Subsequently, the management team meets for a feedback session, during which they are asked to prioritize the broader issues that have been identified. The aim, at this stage, is to end up with a set of about 10 broad issues. This is known as the "natural agenda," the emerging agenda of management's major concerns, on which a successful scenario project might shed new light.

KNOWLEDGE DEVELOPMENT

The real art of good scenario development lies in finding the optimum balance, for the client, between what is familiar and what is new. Erring on either side will reduce the effectiveness of the exercise. If the audience only hears their own familiar problems, without obtaining any new insights from the exercise, they will not consider the scenarios helpful. However, if everything they hear is new, and is perceived as being unconnected to their ongoing concerns, the audience will find the scenarios irrelevant to their needs, and reject them as well.

The natural agenda provides the scenario planner with a definition of what is relevant. It is, then, necessary to develop new insights into the issues identified by that agenda. Such new insights need to be found outside the system to which the client belongs. Searching for those new insights is the knowledge-developmental phase of the scenario-planning process.

An efficient way of gaining this "new knowledge" is through interacting with experts who can throw a new light on a given issue. At Shell, scenario planners maintain a list of what are known as "remarkable people," remarkable because they have something new and unexpected to offer in their area of expertise. By its nature, this is a dynamic list. Names continuously have to be added to replace those whose ideas have become accepted wisdom.

At this point in the process, a scenario team is formed to work on each of the key issues identified by the natural agenda. For each issue a study team of at least two people is formed, which begins to examine the issue and to organize external contacts. Once promising contacts with external experts have been made, those experts are invited to lead workshops where their ideas and insights can be explored by the scenario team. In preparation for the workshop, the experts are asked to write an introductory paper presenting the issue from their perspective. Shell has found that it is worthwhile to have more than one external expert at each workshop. The mixing of different perspectives that results, generally, is a fruitful way to provoke constructive debate and further insights.

This workshop process is repeated several times as the issues on the natural agenda are explored. During this period, the teams accumulate new ideas for the scenarios on the issues that have been identified by senior management. The fundamental and crucial "rule of the game" at this stage is that no structuring of the data should be undertaken. Nobody should try prematurely to make sense out of it. Instead the teams need to remain open to any new or random insights and ideas that may be encountered.

Experience has shown that prematurely created frameworks (or structures) have the effect of closing minds to further input. At this point it's the ideas that *do not fit* that are particularly interesting, and the team needs to keep an open mind to those. This requires real discipline and a high tolerance for ambiguity. Many people have difficulty maintaining that discipline and, for them, it is helpful to set a firm date, marking the end of this "reading period." At a designated time, the focus changes and the process of integrating and structuring what has been learned begins.

STRUCTURING

On a designated date, the whole scenario team goes away for several days, for a workshop "in the green." This part of the process cannot be hurried. The first task is to plough through all of the information obtained, and the insights gained, during the previous phase. The next task is to begin to make some sense of it all. The workshop starts with a large "pile" of ideas and knowledge, which is at that stage entirely unstructured and unrelated. At the end of the workshop a framework must have emerged, a holistic picture in which each bit of information has its own place, and in which there is a logical structure that shows their interconnections.

There is no set procedure for how to do this, there is no sequence of steps that can be followed. A few tools, however, have proven to be useful in practice. These include:

- clustering devices, such as magnetic hexagons;
- cause-effect diagrams, possibly developed using computerized cognitive mapping tools;
- distinguishing predetermineds from uncertainties;
- ranking variables in terms of their importance and predictability;
- holding a discussion to identify which are the critical variables.

Apart from a limited set of tools, the job must be left to the creativity of the team, and, somehow, it seems to work every time.

Although the time it takes differs, experience shows that the group always arrives at a workable result in the end. At some point, somebody suggests a few connections. Others add to it. Suddenly something seems to fit. It is a bit like a figure-ground shift, suddenly a new pattern emerges from all the compiled ideas and knowledge.

Peter Schwartz provides another description of this process in his book *The Art of the Long View:*

> Someone walks in and says: 'As I was lying there last night in the bathtub I had an idea for a scenario.' And he or she lays it out, nearly complete. Someone else across the table says: 'And here is the complement.' This happens so often that many scenario planners have learned to include enough overnight stays to make this happen (Schwartz 1991).

A good way of testing whether one has arrived at a good scenario structure is to try to name the resulting scenarios. Good scenario names express the essence of the scenario in not more than two or three evocative words.

Once this has been achieved, it is relatively straightforward to flesh out plausible, and internally consistent, story lines for each of the scenarios. The hard conceptual task has been completed.

At this stage it is useful to feed back the preliminary scenarios to the client group, to allow them to comment on the usefulness of the result. This sometimes involves multiple iterations until the client is satisfied that the scenarios effectively address their needs and concerns.

QUANTIFICATION

If scenarios are developed for the purpose of evaluating the viability of strategies or projects, the key variables in them need to be quantified. Experience has shown that quantification always is a useful discipline in the development of scenarios, even if it is not required by the client. It often brings to the surface flaws in the logic that did not come out when the scenarios were discussed qualitatively. Quantification is a useful further check on the internal consistency of the stories.

THE SCENARIO TEAM

At the point of scenario construction, a bias in the scenario team may result in information being overlooked. It is important, therefore, to have a wide range of perspectives represented within the team.

Shell has a policy of changing the team almost completely for every scenario round, so that fresh perspectives can be brought to bear. The company goes out of its way to pick a broadly representative group, including economists, energy experts, marketers, engineers, and people from the "softer" disciplines, such as human resources. An attempt also is made to mix genders (which is not all that easy in an energy company) and cultures. In a multinational company like Shell, the latter is particularly important. Cultural domination by British or Dutch participants (the dual parentage of the company) must be avoided. Age and seniority are mixed as well. In this way a team is put together of individuals, each of whom can make a real contribution from his/her different perspective.

PRESENTATION AND COMMUNICATION

Once the scenarios have been finalized, they need to be communicated throughout the organization. This is done using many different techniques, including a printed book, personal presentations and electronic media (including videos, computer shows and multimedia presentations).

The following points apply to all of these modes of presentation:

- it is important to provide an early overview of all the scenarios, and their differences, to serve as a road map for the audience;
- a good scenario presentation provides an understanding of the logic before going into the stories;

- answer the question: "Why these scenarios and not others?";
- show a logical development of the storyline for each scenario, beginning with past history and then moving into the future;
- ensure the internal consistency of each story;
- minimize narrative, pictures bring out the holistic quality of the scenario exercise.

A particularly effective way of transferring the scenarios is by means of workshops, which can be designed either to further develop the scenarios or to work through their implications for action in a specified area.

PROBABILITY

Scenarios are helpful primarily as conceptual devices. Trying to assign subjective probabilities to scenarios does not add anything to it. In fact, experience has shown that attaching probabilities to scenarios reduces their effectiveness. Probabilities focus attention on some scenarios to the detriment of others. It is important to avoid making a choice between scenarios. Managers should consider their projects against all scenarios, not just against the one they believe to be the most probable. To focus on a single scenario is to re-introduce the weaknesses of the single-forecast approach.

Conclusions: Criteria for Good Scenarios

In summary, good scenarios are:

- relevant (rooted in the client's belief structures, addressing their deepest concerns);
- plausible (with a clear cause/effect logic from their historical roots into the future);
- internally consistent (logically relating a variety of seemingly unrelated variables/events);
- challenging to existing mindsets (advancing understanding by introducing new concepts and frameworks).

All four qualities are required. The absence of any one will seriously undermine the effectiveness of the scenario project, and make it either boring and uninformative, or fanciful and unbelievable. Finding the appropriate balance between these four criteria is the main challenge of any good scenario design.

Finally, and above all, the scenario process needs to be built into normal decision-making if it is to realize its full power.

References

Benard, A. 1980. "World Oil and Cold Reality," *Harvard Business Review*, Nov-Dec, 1980.

Eden, C. 1987. "Problem Solving/Finishing," in *New Directions in Management Sciences*. Gower.

Hirschhorn, L. 1984. *Beyond Mechanisation: Work and Technology in the Post-industrial Era*. Cambridge: MIT Press.

Ingvar, D. 1985. "Memories of the Future, an Essay on the Temporal Organisation of Awareness," *Human Neuro-biology*, 4: 127–36.

Kahane, A. 1992. "Scenarios for Energy: Sustainable World versus Global Mercantilism," *Long Range Planning*, Vol 25, No 4, 38–46.

Kahn, H. et al. 1967. *The Year 2000*. New York: Macmillan.

Mensch, G. 1979. *Stalemate in Technology, Innovations Overcome Depressions*. Cambridge: Ballinger.

Mintzberg, H. et al. 1985. "Of Strategies, Deliberate and Emergent," *Strategic Management Journal*, Vol 6, 257–72.

Normann, R. et al. 1993. "From Value Chain to Value Constellation: Designing Interactive Strategy," *Harvard Business Review*, July-Aug, 1993.

Schwartz, P. 1991. *The Art of the Long View*. New York: Doubleday.

Wack, P. 1985. "Scenarios, Uncharted Waters Ahead," *Harvard Business Review*, Sept-Oct, 1985.

———. 1985. "Scenarios, Shooting the Rapids," *Harvard Business Review*, Nov-Dec, 1985.

7 The Information Economy: ICT and the Future of the World Economy

Chris Freeman[*]

THIS PAPER DISCUSSES SOME OF THE DIFFICULTIES OF technological forecasting, with special reference to computer technology. It then takes up the question of defining the "information economy" and argues that the pervasive influence of information and communication technology (ICT) amounts to a change of "techno-economic paradigm" in the world economy. Such a paradigm change involves the transformation of skills, of the capital stock, and of work organization on a vast scale. The paper argues that this helps to explain the "productivity paradox" – why the universal introduction of computers has coincided with a slowdown of productivity growth and a rise of unemployment. All of our societies are engaged in an extensive process of social learning, in an effort to assimilate these new technologies and to develop ways to use them more effectively. Finally, the paper discusses a variety of institutional responses that have been tried to deal with this period of great turbulence and uncertainty, and contrasts the "systems of innovation" in various countries.

The Limits of Forecasting

Those involved in "technological forecasting", in the post-war period have come to recognize that accurate forecasts are impos-

* Christopher Freeman is Professor, and was the founding Director, at the Science Policy Research Unit (SPRU) of the University of Sussex in England. He also works with the Maastricht Economic Research Institute on Innovation and Technology (MERIT) in the Netherlands. He is a leading authority, and the author of numerous books and papers on economic policy and technical change. Professor Freeman also has participated in major policy research programs of the Organization for Economic Cooperation and Development, and the Commission of the European Union.

sible. Human history is a unique process and, by definition, any scientific discovery or radical innovation involves novelty. Consequently there is no way to achieve precision in this area. There are innumerable examples of forecasts that, with the benefit of hindsight, now appear to us to be ridiculous. Trend extrapolation is the commonest technique, but we are all aware that trends cannot persist forever (Table 1). For these reasons, large organizations, such as Shell, have often preferred to use scenarios to envisage a range of alternative possibilities.

Table 1

A TREND IS A TREND, IS A TREND

BUT WHEN AND HOW DOES IT BEND?

DOES IT RISE TO THE SKY?

OR LIE DOWN AND DIE?

OR ASYMPTOTE ON TO THE END?

Institute of Advanced Hindsight

Especially difficult are forecasts for the future of entirely new products, where there is no previous experience of production or of marketing or use. A good example, at the heart of ICT, is the electronic computer itself. It is well known that Thomas J. Watson Sr. (who had as much knowledge of the office equipment market as anyone in the world at that time) firmly believed that there would not be a big market for computers as office machines. Even when IBM was, at last, convinced to begin batch production of the 650 Model, the IBM sales forecasts hopelessly underestimated the market.

When we move from forecasting the future of an individual product, at the very beginning of its product life, to forecasting the diffusion of a product or a technology after some production and marketing experience is available, the situation is not quite so bad. There actually were many quite accurate forecasts, in the 1950s and 1960s, of the diffusion of consumer durables, such as refrigerators, televisions and automobiles. In 1961, for example, the National Institute of Economic and Social Research made a fairly accurate 10-year forecast of the future production and sale of automobiles. In that case, patterns of demand were fairly stable and so was product life: the technology was mature and the pattern of change was incremental.

We therefore need to distinguish between different types of innovation when we are attempting technological forecasting (Table 2). Most difficult to forecast, of course, is the future of a radical innovation, especially when it is at an early stage of development. Much easier to forecast is the future of an incremental innovation, since some trajectory already has been established.

Table 2
Taxonomy of Innovations

INCREMENTAL	Improvement of existing array of products, processes, systems, organizations
RADICAL OR BASIC	Departure from incremental improvement: new factory, new market, new organization
NEW TECHNOLOGY SYSTEM	Economically and technically interrelated clusters of innovations (radical and incremental)
TECHNO-ECONOMIC PARADIGM	A combination of system innovations affecting the entire economy and the typical "common-sense" for designers and managers in all industries

Source: Freeman and Perez (1988).

Techno-Economic Paradigms

Most innovations, however, do not arrive singly, but rather in clusters or systems. They are technically, economically and socially interconnected. A Canadian economist, Keirstead (1948), was

Table 3
Various Ways of Looking at ICT

Approach to information technology	"Information Society"	"IT" sector	Automation	ICT paradigm
Main focus of approach	Knowledge occupations	Micro-electronics, computers, telecommunications	Process innovations	Pervasive technology
Representative work or analysis	Machlup, Bell, Porat	MacIntosh, IT industry, classification systems	Wiener, Jenkins & Sherman, Craft Unions	Diebold, Imsi, Perez, Petit
Major economic consequences	Informatization post-industrial society	Rise of electronics industry	Unemployment and de-skilling as main problems	New industries, new services and transformation of old
Representative strategies and policy proposals	Education	Support for sector: ISDN, etc.	Shorter hours	Diffusion strategies
Approach to software	Software as just another occupation	Emphasis on software industry and hardware suppliers	Software neglected	Emphasis on software users
Implications for technology policy	No special implications for technology policy	Support for electronic industry R&D	Slow down technical change	Generic technology programs linked to diffusion networks

one of the first to recognize the importance of the systemic aspects of innovation, with his concept of "constellations of innovations." When many related technological systems are diffusing through the economy, we are entitled to speak of a change of "techno-economic paradigm."

Steam power and electric power are examples of earlier technologies that had pervasive effects on almost every industry and service, and so provided the basis for a new techno-economic paradigm in their day. Information and communication technology is perhaps the most pervasive technology system ever developed and so is triggering a particularly profound change of techno-economic paradigm. It affects not only every industry and every service activity in the economy, but also every function within each industry (Design, R&D, Production, Marketing, Administration) and their inter-relationships.

Various economists and sociologists had long recognized the growth of information work (e.g., Machlup, Daniel Bell), but they thought of it in terms of occupations (Table 3). For them, the important thing was the shift from blue-collar (manual) work to white-collar (clerical) work. They did not recognize the more radical change being brought about by electronic computers.

Of the various ways of analyzing the diffusion of ICT (Table 3), conceiving it as a change of techno-economic paradigm has proven to be the most fruitful (Perez, Imai, etc.). Two other analytic approaches provide more limited perspectives. The "automation" approach stresses the job destruction effects of the technology, while the analytic approach of the electronics industry emphasizes the job creation effects of the technology. But (as Schumpeter recognized) successive industrial revolutions are a process of creative destruction. They both destroy and create employment. Such industrial revolutions involve a fairly prolonged period of structural adjustment, during which there are basic changes in capital stock and in work organization, as well as in the entire skill profile of the work force and of management. By conceiving ICT as a change of techno-economic paradigm, we better can perceive and understand these dynamics.

Schumpeter (1939) related such changes of paradigm (such successive industrial revolutions) to what he perceived as long cycles in the world economy (Table 4), with the upswings corresponding to the periods of successful diffusion throughout the economy, and the downswings to the periods of painful and difficult adjustment. Carlota Perez (1983) introduced some original modifications to this Schumpeterian framework, and described the key changes of paradigm (from "Fordist" to "ICT") that we currently are experiencing in a way that is illuminating (Table 5).

The ICT Techno-Economic Paradigm

Table 5 summarizes some of the changes from the old "Fordist" style of organizing production to the new information-intensive (ICT) pattern. For example, the introduction of inter-linked computers in design, production and marketing means that far more rapid changes in product mix are feasible and that customized products are more easily produced at low cost. This may be described as "systemation" rather than "automation." In addition, horizontal flows of information and decentralized computing facilitate the elimination of some layers of middle management and lead to flat, rather than pyramidal, organizational structures. Under the ICT paradigm, firms now frequently see themselves as providing a service to their customers, with a variety of changing products and ancillary equipment and supporting software. The distinction between manufacturing and service industries becomes blurred. The role of government also changes significantly under the new paradigm, and increasingly is concerned with coordination, orchestration and the facilitation of consensual solutions.

The magnitude of these changes also provides some clues about the reasons for what Robert Solow has called the "Productivity Paradox" – why is it that, as computers have been adopted everywhere, productivity has slowed and unemployment has increased significantly, especially in OECD countries (Tables 6, 7 and 8)?

Table 4

1ST WAVE (1780s-1840s)	iron*, cotton textiles**, canals
2ND WAVE (1840s-1890s)	coal*, steam engines**, machine tools, railways (iron)
3RD WAVE (1890s-1940s)	steel*, electricity**, engineering, chemicals, railways (steel)
4TH WAVE (1940s-1990s)	oil*, automobiles**, petro-chemicals, aircraft, roads (highways)
5TH WAVE (1990s-?)	micro-electronics*, computers**, telecommunications, data networks

  * Key factor
** Engine of growth

Table 5
Change of Techno-economic Paradigm

"Fordist" – Old	ICT – New
Energy-intensive	Information-intensive
Standardized	Customized
Rather stable product mix	Rapid changes in product mix
Dedicated plant and equipment	Flexible production systems
Automation	Systemation
Single firm	Networks
Hierarchical structures	Flat horizontal structures
Departmental	Integrated
Product with service	Service with products
Centralization	Distributed intelligence
Specialized skills	Multi-skilling
Government ownership, control and planning	Government information, coordination and regulation – "vision"

Source: Perez (1990).

Table 6
Labour Productivity in Business Sector
OECD Countries

Country	1960–73	1973–79	1979–90
Belgium	5.2	2.8	2.4
Canada	2.8	1.5	1.2
Denmark	4.3	2.6	2.3
France	5.4	3.0	2.7
Germany (FR)	4.5	3.1	1.6
Italy	6.3	3.0	2.0
Japan	8.6	2.9	3.0
Netherlands	4.8	2.8	1.5
Spain	6.0	3.3	3.0
Sweden	4.1	1.5	1.5
UK	3.6	1.6	2.1
USA	2.2	0.0	0.5

Source: OECD (1992).

Table 7
Capital Productivity in Business Sector OECD Countries

Country	1960–73	1973–79	1979–90
Belgium	0.6	-1.8	-0.7
Canada	0.6	-0.5	-2.1
Denmark	-1.0	-2.4	-0.7
France	0.9	-1.0	-0.2
Germany (FR)	-1.4	-1.0	-0.7
Italy	0.4	0.4	0.0
Japan	-2.5	-3.4	-1.3
Netherlands	-0.4	-1.0	-0.5
Spain	-3.6	-5.1	-0.9
Sweden	-0.8	-2.3	-1.1
UK	-0.6	-1.5	0.4
USA	0.1	-1.3	-0.7

Source: OECD (1992).

Table 8
OECD Unemployment

Country	Average 1959-67	1979	1992
Belgium	2.4	8.7	9.7
Canada	5.0	7.4	10.4
Denmark	1.4	5.3	10.7
France	0.7	6.0	9.8
Germany (FR)	1.2	3.4	4.8
Ireland	4.6	7.5	16.9
Italy	6.2	7.5	11.2
Japan	1.4	2.0	2.2
Netherlands	0.9	4.1	6.5
UK	1.8	5.3	9.8
USA	5.3	5.8	7.1

Source: OECD.

Table 9
Rates of Growth of Exports in 1980–89

ALL PRIMARY COMMODITIES	2
of which	
Food	3
Raw materials	4
Ores, minerals	4
Fuels	5
ALL MANUFACTURES	8
of which	
Iron and steel	4
Textiles	6
Chemicals	7
Clothing	10
Machinery and transport	8
of which	
ICT goods	13

Source: GATT (1990).

Table 10
Share of Office Machinery and Telecommunications
Equipment in Total Merchandise Exports
(ranked by value of 1989 exports)

Rank	Country	1980	1989
1	Japan	14	28
2	USA	8	13
3	Germany (FR)	5	5
4	UK	5	9
5	Singapore	14	34
6	South Korea	10	22
7	Taiwan	14	25
8	Hong Kong	12	16
9	France	4	7
10	Netherlands	5	7
11	Canada	2.5	4
15	Sweden	6	8
	Brazil	(2)	(3)

Source: GATT: Table IV.40, Vol II.

The share of ICT products and services certainly has increased on a vast scale. They now are the fastest growing group in world trade (Table 9) and account for a very high proportion of total exports from countries such as Japan and the "Four Tigers" (Table 10). They also account for a significant proportion of total employment and of new investment, especially in the service industries. There can be no doubt that ICT is already a pervasive technology.

Therefore, if ICT is becoming so widespread, why are we seeing declines in both capital and labour productivity? What the Perez analysis suggests is that the massive changes, engendered by the conversion to this new ICT techno-economic paradigm, require a prolonged process of learning before we can discover how to make the best use of the new technologies. Productivity declines during this learning process should not be surprising. Many case studies of robotics and FMS diffusion (including studies of the computerization of banks and government offices, for example) point to the learning problems involved. These often lead to an absolute fall in productivity, at least until the problems are solved. A parallel fall in capital productivity was observed a century ago during the diffusion period for electric power.

Adapting National Institutions and Systems of Innovation

Countries have experienced very different levels of success in adapting to the new techno-economic paradigm, and there is much we might learn from those differences. Almost everywhere there has been a problem of skill shortages and skill mismatches, especially in the area of software development and applications. There also have been major problems of incompatibility of standards in manufacturing systems, office systems and telecommunications.

The greatest problems have been in the sphere of work organization. At one time it was fashionable to compare countries in terms of their R&D systems, as in the OECD "Science Policy" Reviews. But it has been recognized increasingly that a "National System of Innovation" is a better unit of analysis than an R&D system. We have to consider the qualitative features of an innovative system as well as the simple quantity of R&D (Table 11). In these areas there are substantial differences in national approaches. The example of Japan has been particularly influential and is often quoted by economists, such as Aoki (1988), Imai (1984) and Sako (1992), as well as by sociologists, such as Ronald Dore (Table 12).

The case of sub-contracting networks illustrates very well the great variety of national institutional arrangements and the extent to which these may affect the diffusion of new technologies. Mari Sako (1992) of the London School of Economics has compared Japanese and British sub-contracting networks within the same industries (Table 13). The contrast is very great: in

Table 11
Some Qualitative Features of
National Systems of Innovation

User-producer relationships
Sub-contractor networks
Science-technology networks
R&D-production linkages
Reverse engineering
Skills and tacit knowledge
Consultancy system and markets
Technology import capability
STS linkages with R&D

Table 12
Social Innovations in the Japanese
National System of Innovation (1970s-1990s)

- Horizontal information flows and communication networks within firms and groups yielding shorter lead times and better processes ("The Factory as Laboratory").
- The firm as a continuous learning and innovating organization by universal training and re-training.
- Capital market providing funds for long-term investment in R&D, training and equipment.
- Collaborative research networks facilitated by "Keiretsu" structure and stimulated/coordinated by central government with long-term strategic perspective ("Vision").
- "Fusion" research facilitated and stimulated by same approach ("Mechatronics," Chematronics") in engineering research associations.
- Links between basic research organizations through increasing performance of basic research in industry.

Table 13
Sub-contracting Networks

	ACR*	OCR**
Dependence	Lo	Hi
Procedure	Bids price contract	Order before price
Disputes	Strict adherence	Case by case
Risk sharing	Lo	Hi
Communication	Narrow minimal	Multiple frequent
Period	Short-term contract life	Long-term commitment
Set-up costs	Lo	Hi
Inspection	Thorough	None
Contract	Detailed clauses	Oral communication
Technology	Not negotiated	Strong interchange

  * ACR Arms length
** OCR Obligated

Source: Sako (LSE)

Britain there is dependence on formal legal contractual arrangements, with rather few high-level contacts; in Japan, oral communication at many different levels is key, with little regard to formal legal arrangements. The British "arms-length" approach was typically short term and involved little, if any, technical collaboration, while the Japanese "obligated" approach typically looked for a long-term partnership with increasing technical collaboration.

Research increasingly has focused on such specific institutional features of "national systems of innovation" (Lundvall, 1992; Mjøset, 1992; Nelson, 1993). One of the most striking, and instructive contrasts between national systems of innovation can be found by comparing Japan with the former Soviet Union

(Table 14). Although the Soviet Union had the highest GERD/ GNP ratio in the world in the 1970s and '80s, it had an extremely inefficient national system of innovation. Very little R&D was done at the enterprise level, and there were strong disincentives to innovation at the company level.

Moreover, even though there were relatively strong institutions in the Academy system, in universities and in industrial branch institutes, they were poorly coupled with the enterprises. Finally, linkages with sub-contractors and with the market were very weak or non-existent. The military-space complex absorbed nearly three-quarters of the available resources. It, therefore, was hardly surprising that the weak civil, national innovation system had a poor record, especially in the 1980s, when ICT became more and more important. A software industry outside the defense sector hardly existed, despite the Soviet Union's great strength in mathematics as a discipline and chess as a hobby.

An almost equally striking contrast can be made between the national innovation systems of Latin America and East Asia. The Asian countries were behind Latin America in the 1950s in their level of industrialization. In the 1960s and '70s they were often bracketed together as the fastest growing "Newly Industrializing Economies" (NIEs), but in the 1980s their paths completely diverged (Table 15). Whereas per capita incomes in the "Four Tigers" grew even faster than in the 1970s (and other countries of southern Asia and mainland China also grew extremely rapidly) growth slowed drastically in almost all Latin American countries, resulting in the so-called "lost decade."

The performance of the Asian countries often is explained in terms of their export orientation and, no doubt, there is considerable truth in this explanation. However, the commodity composition of their exports also merits close attention (Tables 10, 16 and 17). Together with Japan, the Four Tigers have by far the highest share of ICT products in their exports. This was the result of long-term policies to invest in education and training as well as in their telecommunications infrastructure (Tables 18 and 19). The

Table 14
Contrasting National Systems of Innovation – 1970s

JAPAN	USSR
High GERD/GNP* Ratio (2.5%); Very low proportion of military/space R&D (<2 per cent of R&D)	Very high GERD/GNP Ratio (c. 4 per cent); Extremely high proportion of military/space R&D (>70 per cent of R&D)
High proportion of total R&D at enterprise level and company-financed (approx. two-thirds)	Low proportion of total R&D at enterprise level and company-financed (<10 per cent)
Strong integration of R&D, production and import of technology at enterprise level	Separation of R&D, production and import of technology, and weak institutional linkages
Strong user-producer and sub-contractor network linkages	Weak or non-existent linkages between marketing, production, and procurement
Strong incentives to innovate at enterprise level involving both management and work force	Some incentives to innovate made increasingly strong in 1960s and '70s, but offset by other negative disincentives affecting both management and work force
Intensive experience of competition in international markets	Weak exposure to international competition except in arms race

* GERD/GNP = Gross expenditure on Research and Development/gross national product

Table 15
Comparative Growth Rates 1965–89

GDP* % p.a.	1965–80	1980–89
East Asia	7.5	7.9
South Asia	3.9	5.1
Africa (sub-Sahara)	4.0	2.1
Latin America	5.8	1.6
GDP per Capita % p.a.	1965–80	1980–89
East Asia	5.0	6.3
South Asia	1.5	2.9
Africa (sub-Sahara)	1.1	-1.2
Latin America	3.5	-0.5

*GDP = gross domestic product
Source: World Bank Development Report (1991).

Table 16
Shares of Various Countries and Rates of Growth in
Merchandise Exports 1980–88

	Merchandise Exports 1989 $ Bn	Manufacturers Exports 1989 $ Bn	Manufacturers of Merchandise Exports %	Annual Average Growth of Merchandise Exports 1980–88
Hong Kong	73.1	66.8	90.1	15.5
Taiwan	66.2	61.1	90.2	15.0
South Korea	62.3	57.8	90.3	17.0
China	51.6	28.3	54.9	13.0
Singapore	44.7	31.8	72.0	9.0
Thailand	20.1	11.5	57.2	12.0
Mexico	35.6	22.8	64.0	6.5
Brazil	34.4	19.9	57.9	6.5
Venezuela	13.0	4.0*	30.1*	-7.5

* estimated
Source: GATT, International Trade 1989-90, Volume II.

Table 17
Export of ICT Goods

Country	World Market Share in 1980 (%)	Share in 1989 (%)
Japan	21.0	25.5
USA	20.0	18.5
Germany (Fr)	10.0	7.0
UK	6.5	6.5
France	4.5	4.0
Italy	3.5	2.5
Canada	2.0	2.0
Four Tigers	11.0	21.0
Singapore	3.0	6.0
South Korea	2.0	5.5
Taiwan	3.0	5.0
Hong Kong	3.0	4.5

Source: GATT International Trade 1991, Volume II

Table 18
Engineering and Science Students as % of Population

Country	Engineers only	Science+, Maths+, Engineers
Japan	0.34	0.41
Brazil	0.13	0.24
South Korea	0.54	0.76
Taiwan	0.68	0.78
Singapore	0.61	0.73

Table 19
Development in Telecommunications–1988

Country	Telephone lines per person	Per capita sales of equipment ($ US)
Brazil	6	10
Colombia	7	21
Malaysia	7	32
South Korea	24	77
Singapore	34	235
UK	39	166
Japan	39	315
Germany (FR)	46	306
USA	53	389

Source: KISDI

combined result of these differences between the national systems of innovation of East Asia and Latin America is striking (Table 20), and is suggestive of what kinds of institutional approaches are more likely to succeed under the new techno-economic paradigm.

Some observers expect that the United States and Canada now may begin to improve their performance relative to Japan, and that the Latin American countries may improve relative to East Asia. President Clinton, for example, recently has announced a whole series of measures designed to accelerate the pace of technical change in the United States. These measures range from energy-efficient federal buildings to advanced manufacturing extension centers, which are able to assist firms with anything from the adoption of "agile" techniques to "information superhighways."

It remains to be seen, however, whether these measures and (more importantly) changes made by industry itself, will prove sufficient to reverse the adverse features of the American national

Table 20
Divergence in National Systems of Innovation in the 1980s

EAST ASIA	LATIN AMERICA
Expanding education system with high levels of participation in tertiary education, and with a high proportion of engineering graduates	Deteriorating education system with proportionately lower output of engineers
Rapid growth of scientific and technical activities at enterprise level, especially R&D	Slow growth, stagnation or decline of enterprise-level R&D
Industrial R&D typically rises to >50 per cent of all R&D	Industrial R&D typically remains at <30 per cent of total
Development of strong science-technology infrastructure	Weakening of science-technology infrastructure
Strong influence of Japanese models of management and networking organization	Continuing influence of American management models
High levels of investment and major inflow of Japanese investment	Decline in foreign investment and generally lower levels of investment
Heavy investment in advanced telecommunications	Slow development of modern telecommunications
Strong and fast-growing electronic industries with high exports	Weak electronic industries with low exports
Growing participation in international technology networks and agreements	Low level of international networking in technology

Table 21
MIT Report "Made in America" (1989)
(Eds.: Dertouzos, Lester, Solow)
"Pervasive Ills of the U.S. Economy"

Outdated strategies	Mass production mentality Parochialism
Short-term horizons	Capital market R&D
Organizational weaknesses in development and production	Lead times Quality
Neglect of human resources	Education Training
Failures of cooperation	Within firms Labour relations Networks
Government and industry at cross purposes	

system of innovation that were highlighted in the MIT Report (Dertouzos et al. 1989), "Made in America" (Table 21).

Japan, too, has deep problems, including the collapse of asset values and the need for continually expanding markets for Japanese mass-production industries. Most of Japan's major electronic and automobile firms suffered a serious decline in profitability in 1992–3. Many observers also point to conformism in Japanese society as a possible source of weakness, now that Japan has reached the world technological frontier. Diversity and non-conformism are essential to radical innovation and scientific advancement. Moreover, the growth of protectionism and the instability of world capital markets and exchange rates also create new dangers for Japanese trade.

Conclusions

One important conclusion we can draw from all of this is the importance of learning from the very different ways in which national social institutions have adapted (or not) to the new techno-economic paradigm, and which adaptations of social institutions seem to work best.

To a very large degree, it is on that process of institutional adaptation, on that social learning process, that economic success will depend in this new era.

Such a learning process will be especially important for Third World development, given the continued divergence in growth rates and related instabilities. One positive sign is that the World Bank has begun to recognize the importance of intangible investment (for example, in training and institutional development), and has begun to devote resources to this type of investment in some Third World countries. But this investment will have to go a lot further if the countries of Latin America and Africa are to have any hope of catching up with East Asia. What is needed is a wider set of institutional changes, designed to strengthen the autonomous capability of Third World countries for innovation and diffusion. Canada's International Development Research Centre (IDRC) has been a pioneer in the development of such approaches.

In this effort to develop social institutions and approaches more appropriate to the new techno-economic paradigm, it will be essential not to forget long-term, global, environmental issues. Indeed, ICT has tremendous potential to aid in the development of more sustainable approaches to development (Freeman, 1992). I hope that at least one of your scenarios will incorporate this possibility. This is above all an area where international cooperation is essential, and where Canada is in a unique position to provide leadership.

References

Aoki, M. 1988. *Information, Incentives and Bargaining in the Japanese Economy*. New York: Cambridge University Press.

Bell, D. 1974. *The Coming of Post-industrial Society*. London: Heinemann.

Dertouzos, M., R.K. Lester, and R. Solow. 1989. *Made in America*. Cambridge: MIT Press.

Dore, R. 1973. *British Factory–Japanese Factory: the Origins of National Diversity in Industrial Relations*. Berkeley: University of California Press.

Dore, R. 1987. *Taking Japan Seriously*. London: Athlone Press.

Freeman, C. 1992. *The Economics of Hope*. London: Pinter.

———— and C. Perez. 1988. "Structural crises of adjustment: business cycles and investment behaviour," 3 in Dosi, G. et al., eds. *Technical Change and Economic Theory*. London: Pinter.

GATT. 1991. *International Trade 1989–1990*. Geneva: GATT.

Imai, K. and H. Itauri. 1984. "Inter-penetration of organization and market: Japan's firm and market in comparison with US," *International Journal of Industrial Organization*, 285–310.

Jenkins, C. and B. Sherman. 1979. *The Collapse of Work*. London: Eyre Methuen.

Keirstead, B.S. 1948. *The Theory of Economic Change*. Toronto: Macmillan.

Lundvall, B.A., ed. 1992. *National Systems of Innovation*. London: Pinter.

Machlup, F. 1962. *The Production and Distribution of Knowledge*. Princeton: Princeton University Press.

Mjøset, L. 1992. *The Irish Economy in a Comparative International Perspective*. Dublin: NESC.

Nelson, R., ed. 1993, forthcoming. *National Systems of Innovation: An International Comparison*. Oxford: Oxford University Press.

OECD. 1992. *Economic Outlook*. Paris: OECD.

Perez, C. 1983. "Structural change and the assimilation of new technologies in the economic and social system," *Futures*, Vol. 15, No. 5, 359–75.

Sako, M. 1992. *Contracts, Prices and Trust: How the Japanese and British Manage their Sub-Contracting Relationships*. Oxford: Oxford University Press.

Schumpeter, J.S. 1939. *Business Cycles,* 2 Vols. New York: McGraw Hill.

Wiener, N. 1949. *The Human Use of Human Beings: a Cybernetic Approach.* New York: Houghton.

World Bank. 1991. *World Development Report.* New York: Oxford University Press.

Tables

1. Institute of Advanced Hindsight quote.
2. Taxonomy of Innovations
3. Various Ways of Looking at ICT
4. Cycles in the World Economy
5. Change of Techno-economic Paradigm
6. Labour Productivity in Business Sector, OECD Countries, 1960–90
7. Capital Productivity in Business Sector, OECD Countries 1960–90
8. OECD Unemployment
9. Rates of Growth and Exports in 1980–90
10. Share of Office Machinery and Telecommunications Equipment in Total Merchandise Exports
11. Some Qualitative Features of National Systems of Innovation 1970s–90s
12. Social Innovations in the Japanese National System of Innovation 1970s–90s
13. Sub-contracting Networks
14. Contrasting National Systems of Innovation – 1970s
15. Comparative Growth Rates 1965–89
16. Shares of Various Countries and Rates of Growth in Merchandise Exports 1980–88
17. Export of ICT Goods
18. Engineering and Science Students as % of Population
19. Development in Telecommunications – 1988
20. Divergence in National Systems of Innovation in the 1980s
21. MIT Report, Pervasive Ills of the U.S. Economy

8 Postmodernism, Pluralism, and the Crisis of Legitimacy

Walter Truett Anderson[*]

We must reconcile ourselves to a paradoxical-sounding thought: namely, the thought that we no longer live in the 'modern' world. The 'modern' world is now a thing of the past. Our own natural science today is no longer 'modern' science. Instead...it is rapidly engaged in becoming 'postmodern' science: the science of the 'postmodern' world, of 'postnationalist' politics and 'postindustrial' society – the world that has not yet discovered how to define itself in terms of what it is, but only in terms of what it has just-now ceased to be.[106]

IF THE WORLD IS ENTERING an historical era significantly different from the modern era that shaped society and governance as we have known them, we must attempt to understand what implications this transition may have for the various concepts of authority that underlie public and private institutions. Not only are specific authority systems such as church and state, in crisis, but so is authority itself. This is not to say that these institutions are on the verge of collapse, but that their foundations are being challenged by the main themes of contemporary postmodern thought.

[*] Walter Truett Anderson is a political scientist and the author of numerous books and articles on issues of governance, technology and cultural change. His most recent book is *Reality Isn't What It Used To Be* (San Francisco: Harper/Collins, 1992). Dr. Anderson is a Fellow of the World Academy of Art and Science and is Chairman of the Board of Trustees of the Saybrook Institute.

106 Toulmin, Steven. *The Return to Cosmology: Postmodern Science and the Theology of Nature* (Berkeley: University of California Press, 1982), 254.

What are these themes? What, for that matter, is postmodern thought?

Several answers can be put forward, and it is typical of the postmodern condition that there is no final arbiter. Some schools of thought (in architecture, for example) call themselves "postmodern," and we can find various discussions of the condition of "postmodernity," but these are not quite the same as a coherent dogma or doctrine. Postmodern thought is, rather, a number of attempts to engage the zeitgeist. We should perhaps note here the distinction between the term "postmodernity," which has to do with the condition in which we find ourselves, and "postmodernism," which refers to various movements that aspire to serve as the cutting-edge of this condition.

Definitions of Postmodern

Some definitions of postmodernity or postmodernism are widely cited, and have a certain canonical status in various dialogues and arguments.

Among these is the one offered by David Harvey in his book *The Condition of Postmodernity.* Harvey defines postmodernity as the situation in which the world finds itself after the breakdown of the "Enlightenment project":

> The Enlightenment project...took it as axiomatic that there was only one possible answer to any question. From this it followed that the world could be controlled and rationally ordered if we could only picture and represent it rightly. But this presumed that there existed a single correct mode of representation which, if we could uncover it (and this was what scientific and mathematical endeavours were all about), would provide the means to Enlightenment ends.[107]

---

107   Harvey, David. *The Condition of Postmodernity* (Cambridge: Basil Blackwell, 1989), 27.

Another frequently quoted definition of postmodernism comes from Jean-Francois Lyotard, who, in his book *The Postmodern Condition,* says that all modern systems of knowledge, including science, legitimate themselves with reference to a "metanarrative" or "grand discourse" about the course of history. He cites as examples the Hegelian metanarrative of the Spirit, the Marxist metanarrative of revolution, and the Enlightenment metanarrative of rational progress. And he proceeds to define postmodern as "incredulity toward metanarratives."[108]

Jurgen Habermas is seen primarily as a critic of postmodern thought, but in the process he also has become one of its definers. He recognizes the problem of a "legitimation crisis," caused by the forces of which Harvey and Lyotard speak, and advocates a renewal of the Enlightenment project in the name of "communicative action." He has contributed to framing the debate about the political implications of postmodernity.

The postmodern era has intensified debate between those who still cling to some system of absolute truth and those who are more inclined to recognize all truths as, in some measure, socially constructed. This polarization is variously characterized as objectivists vs. constructivists, absolutists vs. relativists, or fundamentalists vs. revisionists. Richard Rorty, an increasingly important participant in the dialogue about postmodernity, speaks of "metaphysicians" and "ironists" – that is, those who see truth as found and those who see it as made. Metaphysicians, he says, "believe that there are, out there in the world, real essences which it is our duty to discover, and which are disposed to assist in their own discovery." Ironists, according to Rorty, are "always aware that the terms in which they describe themselves are subject to change, always aware of the contingency and fragility of their final vocabularies, and thus of their selves."[109]

108 Lyotard, Jean-François. *The Postmodern Condition: A Report on Knowledge* (Minneapolis: University of Minnesota Press, 1984).
109 Rorty, Richard. *Contingency, Irony and Solidarity* (Cambridge: Cambridge University Press, 1989), 73.

Social Coherence: Premodern, Modern, Postmodern

The dialogue about postmodernity has to do with the human need for universality (or, at the very least, for social coherence). Human beings are social creatures, and our beliefs and values – indeed, our very sense of who and what we are – are formed by the social environments in which we live.

In premodern societies, it was possible for people to live their entire lives within the context of a single, coherent system of beliefs and values. This is not to say that premodern societies necessarily were simple or primitive, only that the majority of people who were members of those societies, were relatively free from the experience of "culture shock," from the experience of close contact with other people who had entirely different systems of value and belief: different world views, different realities.

Modernism begins with culture shock, and with the attempt to create and institutionalize larger (and less vulnerable) systems of value and belief, which are believed to hold true across all cultures. Some observers would place the beginnings of modernism as far back as the time of Socrates and Plato, who were engaged in finding essential truths, truths greater than those of their tribal gods. Other great institutionalized belief systems – philosophical, religious, ideological, and various combinations of the three – have dominated modern history, and frequently have competed with one another. Although all of these have laid claim to absolute, cosmic, transcendent truth (and thus to being able to serve as the source of universal values and beliefs that are not merely contingent upon culture) none has been able to gain universal agreement.

Premodern societies had an experience of universality, but no concept of it; modern civilization has had a concept of universality, but no experience of it. Now, in the postmodern era, the very concept of universality is, as the deconstructionists say, "put into question."

How did we get here? One might reasonably respond that the postmodern condition is created by mobility, globalization, and technological change. All of these answers would be correct. Postmodernity is the result of a vastly increased exposure to otherness: because, in traveling, you put yourself into a different reality; because a different reality comes to you; and because, with no physical movement at all (only the flow of information) cultures now interpenetrate. It now becomes increasingly hard to live one's life within the premodern condition of an undisturbed society, or within the modern condition of a strongly institutionalized belief system.

Main Currents of Postmodern Thought

Contemporary cultural life is crowded with schools and movements that, in various ways and languages, deal with the issues of postmodernity, or describe themselves as postmodern. Some of these are now beginning to flow together into a sort of postmodern synthesis, but there remains a wide and rather bewildering variety of discourses.

One of the oldest schools of thought that specifically addresses these concerns is the sociology of knowledge, which dates back to the 1930s, and which is admirably presented in Berger and Luckmann's book *The Social Construction of Reality*.[110] For many people, however, postmodern thought really dates from the period following the student upheavals in Europe in the late 1960s, with its turn to "post-structuralism." This period saw a strong surge of interest in the work of Michel Foucault (who undertook the "archaeological" documentation of the creation of various realities, such as the idea of madness), and in the "deconstructionist" literary criticism of Derrida. As this interest spread across the Atlantic, in the 1970s, the postmodern era began in many North American universities.

Other thinkers also have become voices in the postmodern conversation: anthropologists such as Gregory Bateson and

---

110 Berger, P.L., and T. Luckmann. *The Social Construction of Reality* (New York: Doubleday, 1966).

Clifford Geertz, linguists such as George Lakoff, "constructivist" cognitive scientists such as Marvin Minsky, philosophers such as Richard Rorty. And, since the question of how societies construct gender roles is of immediate and intense concern for women, postmodern themes are a central part of contemporary feminist scholarship.

Postmodern philosophy is linked to the "linguistic turn" taken by thinkers such as Wittgenstein. Richard Rorty, lucidly summarizing one of the central themes of this emphasis on language, says:

> We need to make a distinction between the claim that the world is out there and the claim that truth is out there. To say that the world is out there, that it is not our creation, is to say, with common sense, that most things in space and time are the effects of causes which do not include human mental states. To say that truth is not out there is simply to say that where there are no sentences there is no truth, that sentences are elements of human languages, and that human languages are human creations.[111]

Today, postmodernism has become an academic growth industry, with new volumes appearing regularly from the university presses. It also has become a recurrent theme in high and low culture, and has made it increasingly hard to tell which is which.

According to architect Charles Jencks, the postmodern era commenced at 3:32 p.m. on July 15, 1972, when the vast Pruitt-Igoe housing development in St. Louis, which had been praised as a perfect example of LeCorbusier's "machine for living", was dynamited as an uninhabitable environment for the low-income people it had housed. That collapse coincided with the collapse of doctrinaire "high modernism" and its tendencies toward standardization. Jencks says: "Modern architecture, as the son of the Enlightenment, was an heir to its congenital naiveties...."[112]

111 Rorty, op. cit., 4–5.
112 Jencks, Charles. *What is Postmodernism?* (London: Academy Editions, 1989).

The collapse opened up a world of new possibilities, including a period of infatuation with "vernacular" architecture (such as Las Vegas casinos). Postmodern architects reject the notion that they have to swear allegiance to any particular style. They embrace eclecticism (the greatest sin of modernism) and cheerfully combine different architectural languages. In fact, Jencks speaks of "double-coding" – the mixture of monumental and high-tech modes, or of high and low art – as characteristic of postmodern architecture, expressing the "pluralism of culture" and embodying a recognition that rules of style are socially constructed.

Similar themes – an increasing plurality of styles, an incredulity toward the reign of any school or style, a breakdown of the boundary between high and low art – are visible in much of contemporary art and culture. Jim Collins, in his book *Uncommon Cultures*, asserts that, although we still speak of "the culture" or "the dominant culture" as though it were a recognizable and more or less monolithic entity in modern societies, no such entity exists.

> We need to see popular culture and Postmodernism as a continuum because both reflect and produce the same cultural perspective – that 'culture' no longer can be conceived as a Grand Hotel, as a totalizable system that somehow orchestrates all cultural production and reception according to one master system. Both insist, implicitly or explicitly, that what we consider 'our culture' has become discourse-sensitive, that how we conceptualize that culture depends upon discourses which construct it in conflicting, often contradictory ways, according to interests and values of those discourses as they struggle to legitimize themselves as privileged forms of representation.[113]

This thesis says something rather more serious than Yeats' famous "the center cannot hold." It says that there is no center.

---

113 Collins, J. *Uncommon Cultures: Popular Culture and Postmodernism* (New York: Routledge, 1989), xiii.

Languages of Truth and Reality in Public Dialogue

The Enlightenment project was an attempt to give one mode of approaching truth (one mode of verifying reality) a position superior to (in fact, supplanting) other modes such as social tradition or religious revelation. That mode (scientific rationality) has not completely lost its privileged place in the postmodern era; but it now has to exist alongside other, and in some cases significantly different, ways of thinking.

I propose that we can identify at least four different concepts of reality – different epistemologies, sensibilities, world views, or what, in postmodern terminology, would be called "discourses" – that function in contemporary public life. Each of these has different ideas of what truth is, how it is to be found, and how it may be verified or evaluated. These are:

- the postmodern/constructivist, in which truth is regarded as socially constructed;
- the scientific/rational, in which truth is "found" through disciplined inquiry and scientific method (and findings are subject to the testing of replication);
- the social/traditional, in which truth is regarded as embodied in the cultural heritage of a given society;
- the neo-romantic, in which truth is to be found in the soul, in nature, in passion or in introspection.

The scientific/rational and social/traditional, taken together, are the power structure; the alliance between them is sometimes fractious, as in the debate between evolution (a major tenet of the scientific world view) and creationism (a backward but respectable cousin of western Christian civilization) but, on the whole, they support one another. They are the twin pillars of modernism.

Modernism now equates with a certain kind of conservatism, with the urge to hold onto the institutions of modernity and the world view that built them. Neo-romanticism – expressed now in much New Age spirituality and radical environmentalism – is reactionary, hankering back to a supposed golden era before the Industrial Revolution and the Enlightenment.

Personal Identity in the Postmodern World

Since human identity is constructed in the context of society, the fragmentation of culture in the postmodern world is reflected in a fragmentation of the self.

Life in premodern societies undoubtedly had many kinds of stress, both psychological and physical, but identity crisis was not one of them. The experience of living totally within a single community (with its roles clearly defined and celebrated in rites of passage, its values and beliefs continually reinforced) allowed individuals to develop a strong sense of who and what they were – a condition in which individual and community were inseparable.

For many people in modernizing social environments (especially those who remained within relatively remote villages or in communities such as monasteries) social reality may have been equally stable. But, for most, the experiences of modernization bring increasing contact with other realities, and so require increasingly heroic efforts to create institutions and belief systems capable of sustaining a sense of truth and personal identity.

Postmodern life brings an even more diverse, and often contradictory, barrage of cultural stimuli. The postmodern individual is, in Kenneth Gergen's term, the "saturated self," a member of many communities and networks, a participant in many discourses, an audience to messages from everybody and everywhere – messages that present conflicting ideals and norms and images of the world, even different beliefs about belief. Gergen speaks of a condition he calls multiphrenia, a "fragmenting and populating of self-experience" in which we must find a way to integrate the different identities we construct for ourselves in different contexts.[114]

---

114 Gergen, Kenneth J. *The Saturated Self: Dilemmas of Identity in Contemporary Life* (New York: Basic Books, 1991).

In psychology, postmodernism is manifest in new attempts to define the human personality as more diverse, changeable and multi-dimensional; and in new psychotherapies which attempt to help individuals and families grapple with the tensions of life in "saturated" cultures. There are now numerous schools of postmodern or constructivist therapy (and a growing body of theoretical work) that draw heavily on postmodern thought.

Postmodern Politics

The modern era was dominated by conflict between belief systems: between religions, between religion and science and, most notably, between political ideologies. The postmodern era is characterized by conflicts within belief systems, as each religion and ideology develops its schisms between its absolutists and its relativists. In a sense, each institutionalized belief system is having its own crisis of legitimized authority, as many of its members come to regard its truths as being socially constructed – by human beings, in response to specific historical conditions and sets of values – and so subject to being reconstructed, in the light of changed conditions and understandings.

Sociologist James Davison Hunter has written of the prevalent "culture wars" which, he says, rage through many institutions and subject areas – the family, art, education, law, politics – and which are essentially different forms of "political and social hostility rooted in different systems of moral understanding."[115] Hunter defines the polarizing stress as being a split between "impulses toward orthodoxy" and "impulses toward progressivism." This turns out to be more or less the same as what others have described as a conflict between objectivists and constructivists, or between absolutists and relativists, or between fundamentalists and revisionists, or between metaphysicians and ironists.

Hunter describes orthodoxy as "the commitment on the part of adherents to an external, definable, and transcendent authori-

---

115 Hunter, James Davison. *Culture Wars: The Struggle to Define America* (New York: Basic Books, 1991).

ty;" and progressivism as "the tendency to resymbolize historic faiths according to the prevailing assumptions of contemporary life." However its antagonists may be defined, the culture wars, as Hunter describes them, appear to be flaring across an astonishingly wide social battlefield, and to be revealing crises of legitimacy wherever authority exists.

Hunter's subject is the domestic culture wars – his book is subtitled *The Struggle to Define America*. But it is not hard to extend the same description and analysis to the conflicts between orthodox/fundamentalist Muslims and their progressive/secularist counterparts in countries such as Egypt, or between fundamentalist Hindus and the secularist Hindu political establishment in India, or between doctrinaire Marxists and free-market revisionists in the former Soviet empire, or between "traditionalists" and "moderns" who contend with one another in the politics of indigenous tribal societies, or even between the "fundis" and the "realos" who battle for the soul of the Green political movement in Germany.

The postmodern conflict has become a global one, and globalization itself is one of the issues. Progressivism generally tends toward a greater willingness to adapt to a changing and pluralistic global community, while orthodoxy tends toward particularism and separatism. The Islamic fundamentalists in Algeria, tearing down television antennas on the roofs of houses in order to protect their countrymen from the corrupting influence of European television, clearly see the outer world as their enemy.

Life in the Post-postmodern World

In summarizing, let us examine three somewhat over-simplified scenarios for the future:

BACK TO BASICS

The world separates into a number of distinct social entities. Different regions become bastions of fundamentalist Christianity, fundamentalist Islam, Marxism, clearly defined ethnic groups such as Basques, American Indian tribes, Palestinians: each group maintaining its traditions and lifestyles with minimal change, dilution or outside interference. (This scenario is popular with cultural preservationists and enthusiasts for the currently fashionable agenda of "devolving" global society into smaller social and political units.)

TOMORROW THE WORLD
Global civilization comes together under one belief system. Peace and stability are achieved as all learn to understand reality according to the same teachings. (Although most of us regard this scenario as highly unlikely, many people still hope to unite the world under one Christian, Marxist or otherwise monolithic order.)

A PLURALITY OF PLURALISMS
All regions of the world become pluralistic, with people of different races, religions, world views and traditions living in close contact with one another and exposed to global events. There are not only many beliefs, but many beliefs about belief. People inhabit cultures in different ways, improvise, and create new forms. "Culture wars" between traditionalists and innovators continue to be a familiar part of social and political life everywhere.

Conclusion: Postmodern Pragmatism and the next Enlightenment Project

People frequently hasten to dismiss the postmodern diagnosis of our time as a prescription for a state of valueless relativism, in which all values and beliefs are to be regarded as equal because they are equally lacking in transcendent justification. I submit that, although there are many weaknesses and flaws in postmodern thought, this is not one of them. In the postmodern context we do not cease to value or to evaluate, but we do find ourselves compelled to take a new look at how we go about it: to evaluate, in a sense, evaluation.

Evaluation and meaning-making appear to be integral parts of human cognition. Human societies may create many different values and beliefs, but nobody has ever discovered a society, or a functioning individual, who did not have values and beliefs (and opinions).

Furthermore, even the most fervent postmodernist remains a product of his or her culture; we may come to understand that culture in a different way, but no one stands completely outside of culture. The postmodern experience seems to be one of participating in numerous cultures, and to some extent, even internalizing parts of them. We do not find that we are left with nothing, but that (equally bewildering) we are left with everything.

The challenge of postmodernism is to learn to live without the idea that our particular values and beliefs (and opinions) are rooted in any absolute, transcendent, super-human and universal truth. We come instead to see them as contingent products of our historical experience and of the time and place in which we live. And none of us forfeits the right (indeed, the responsibility) to participate actively, even passionately, in the construction of our own social reality.

But on what basis, other than mere personal whim, can we evaluate competing ideas about what this social reality should be? Richard Rorty proposes a rediscovery of pragmatism, which essentially is a decision to evaluate ideas on the basis of their effects rather than on the basis of their congruence with some absolute doctrine or metanarrative. He also acknowledges that this is easier said than done:

> If one takes the core of pragmatism to be its attempt to replace the notion of true beliefs as representations of 'the nature of things' and instead to think of them as successful rules for action, then it becomes easy to recommend an experimental, fallibilist attitude, but hard to isolate a 'method' that will embody this attitude.[116]

116 Rorty, Richard. *Objectivity, Relativism and Truth* (Cambridge: Cambridge University Press, 1991), 65–6.

Although postmodern pragmatism may not be any easier (actually it may be more difficult) than claiming the authority of Marx or Jesus, it does offer a promising way to understand public dialogue, and to commence a new conversation. This conversation may, in time, turn out to be a very different sort of Enlightenment project – one that recognizes, and even celebrates, the incredible diversity of human thought, sees the mind as multi-epistemological, and does not expect to progress toward a world in which there is only one right answer to any question.

9 Communitarianism[*]

Amitai Etzioni[**]

What is Communitarianism?

Communitarianism is a social movement that aims at changing our moral and civic environment. It is part change of heart, part renewal of social bonds, part reform of public life.

Change of heart is the most basic aim. Without stronger moral voices, public authorities are over-burdened and markets cannot work. Without moral commitments, people act without consideration for one another. In recent years, too many of us have been reluctant to lay moral claims on one another. It is a mistaken notion that just because we desire to be free from governmental controls, we should also be free from responsibilities to the common good, or indifferent to the community.

Whose Values Should the Renewed Moral Voices Reaffirm?

Let's start with those values we all share. Nobody seriously maintains that lying is better than telling the truth. Using force to intimidate fellow human beings – whether it is a police officer indiscriminately clubbing a civilian who is already shackled, or rioters pulling innocent people out of their cars – is something we

---

[*] Drawn directly on *The Spirit of Community*, by Amitai Etzioni.

[**] Amitai Etzioni is a Professor at George Washington University, and also has served as Professor at Harvard and Columbia Universities. He is the editor of *The Responsive Community*, a Communitarian journal, and is the author of 14 books and numerous articles on issues of social organization and change. His most recent book is *The Spirit of Community: Rights, Responsibilities and the Communitarian Agenda* (Crown Books, 1993).

deem to be unacceptable. Sexual harassment occurs, and while we may disagree about what exactly is encompassed by this term, we all agree that it should be considered morally inappropriate. And so on.

In the 1950s we had a well established society, but it was unfair to women and minorities and a bit authoritarian. In the 1960s we undermined the established society and its values. In the 1980s we were told that the unbridled pursuit of self-interest was a virtue. By the 1990s we have seen the cumulative results. There is now almost universal agreement that the resulting world of massive street violence, the failing war against illegal drugs, unbridled greed, and so on, is not the future we wish for our children and ourselves.

The Future

FAMILY

To shore up the moral foundations of our society, we start with the family. The family always was entrusted with laying the foundations of moral education. In the renewed communities we envision, the upbringing of children is not a job for mothers alone, but for both parents. There is no contradiction between treating women and men as equals, and calling for greater attention to, investment in, and above all, a higher valuation of children.

SCHOOLS

Schools are more than places in which people acquire skills and knowledge: they are places in which they acquire (or fail to acquire) education. Education includes the reinforcement of values gained at home, and the introduction of values to children whose parents neglected their character formation and moral upbringing.

NEIGHBOURHOODS

These are social webs that are provided by communities in localities, at work and in ethnic clubs and associations. They bind individuals, who otherwise would be on their own, into groups of people who care for one another, and who help to maintain a civic, social and moral order. For these communities to be able to make their contributions, they need to be strengthened. This will require a new respect for the role that institutions, such as local schools, have in sustaining communities. It also will require that government refrain from usurping the functions of communities; that planners make spaces more community-friendly; and that all of us invest more of ourselves in one another.

NATIONAL SOCIETY

We need to ensure that local communities will not adopt values that we, as a national society, abhor (such as burning books). Our national society needs to maintain encompassing bonds that keep the many groups, of which it is composed, from turning hateful and violent toward one another. We readily can accommodate, indeed be enriched by, the cuisine, music and religious practices of the great variety of sub-cultures that make up America. But all of these sub-groups need to subscribe to a set of overall values – to the democratic process, to the Constitution and the Bill of Rights, and to a commitment to be respectful of one another – if our national society is to thrive.

Rights and Responsibilities

We need to concern ourselves with the civic order. Individuals' rights need to be balanced with social responsibilities. For example, if people want to be tried before juries of their peers, they should be willing to serve on such juries. If people want elected officials that respond to their values and needs, they should be willing to involve themselves in the primaries in which the candidates are chosen. Voting is not enough. We also have to dedicate more time and energy to participating in local politics and institutions, from the community hospital to the local school board.

We need to remind one another that no rights are absolute. Even freedom of speech, we all know, is denied to people who want to shout fire in a crowded theater when there is no fire. To make society work again, in the face of serious new threats, we should be willing, for example, to require mandatory drug testing for those who have the lives of others in their hands, or to set up sobriety checkpoints to stop drunk drivers, or to ask people, whose blood is being tested, to allow it to be checked for the HIV infection.

The Public Interest

Special interests need to be countered, and their money kept from corrupting our elected officials. The political energy required to reform the political system, so that it better protects the public interest, can only come from aggrieved citizens banding together to clean up politics.

During a dinner discussion of the Communitarian agenda, Dr. Joan W. Konner, the dean of the School of Journalism at Columbia University, puzzled over Communitarianism. "It appears to be one part church sermon, one part re-assertion of old values, one part political campaign and one part social movement," she said. I could not have put it better myself. The Communitarian agenda, of necessity, is as complex and encompassing as the problems we face: beware of politicians promising simple solutions. Our aim is to change values, to alter mind-sets, and to promote public policy that serves the common good.

10 The Learning Society in the Information Age*

Daniel P. Keating**

The Information Age: Challenges for Contemporary Societies

THE RAPID SOCIAL AND ECONOMIC CHANGES we are encountering, as we approach the 21st Century, present complex and unprecedented challenges to contemporary societies. There is a high probability that these changes herald fundamental structural rearrangements. Societies now must cope simultaneously with global economic competition, the demand for new competencies within the population, the provision of opportunities for health and well-being across the population, and the maintenance of the social fabric for nurturing, socializing, and educating the next generation.

As the pace of social change accelerates, it becomes increasingly important that we attend to the basic requirements for healthy human development. There lay the foundations for future economic prosperity and population health. Yet, the pace, magnitude, and complexity of these changes are felt by many to be overwhelming and uncontrollable, and that very perception of lack of control may diminish further our ability to respond, and

* In this paper, I draw upon an earlier Working Paper of the CIAR Human Development Program entitled "The Learning Society." Robbie Case and I coordinated the writing of that document on behalf of a CIAR Task Force. My Introduction to that document is especially relevant for this paper.

** Daniel P. Keating is a Royal Bank Fellow at the Canadian Institute for Advanced Research, and Director of the CIAR Program in Human Development. He also is Professor in the Department of Applied Psychology at the Ontario Institute for Studies in Education, and is a member of the Graduate Faculty at the University of Toronto.

to adapt, to the changes. This underlying dynamic, of accelerating change and decreasing control makes it difficult to engage in thoughtful planning, and increases the costs of social divisiveness (Kaplan, 1994).

One way out of this vicious circle might begin with a deeper understanding of the fundamental processes of human development. Such an understanding starts with a recognition of the fundamentally social nature of the human species, and of the powerful impact that social environments have on human development.

A FRAMEWORK FOR UNDERSTANDING HUMAN DEVELOPMENT

Homo sapiens is a social species. Throughout our lives, we play, work, interact, learn, and reproduce in social groups. We develop in social relationships from the earliest period of life, and we remain dependent longer on caretaking for our survival than any other primate. At our core, then, we need social groups to survive.

The nature of our early experiences – most of which occur through social interactions – plays a critical role, throughout life, in how we cope, how we learn, and how competent we become. The nature of the social environment in which we develop is thus a key determinant of our quality of life. These influences are powerful throughout the lifespan, but particularly so in early life. Diverse life outcomes (positive and negative) are closely associated with identifiable differences in social experiences.

In turn, the quality of the human social environment is a function of the competence that is available within the society. The nurture, education, and socialization of new members of the group depend on the skills possessed by more mature members, and on social arrangements that facilitate high-quality interactions between generations.

Almost all of this is equally true for our primate cousins. This is perhaps not surprising in light of the genetic similarity between humans and non-human primates – a 95 per cent or higher overlap of the genetic code in most comparisons. Among *Rhesus macaques* (like us, a social species), for example, the quality of early attachment relationships, the opportunity for broad social interaction within the troop, and the stability of the troop during critical developmental periods, all play a role in eventual competence and coping skills (Suomi, 1991).

But we face additional challenges, unknown to other species, and even to our own quite recent ancestors. Although we share much in common with our primate cousins, humans are unique in having developed a capacity for conscious self-reflection, cultural transmission of skills and knowledge through language and other symbolic means, cumulative technological development and, most recently, civilization. In evolutionary terms, these are quite recent changes in our lives (Keating & Mustard, 1993).

Because large numbers are sometimes hard to grasp in the abstract, we can get a better sense of how recent are all of these changes in human development, by using an analogy to a calendar year. If we were to take 100,000 years as an estimate of the time elapsed since the emergence of fully modern humans, and place it on the scale of a single year, we would note that our species first moved into small urban centers, supported by agriculture, at about the end of November, and started an industrial revolution on the afternoon of New Year's Eve. Just a few minutes ago, we launched experiments in instantaneous global communication, information technology, and multicultural metropolism.[117]

The origins and mechanisms of this evolutionary process remain controversial, but several important features have gained fairly broad consensus. First, we might note that not all of our complex social arrangements and behaviors are a function of cultural experiences alone; other primates also are social strategists

---

117 It has been suggested that this analogy overemphasizes the accelerative function, treating time as if it were simply linear. Various log transforms would show different patterns, some with non-exponential acceleration. On the other hand, humans are temporal by both biology (in growth rates and lifespan) and culture (with precise timekeeping artifacts and social practices). Thus, the widespread perception of change as explosive may well reflect the true state of affairs, at least as it pertains to humans. Harvey (1989) offers a detailed critique of this notion of time-space compression in society.

of the first order (Tomasello, Kruger, & Ratner, 1993). Much of our intuitive understanding of how to function in groups has a lengthy evolutionary history. To this already rich social mix, however, we added new language capabilities (Donald, 1991) that yielded apparently infinite potential for complex communication (Chomsky, 1965). Language enables much more complex social communication, and perhaps arises initially out of a need to maintain cohesion in larger groups (Donald, 1991; Dunbar, 1992).

That larger group size may have contributed economic benefits, by enabling better organization and specialization of work (Schick & Toth, 1993), and permitting more effective exploitation of harsh habitats and a primitive form of shared risk. The teaching and learning of special skills also were enhanced by language, and technological development ensued (first with stones, and then with transformed materials such as iron and bronze). Here we might recognize early versions of continuous improvement and diffusion of best practice, two contemporary hallmarks of successful learning organizations! This unification of instrumental and symbolic functions apparently is unique to *Homo sapiens*, and has been proposed as the starting point of fully human intelligence (Vygotsky, 1978).

We are different from other primates in another critical way. We drew on our increasing symbolic and instrumental sophistication (that is, on language and tool use) to establish connections between troops and tribes. We can date the origins of this pattern rather precisely to about 40,000 years ago (Stringer & Gamble, 1993). The evidence for this lies in the remarkable explosion of symbolic forms (particularly art), and in the rapid spread of more complex stone technologies, which previously had been unchanged for a million years or more (Schick & Toth, 1993).

The accelerating pace of technological and social change, thus, is based on our unique penchant for collaborative learning across formerly rigid group boundaries. Our ability to encode and enhance this learning through progressively more efficient cultural means – oral histories, writing, and now information technologies – contributes directly to this acceleration. Note, too, that changes in the means of communication have non-trivial consequences for cognitive activity: how we think, what we know, and how we learn.

A well understood example of this is the connection between the practice of literacy and the development of logic, argument, reflection, and metacognitive understanding (Olson, 1994; Scribner & Cole, 1981). As literacy spreads, so do literate habits of mind. This combination of a new technology with a new set of capabilities in the population, creates a potent new medium for discourse among previously isolated groups and individuals.

In concert with changes in social communication (such as language and literacy), we have continued to discover new means for extracting material subsistence from the earth. The agricultural revolution first made possible the congregation and settled existence of large groups of humans in specific places over a long period of time (that is, cities). Such concentrations appeared to enhance the exchange of ideas and techniques, and to lead to more rapid growth in technical innovation and, thus, productivity (Harvey, 1989; Jacobs, 1993).

We know relatively little about forms of governance in prehistoric *hominid* or human troops (and may never know much), but we do know that large-scale human settlements were accompanied by increasingly formal arrangements for the distribution of work and its resulting wealth, and for the maintenance of social structures. The production demands of agricultural societies were such that a relatively large proportion of the population was needed to contribute physical energy directly to the system. As a result, various forms of strict social domination formed the most frequent political pattern, including slave and feudal systems.

The next major revolution in social forms occurred very recently. The industrial revolution removed human labour from the direct energy loop required for material production (Rosenberg & Birdzell, 1986), but created a demand for an ever more complex division of labour. Here, again, we see the ongoing, mutually causal interplay between technological and social innovation. This may be difficult to visualize initially, since we are more accustomed to linear models, in which an isolated cause yields a specific outcome (Keating, in press; Senge, 1990). But as we trace major transformations in our species' history, we can see that changes in technology generated demands and opportunities for changes in societal functioning, and changes in society generated demands and opportunities for technological innovation.

Unique among species, then, we have created what systems theorists call an iterative feedback loop between our ways of using material resources and the ways in which we organize our social lives. This new pattern of cultural and social change continually reshapes the ecological habitats in which we live and work, and in which subsequent generations develop (Keating & Mustard, 1993).

Another such transformational moment seems to be upon us, arising from already existing information technologies: instantaneous global communication, unlimited knowledge storage and retrieval, sophisticated techniques for data analysis and simulation, and artificially intelligent design with robotic manufacture (Keating & Mustard, 1993; Lipsey, 1993; Romer, 1990). The fundamental task for contemporary societies, then, is to adapt effectively to these new realities:

> ... the two dominant issues facing countries like Canada are (1) to build the new kind of economy that can create wealth from ideas, and (2) during a period of profound economic change with diminished resources, to sustain the healthy social environment that is best for human development (Keating & Mustard, 1993, pp. 101–2).

Different cultures and societies have arrived at different solutions to the dilemmas of contemporary social organization (Rohlen, 1992). The comparative study of these varying adaptations suggests that some solutions work better than others for particular issues. But cultural forms are not interchangeable parts;

what works in a particular setting may not easily transfer to a different cultural pattern. As well, demands shift over time, and some contemporary societal successes may owe as much to historical contingency as to cultural adaptability. To adapt well in the face of these challenges, we will need to become learning societies. To understand this better, we can look first at notions emerging from recent research on how individuals and groups learn.

NEW NOTIONS OF LEARNING
Many of the key issues are brought into focus if we use the new notions of learning arising from recent research in the human sciences, from neuroscience to cultural anthropology (Task Force on Human Development, 1992). In recent years we have begun to develop a clearer picture of the critical importance of the quality of the social environment for an individual's development of competence, coping, health, and well-being (Keating, 1993; Keating & Mustard, 1993). In other words, the ways in which we learn and adapt are shaped in a mutual interaction between the individual and the environment. This is true for visual and other sensory systems, which have critical periods in early life that set the stage for their lifelong functioning (Cynader, Shaw, Prusky, & Van Huizen, 1990). There may be similar critical or sensitive periods for other fundamental social, cognitive, and behavioral systems, such as patterns of attachment to parents (or other caregivers) in the first two years of life, or central conceptual structures in domains like mathematics in the preschool years (Case, 1992).

Another crucial part of this equation is our species' characteristic of neoteny, a delay in the attainment of maturity that provides an extended period of plasticity for learning. This enables us to adapt to an extremely wide range of habitats. For example, we quickly come to regard as commonplace what earlier generations would have seen as supernatural: making sense from arbitrary visual symbols, flying through the air, having a pleasant chat with someone half a globe away, or viewing that globe from afar as it spins through space. These changes, in turn, create new patterns and possibilities for action, communication, and thought.

The social and technological transformations we are going through alter the contexts of individual development. But we should not assume that unguided changes automatically will have positive consequences for population health, competence, and coping. If we fail to provide adequate support for human development, especially in early life, then we may expect to encounter a long-term reduced capability for learning and adaptation in the population overall (Ross, 1993).

Despite the dramatic changes in our habitat, most of our basic biological needs remain relatively constant. The development of healthy humans still depends on their attainment of competence and their ability to cope with, and to learn from, change, stress, and novelty. Many kinds of social environments can support healthy development, but all the successful ones share key features that we are learning to identify. We also are learning, sadly, about the kinds of social environments that create enormous risks for healthy development (Keating, 1993; Offord et al., 1992; Ross, 1993; Tremblay et al., 1992).

Following traditional Western folklore that viewed knowledge and expertise as an exclusively individual possession, most of our research on learning has focused on the individual. More recently, researchers have begun to focus on the social aspects of learning (Resnick, Levine, & Teasley, 1991), particularly collaborative learning. Although there are many variants of this notion, only a few of which have been studied carefully, one common core is the recognition that knowledge and its acquisition are inherently social.

Instead of empty vessels awaiting the infusion of knowledge, learners (even the youngest ones) now are seen as actively constructing their internal world from their interactions with the external world, and especially with other people (Gardner, 1991). Working within groups on meaningful tasks seems to engender the kinds of interactions that are most likely to advance individual learning (Resnick et al., 1991).

Efforts to apply the new information technologies more effectively also have contributed to an increasing recognition of the social nature of knowledge. Recent research on the dynamics of the workplace (especially for knowledge work), for example, suggests that it typically functions as a learning community or "community of practice," and that connected networks of expertise within the workplace generally are more productive than experts working alone or in small enclaves (Brown & Duguid, 1991; Lave & Wenger, 1991). In addition, there is considerable evidence that the use of networks in school situations (for example, cooperative learning, discourse-centered instruction, or computer-supported intentional learning – Scardamalia et al., 1989) raise both group and individual performance levels.

Discovering ways to enhance both individual and organizational learning will become keys to societal adaptation. Diversity is a key factor at both levels. With respect to individual learning, for example, when individuals experience a broader, and more diverse range of tasks and challenges, their cognitive complexity and ability to solve problems increases and grows more flexible (Kohn & Schooler, 1983). Similarly, with respect to organizational learning, if workplace constraints are quite narrow (as in the traditional manufacturing assembly line), then workplace skills and attitudes are likely to develop similarly across the population working within those constraints. There will not be much diversity nor a very high capacity for organizational learning. On the other hand, if the constraints are broadened (for example, to encourage a focus on the higher-order goals of the organization as well as on the specific task at hand) a collectively more diverse range of skills and talents will emerge across the organization, and its capacity to learn and to adapt will increase.

In sum, the capability of any group to learn and to adapt is based on two factors: the total amount of ingenuity available within the group, that is, how effectively the individuals learn and adapt; and the ability of the group (or society) to function as a learning organization.

THE LEARNING SOCIETY

It seems likely that tomorrow's successful societies will be those that find innovative ways of supporting human development, both individually and collectively. As it happens, we now are in a position to make effective use of a considerable body of research on human development to help us to understand the critical factors that have the greatest impact. We can group these factors as follows:

- how individuals develop, which in turn comprises the human resources of the society (population health, well-being, coping, and competence);[118]
- how a society, through its institutions and practices, organizes the human resources available to it;
- how the society learns from experience in both cases, and includes this knowledge in adapting its institutions and practices.

Societies that do well on these dimensions are likely to become learning societies: purposeful enough to be successful in a global economic competition; strong enough to participate in global economic partnerships; and innovative in response to changing social, political, and economic conditions. As the "price" of information decreases, what will distinguish more from less successful societies is their relative ability to learn from universally available information; that is, to adapt quickly and productively to rapidly changing conditions.

Healthy Communities: Foundations of a Learning Society

The scientific story here is quite simple at one level, but can be expanded to reveal considerable complexity. In a nutshell, it is that the quality of the social environment is principally responsi-

118 Some have used the notion of human capital to convey the same idea. Both metaphors attempt to place the human talents of a population into an economic discourse, to indicate its value. This is a good starting point. But the limits of the analogy should also be noted; human talents are neither capital nor resources in the strict sense. Finding common ground and a common language to understand these relationships is itself a daunting task.

ble for overall population health, well-being and competence, and for the learning capacity both of individuals and of society. In health, for example, the social class gradient (the degree of social disparity) accounts for more of the difference in health outcomes between countries than does health care expenditure. These are not just poverty effects, since they obtain throughout the middle class as well. Moreover, countries with steep gradients (high degrees of social disparity) have overall poorer health outcomes than those with flatter gradients (Keating & Mustard, 1993). Similar findings appear to hold for educational achievement outcomes.

DEVELOPMENTAL PATHWAYS TO HEALTH AND COMPETENCE
Discovering the connections between broad social environmental factors and outcomes of health and competence is an important first step. These are central markers or indicators of how various sectors of the population are functioning. In addition to monitoring these outcomes, however, we need to get a better grasp of the developmental processes that underlie them. Otherwise, we may be induced to make decisions on the basis of spurious or superficial connections.

One such developmental process that it is important to understand is the evolution of antisocial behavior in children. Antisocial behavior in childhood often has its roots in the dynamics of the home. In the Ontario Child Health Study, 5.5 per cent of children 4 to 16 years of age were classified as conduct disordered; that is, they had clinically important levels of antisocial behavior. Children with this disorder have a lowered life quality, disturbed social relationships, and poor school performance. The onset of antisocial behavior in childhood very often heralds a lifetime of serious psychological disturbance. For instance, in the Ontario Child Health Study, approximately 60 per cent of children age 8 to 12 who were classified as conduct disordered retained that classification four years later. And, in clinical samples, approximately 40 per cent of children or early adolescents with persistent antisocial behavior have been found to have serious psychosocial difficulties in adult life, including psychopathy, criminality, and alcohol and drug abuse. The societal costs resulting from conduct disorder and its sequelae, thus, are very high (Offord et al., 1992).

Knowledge of the developmental pathways by which antisocial behavior arises is of prime importance if effective intervention programs are to be realized, and if the socially marginal life courses of many of these children are to be avoided. One of those developmental pathways, that has been well documented (Offord et al., 1992), begins with a preschool child who has a difficult temperament, and who grows up without encountering consistent parental limits. When such a child enters school, he often exhibits aggressive patterns of behavior, which lead to a downward spiral of alienation and school failure in the early elementary years. By early adolescence, the child often has found a deviant peer group with whom to associate (Offord et al., 1992).

Finally, when the antisocial adolescent becomes a father or mother, the whole pattern may repeat. Indeed, one of the best predictors of this developmental pathway is the parents' own personal adjustment before the birth of the child. Youths who have had important social adjustment problems tend to mate with individuals who also have had adjustment problems (Rutter, Quinton, & Hill, 1990). They are at high risk of becoming parents early in life, and of providing less care to their children (Quinton & Rutter, 1988; Serbin, Schwartzman, Moskowitz, & Ledingham, 1991). We need to find ways to break this intergenerational reproduction of social failure (McCord & Tremblay, 1992; Offord & Racine, 1991).

It is important to note, however, that the foregoing pattern is not an immutable one. Early developmental stimulation may be a promising avenue for interrupting this negative cycle (Weikart & Schweinhart, 1992). Other factors, such as attachment to a supportive adult, other than the parents, can mitigate these effects and generate a different developmental pathway (Werner, 1989; Werner & Smith, 1992). Much work is needed to refine our knowledge about developmental pathways, and about the "points of leverage" that can be applied to transform an unsuccessful developmental trajectory into a successful one (Keating, 1990).

One such point of leverage for redressing early difficulties is suggested by experimental studies with non-human primates (*Rhesus macaques*). In these studies, macaque infants who are genetically susceptible to hyper-reactivity to stress, have been cross-fostered to highly nurturant mothers. These infants do not follow their predicted pattern of low troop status and/or early death. Instead, they are generally indistinguishable from the broad population, and in fact are slightly more likely to become troop leaders (Suomi, 1991).

Note that cross-fostering is but one form of surrogate nurturing of the young, a phenomenon that occurs in various forms in most primate species, including *Homo sapiens*. Recall that a key buffering or protective factor for high-risk children, found in many studies, is a supportive relationship with a non-parental adult. In particular, support from extended families, or other social connections, has a beneficial effect on the quality of nurturance, especially for high-risk mothers (Booth, Spieker, Bernard, & Morisset, 1992). Thus, there are many possible ways to ensure that virtually all children receive adequate nurturance. To the extent that societal changes have compromised these historic sources of support for families with children, we need to devise new ways to provide these critical supports for healthy human development.

Many developmental pathways could be similarly described, both for dysfunctional and for more optimal outcomes. As we improve our ability to monitor and to understand these pathways, we may be able to learn how to respond more effectively in order to prevent problems and to optimize development. Doing so will be a key to protecting and enhancing the learning capacity both of individuals and of society, and it is on that learning capacity that both economic prosperity and the quality of societal life will depend.

SOCIAL ENVIRONMENTS AND HUMAN DEVELOPMENT

The good news from all this is that we now understand more clearly the impact of the social environment on the development of health, well-being, coping and competence, and we have identified many of the key factors (Hertzman, 1993; Keating, 1993). The bad news is that many children and adolescents are not growing up in highly supportive environments. For some of these children, poverty is the central problem. But these difficulties increasingly are being observed among the working and professional/managerial classes as well, largely because of shifts in labour market configuration (Maxwell, 1993; Ross, 1993). For example, the proportion of children under age 13, who live in a home with two parents, one of whom is at home full time, is small and decreasing (Lero et al., 1992). Generally, the quality and affordability of alternative care for these children is inadequate, leaving a substantial proportion of the infant/toddler population subject to sub-optimal care (Pence & Goelman, 1991).

Although there is justifiably great concern about how social changes are affecting the nurturance of infants and young children, it also is important to recognize that subsequent developmental histories also have a strong effect (Keating, 1990, 1993). In particular, the transition to school, the onset of adolescence, and the transition to work occur in social environments that impact on individual health and competence, and on the capacity to learn.

Learning societies will need to support lifelong learning throughout the population, especially as the time available for social adaptation to technological and other changes shrinks from eras to generations, to individual lifetimes. Japan and much of Europe appear to foster lifelong learning much better than do the UK, the US, or Canada. But Japan and Europe differ quite sharply from each other in how they accomplish this (Rohlen, 1989; Streeck, 1990). Finding better ways to shape the social environment, so that it can provide more effective support at these crucial transition points, should greatly enhance the ability of our population to learn and to adapt throughout life.

LEARNING TO DEVELOP HUMAN RESOURCES

Some may argue that health, well-being, competence, and coping are issues of individual behavior, rather than of societal practice or governmental policy. But that ignores the fact that, in a high-technology, high-skill, high-wage economy, two kinds of costs become prohibitive for a society:

- too shallow a base of expertise and talent to support innovation;
- too many resources required to contain (security, corrections) and maintain (welfare) marginalized segments of the population.

In addition, as Putnam (1992) demonstrates, we are coming to understand that economic benefits accrue to regions with highly civic societies. There is a legitimate public interest in addressing these issues.

While there are no magic solutions, and we still have much to learn, we can suggest a few guidelines for developing human resources in a learning society:

- Both to avoid negative outcomes and to optimize positive ones, intervention earlier in life is better. Because families with young children often are particularly vulnerable in periods of rapid social and economic change, we need to pay particular attention to these critical periods in early life.
- Societies need useful information on how the population is doing, and where problems are occurring. This monitoring needs to occur at a variety of levels (national, provincial, community) because distinctive patterns emerge at each level. To leverage this knowledge effectively, a learning society will need to build networks among these multiple monitoring activities. And we need on-going research that models both the outcome indicators and the developmental processes and pathways that underlie them.
- Social policies that support lifelong learning need to be created. In particular, barriers between school and work, or between levels of schooling, need to be replaced with sensible bridges.

- Local communities need to be engaged in the generation of local solutions, for several reasons:
  - the problems are not the same in every community;
  - local solutions engage a wider variety of the population, in itself a sign of community health;
  - fiscal resources will need to come from a variety of sources, not just government.

But these community initiatives need to be able to build on each other, rather than requiring re-invention on every occasion. To that end, governments can play a key role by reserving public spaces on the information highway to enable within-community and community-to-community exchange. We need to apply the notions of continuous improvement and diffusion of best practice beyond the corporate sector.

Collaborative Learning Organizations: The Human Advantage

Social policy analysts generally have become familiar with many of the foregoing issues, especially as the critical nature of human resources for economic growth has become more apparent. Less attention, however, has been paid to a closely related and equally critical human developmental factor: how those human resources can best be organized.

INNOVATION AND PROSPERITY IN THE INFORMATION AGE
In reconstructing our species' history, we often have focused on the technological and material aspects of revolutionary transitions:

- learning how to make and refine tools, beginning with stone;
- learning how to cultivate food resources, both plant and animal;
- learning how to make use of transformed materials, such as bronze and iron;
- learning how to harness energy from non-animal sources;

- learning how to engineer complex materials to do complex tasks, in industrial uses; and, most recently,
- learning how to use electromagnetic channels to communicate instantaneously, to analyze problems whose complexity made them previously unassailable, and to create artificially intelligent systems to execute increasingly complex tasks.

What is less obvious, but equally true, is that each of these major revolutions depended, in part, on new forms of social interaction (Rosenberg & Birdzell, 1986). From inter-tribal trade, to the congregation of large groups of humans in urban settings, to the invention of ways to share risk through capital investment, *Homo sapiens* repeatedly have generated new social practices and institutions at a pace similar to that of technological innovation. It seems likely that we are once again entering such a transformation:

> Although we do not fully understand the determinants of economic growth and prosperity, we do know that technological innovation is a driving force, and that periods of major technological change cause changes in a nation's or region's prosperity base and its society. All of the evidence indicates that we are in such a major techno-economic and social change (Keating & Mustard, 1993, p. 90).

The capacity for innovation, thus, is likely to become even further entrenched as a key determinant of economic prosperity. But, especially in the information revolution, the capacity for innovation is driven both by the pool of human ingenuity that is available, *and* by how well that ingenuity can be magnified by effective organization. This is the key idea of the "learning organization."

LEARNING ORGANIZATIONS: KEY PRINCIPLES
The development of information technology that can support learning organizations is relatively recent. As a result, we have

many descriptions and case studies of learning organizations, but little comparative or systematic research. Nonetheless, key elements, noted by thoughtful observers, can be summarized. They all start with the recognition that learning occurs not just within individuals, but also within groups and organizations of all sorts.

A first characteristic of collaborative learning organizations is that they tend to emphasize coordinated group effort toward commonly shared goals, rather than purely individual accomplishment. This requires that enough people in the organization choose to participate actively in its success, and this, in turn, generally depends on the degree to which those individuals believe that they will receive a reasonable return for their investment of effort. As a result, effective learning organizations often require shallower gradients (less disparity) in the distribution of group-generated resources among members of the organization.

Societies with cultural traditions that emphasize a balance between the individual and the collective are likely to be better prepared to organize in this fashion, as compared with societies that place a stronger emphasis on the individual apart from society (such as the United States and, to a lesser extent, Canada). The current search for communitarian models (Bellah, Madsen, Sullivan, Swidler, & Tipton, 1991; Etzioni, 1993) reflects this perceived need to strengthen the basis for collaborative effort by citizens within society. Indeed, in some recent studies, higher levels of civic participation have been found to lead to better economic growth and prosperity (Putnam, 1992).

Second, there is an active commitment to continuous improvement and to the diffusion of best practices throughout the organization. Part of each individual's contribution is to discover ways of doing the task better or more efficiently. In addition, the organization seeks to understand and analyze the dynamic system within which it is functioning (Senge, 1990).

Third, collaborative learning organizations are characterized by horizontal networks of information flow rather than vertical/hierarchical structures for top-down decision making. In vertical systems, there are "checks" on the flow of information at many points, both on the way up and on the way down. Decentralized decision-making, on the other hand, yields a more nimble organization, as information is channeled more flexibly along the most effective route. Such horizontal systems, to operate effectively, require a widely shared understanding of the organization's goals. One might say that it requires a coherent, shared conceptual framework among the members of the organization.

This horizontal network, when effective, brings together all the expertise of an organization. The more diverse that expertise, the more contact points there will be with the external world to which the group needs to adapt. Diversity can increase significantly the learning capacity of an organization or society. For example, in North America, one frequently overlooked learning resource is multicultural diversity. Too often that diversity is viewed as a difficulty to be overcome, rather than as a strength. Although some advantage may accrue in the short term to more monocultural societies (such as Japan), the diverse storehouse of useful cultural solutions contained in North American society constitutes an invaluable asset that should greatly enhance our capacity to learn and to adapt in the future.

We need to discover how best to organize learning communities in the information age. Supporting effective learning by organizations, in all sectors of society, will be a critical factor in the building of a learning society.

Building the Learning Society

Can we design a coherent strategy for becoming the kind of learning society we have described? We hardly need to be reminded of the catastrophic failures of grand central plans for society in this century (Harvey, 1989). We are wise to be leery of grand social designs. In addition, as the complexity of available information expands, and as the rate of change accelerates, it becomes even more obvious that there can be no central blueprint to specify the steps for building a learning society. Instead, it is useful to think of the learning society we hope to achieve not as a static structure toward which we are headed, but rather as a process of continuous improvement.

THE CHANGING ROLE OF GOVERNANCE:
ORGANIZING FOR ADAPTATION

Although difficult to build, successful learning societies benefit from progressive self-renewal. And the active participation of the whole population in lifelong learning, in a series of learning organizations and networks (at home, in school, at work, in the community), is perhaps the best safeguard against future grand social designs.

The role of governance in all of this clearly is central, and major changes in the styles and forms of governance will be needed if we are to achieve a learning society. But what changes? In approaching this question, we need to recognize explicitly that we are involved in an experiment with civilization, willingly or not, and that our only positive choice is to learn as much as possible, and to work together to do so. Governance, in a learning society, will need to be more concerned with empowerment than power, and will need to fulfill an educative function about our collective tasks. If our analysis is broadly correct, then, it suggests at least three important new roles for governance:

- maintaining healthy communities for the effective development of human resources;
- supporting learning networks for the effective organization of those resources;
- forging the kind of consensus on common goals, across society, that can enable the learning society to become a reality.

BUILDING HEALTHY COMMUNITIES

One important task for governance in this domain is to establish mechanisms for monitoring important human developmental outcomes, and for incorporating this knowledge into policy and planning, both public and private. No modern government or business would finalize decisions in the absence of economic information, and most new initiatives to change the physical world require an estimate of environmental impact. Yet we do not systematically do this for human developmental indicators. We should.

Fortunately, we do not need to build such indicators and monitoring mechanisms from scratch. A surprising number of these already exist, and a relatively small investment in coordination, and in filling some gaps, could produce very significant benefits.

BUILDING LEARNING NETWORKS

Second, learning societies will need to find ways to organize human ingenuity in more productive ways. A broad social goal should be to maximize learning, both by individuals and by groups (firms, organizations, communities, and so on). Increasingly, governments will need to coordinate rather than control such learning activity. They will need to encourage new learning partnerships across traditional divides (such as school and work, management and labour, private and public sector).

BUILDING SOCIAL CONSENSUS

Third, we need to recognize that Canada, as a multicultural society, cannot rely on historically shared cultural or institutional traditions to supply the social consensus needed to underpin legitimate and effective government action. Instead, that social consensus needs continually to be constructed from among the diverse perspectives and traditions that make up our society. Such a consensus cannot be constructed through the denial of conflict, or even through its management, but rather needs to be based on a process of learning from conflict, and from our diversity. It is essential that we find better ways to accomplish that.

Of these three key tasks, perhaps the most critical is the forging of a social consensus. Such a consensus may emerge to support the notion of building a learning society, and such a consensus would provide an essential foundation for future economic growth, population health, and human development.

References

Bellah, R.N., R. Madsen, W.M. Sullivan, A. Swidler, and S.M. Tipton. 1991. *The good society.* 1st ed. New York: Knopf.

Booth, C.L., S.J. Spieker, K.E. Bernard, and C.E. Morisset. 1992. Infants at risk: The role of preventive intervention in deflecting a maladaptive developmental trajectory. In J. McCord and R.E. Tremblay, eds., *Preventing antisocial behavior: Interventions from birth through adolescence,* 21–42. New York: Guilford Press.

Bronfenbrenner, U. 1992. Child care in the Anglo-Saxon mode. In M.E. Lamb, K.J. Sternberg, C.-P. Hwang, and A.G. Broberg, eds., *Child care in context: Cross-cultural perspectives.* Hillsdale, NJ: Erlbaum.

Brown, J.S., and P. Duguid, 1991. Organizational learning and communities of practice: Toward a unified view of working, learning, and innovation. *Organizational Science, 2,* 40–57.

Case, R. 1992. *The mind's staircase: Exploring the conceptual underpinnings of children's thought and knowledge.* Hillsdale, NJ: Erlbaum.

Chomsky, N. 1965. *Aspects of the theory of syntax.* Cambridge, MA: MIT Press.

Cynader, M., C. Shaw, G. Prusky, and F. Van Huizen. 1990. Neural mechanisms underlying modifiability of response properties in developing cat visual cortex. In B. Cohen and I. Bodis-Wolliner, eds., *Vision and the brain: The organization of the central visual system.* New York: Raven Press.

Donald, M. 1991. *Origins of the modern mind: Three stages in the evolution of culture and cognition.* Cambridge, MA: Harvard University Press.

Dunbar, R. 1992. Why gossip is good for you. *New Scientist, 136,* 28-31.

Etzioni, A. 1993. *The spirit of community: Rights, responsibilities, and the communitarian agenda.* New York: Crown Publishers.

Gardner, H. 1991. *The unschooled mind.* New York: Basic Books.

Harvey, D. 1989. *The condition of postmodernity.* Cambridge: Blackwell.

Hertzman, C. October 1993. *Developmental pathways to health.* Paper presented at the CIAR/Honda Forum on Determinants of Health, Toronto, ON.

Jacobs, J. 1993. *The death and life of great American cities.* New York: Random House.

Kaplan, R.D. Feb 1994. The coming anarchy. *Atlantic Monthly,* 44–76.

Keating, D.P. 1990. Charting pathways to the development of expertise. *Educational Psychologist*, 25(3 and 4), 243–67.

―――. 1993. *Developmental determinants of health and well-being in children and youth.* Report to the Steering Committee on Children and Youth. Toronto, ON: Premier's Council on Health, Well-Being, and Social Justice.

―――. In press. Understanding human intelligence: Toward a developmental synthesis. In C. Benbow and D. Lubinski, eds. *From psychometrics to giftedness: Essays in honor of Julian Stanley.* Baltimore, MD: Johns Hopkins University Press.

―――and J.F. Mustard. 1993. Social economic factors in human development. In D. Ross, ed. *Family security in insecure times,* Vol. 1, 87–105. Ottawa, ON: National Forum on Family Security.

Kohn, M.L., and C. Schooler. 1983. *Work and personality: An inquiry into the impact of social stratification.* Norwood, NJ: Ablex.

Lave, J., and E. Wenger. 1991. *Situated learning: Legitimate peripheral participation.* Cambridge: Cambridge University Press.

Lero, D.S., H. Goelman, A.R. Pence, L.M. Brockman, and S. Nuttall. 1992. *Parental work patterns and child care needs.* Ottawa, ON: Statistics Canada.

Lipsey, R.G. Feb 1993. *Notes on globalisation and technological change and Canadian trade policy.* Canadian Institute for Advanced Research, Economic Growth working paper #8. Toronto, ON: CIAR.

Maxwell, J. 1993. Globalization and family security. In D. Ross, ed., *Family security in insecure times,* Vol. 1, 19–55. Ottawa, ON: National Forum on Family Security.

McCord, J., and R.E. Tremblay, eds. 1992. *Preventing antisocial behavior: Interventions from birth through adolescence.* New York: Guilford Press.

Offord, D.R., and Y.A. Racine. 1991. Children at risk: Schools reaching out. *Education Today, 3,* 16–18.

―――et al. 1992. Outcome prognosis and risk in a longitudinal follow-up study. *Journal of the American Academy of Child and Adolescent Psychiatry, 31*(5), 916–23.

Olson, D.R. 1994. *The world on paper: The conceptual and cognitive implications of writing and reading.* Cambridge: Cambridge University Press.

Pence, A.R., and H. Goelman. 1991. The relationship of regulation training and motivation to quality of care in family daycare. *Child and Youth Care Forum, 20*(2), 83–101.

Putnam, R.D. 1992. *Making democracy work: Civic traditions in modern Italy.* Princeton, NJ: Princeton University Press.

Quinton, D., and M. Rutter. 1988. *Parenting breakdown: The making and breaking of intergenerational links.* Brookfield: Avebury.

Resnick, L.B., J.B. Levine, and S.D. Teasley, eds. 1991. *Perspectives on socially shared cognition.* Washington, DC: American Psychological Association.

Rohlen, T.P. 1989. Order in Japanese society: Attachment, authority, and routine. *The Journal of Japanese Studies, 15,* 5–40.

Rohlen, T.P. 1992. Learning: The mobilization of knowledge in the Japanese political economy. In S. Kumon and H. Rosovsky, eds., *The political economy of Japan: Volume 3. Cultural and social dynamics.* Stanford, CA: Stanford University Press.

Romer, P.M. 1990. Endogenous technological change. *Journal of Political Economy,* 158–61.

Rosenberg, N., and L.E. Birdzell. 1986. *How the West grew rich: The economic transformation of the industrial world.* New York: Basic Books.

Ross, D., ed. 1993. *Family security in insecure times.* Ottawa, ON: National Forum on Family Security.

Rutter, M., D. Quinton, and J. Hill. 1990. Adult outcome of institution-reared children: Males and females compared. In L.N. Robins and M. Rutter, eds., *Straight and devious pathways from childhood to adulthood.* Cambridge, MA: Cambridge University Press.

Scardamalia, M., C. Bereiter, R.S. McLean, J. Swallow, and E. Woodruff. 1989. Computer supported intentional learning environments. *Journal of Educational Computing Research, 5,* 51–68.

Schick, K.D., and N. Toth. 1993. *Making silent stones speak: Human evolution and the dawn of technology.* New York: Simon & Schuster.

Scribner, S., and M. Cole. 1981. *The psychology of literacy.* Cambridge, MA: Harvard University Press.

Senge, P.M. 1990. *The fifth discipline: The art and practice of the learning organization.* New York: Doubleday.

Serbin, L.A., A.E. Schwartzman, D.S. Moskowitz, and J.F. Ledingham. 1991. Aggressive, withdrawn and aggressive-withdrawn children in adolescence: Into the next generation. In D. Pepler and K. Rubin, eds., *The development and treatment of childhood aggression.* Hillsdale, NJ: Erlbaum.

Streeck, W. 1990. *Vocational training: Reflections on the European experience and its relevance for the United States.* Madison, WI: Center on Wisconsin Strategy, University of Wisconsin.

Stringer, C., and C. Gamble. 1993. *In search of the Neanderthals: Solving the puzzle of human origins.* London: Thames and Hudson.

Suomi, S.J. 1991. Early stress and adult emotional reactivity in rhesus monkeys. In *The childhood environment and adult disease.* Ciba Foundation Symposium 156. Chichester: Wiley.

Task Force on Human Development. 1992. *The learning society.* Canadian Institute for Advanced Research, Research Publication #6. Toronto, ON: CIAR.

Tomasello, M., A.C. Kruger, and H.H. Ratner. 1993. Cultural learning. *Behavioral and Brain Sciences, 16,* 495–552.

Tremblay, R.E., F. Vitaro, L. Bertrand, M. LeBlanc, H. Beauchesne, H. Boileau, and L. David. 1992. Parent and child training to prevent early onset of delinquency: The Montréal longitudinal-experimental study. In J. McCord and R.E. Tremblay, eds., *Preventing antisocial behavior: Interventions from birth through adolescence,* 117–38. New York: Guilford Press.

Vygotsky, L. 1978. Mind in society: The development of higher psychological processes. In M. Cole, V. John-Steiner, S. Scribner, and E. Souberman, eds., *Mind in society: The development of higher psychological processes.* Cambridge, MA: Harvard University Press.

Weikart, D.P., and L.J. Schweinhart. 1992. The high/scope preschool program outcomes. In J. McCord and R.E. Tremblay, eds., *Preventing antisocial behavior: Interventions from birth through adolescence,* 67–86. New York: Guilford Press.

Werner, E.E. 1989. Children of Garden Island. *Scientific American, 260,* 106–11.

Werner, E., and R. Smith. 1992. *Overcoming the odds: High risk children from birth to adulthood.* New York: Cornell University Press.

11 A Critique of the "Information Society" Concept

Daniel Yankelovich[*]

THE GOVERNING IN AN INFORMATION SOCIETY project is taking place at a time when public confidence in our institutions of
governance, both in Canada and in the United States, is low and is
sinking lower. Indeed, in all of the advanced industrial democracies, governments seem unable to come to grips with the great
social and political issues that are of deepest concern to people. As
public insecurities mount about job security, personal safety,
growing inequality and declining morality (and the apparent
inability of government to cope with them) institutional legitimacy erodes. That erosion is not confined to government; opinion polls show that it has spread to education, the media, the
professions and other institutions.

The informing insight of the Governance project (one might
almost call it a revelation) is that the principal cause of the government's loss of legitimacy is an obsolete framework within
which issues are defined and addressed. Participants in the project are working to free themselves, and their colleagues in government, from the distortions imposed by a dysfunctional way of
thinking about, and acting upon, the great issues of our times.

[*] Daniel Yankelovich, a leader in the development of public opinion research, is
the founder of Yankelovich, Skelly and White, the Chairman both of DYG, Inc.
and of WSY, Inc., and the founder and President of the Public Agenda
Foundation. Previously he was a Professor at New York University and at the
Graduate Faculty of the New School for Social Research. Mr. Yankelovich is the
author of numerous books and articles on issues of governance and public
opinion, the most recent of which is *Coming to Public Judgement: Making
Democracy Work in a Complex World* (Syracuse: Syracuse University Press,
1991).

As an alternative to government's outmoded framework, the project offers the concept of the "information society." The project's main premise can be stated as follows:

> The most urgent problems of governance in Canada, the United States and other advanced industrial democracies no longer yield to pre-information age frameworks. When these same problems, however, are examined in the light of information society frameworks, new possibilities arise. Fresh thinking can be brought to bear, solutions that did not exist even a few years ago suggest themselves, and implementation can be carried out in a cost-effective manner. The new information society framework can, therefore, lead to a genuine re-invention of government and restoration of public confidence.

Clearly, the success or failure of the project hinges on the viability of this premise. I believe that the premise, properly understood, is sound and will yield new solutions to old intractable problems. But the qualification, "properly understood," is critical. The information society concept, as now formulated, is loaded with ambiguities, both superficial and profound.

In practice, the Governance project tends to use the label "information society" as a shorthand way of referring to a vast array of changes in the world view of the advanced industrial democracies. The key to the correct understanding of the information society concept is, therefore, to comprehend what this emerging world view is and to identify within it the specific features most relevant to revitalizing government.

In what follows, I will discuss the ambiguities in the information society concept (both the superficial and the deeper ones), briefly characterize the broader shift in culture, which is the context for the Governance project's work, and then focus the main body of the paper on two features of the emerging world view that promise to lead most directly to more effective ways of governing

The Surface Ambiguity

The superficial ambiguity in the information society concept is semantic. To the public at large, the label "information society" implies that the driving force behind the great transformations of our age, such as the global economy, is information: more of it, delivered more quickly, and packaged more powerfully as it barrels down the information highway.

In the Canadian project, however, the label "information society" refers to a broader set of transforming changes than those wrought by information and information technology alone. Unless we understand the supple and flexible way the project has gradually enriched the concept of the information society as it has progressed with its work, we could easily be misled into the simplistic view that by information society the project simply means a society in which information is more abundant. In its day-to-day work, the Governance project encompasses a number of trends and transformations that include, but are not confined to, information or information technology.

One such trend, for example, is the breakdown of boundaries that heretofore have rigidly separated various branches of knowledge from each other. In recent years these boundaries have grown progressively more blurred and indistinct, even in such conservative institutions as universities. As one observer remarked: "We are beginning to recognize that God did not create the universe according to the departmental structure of our research universities."[119] (This trend partly relates to information, but it relates even more profoundly to new ways of thinking and knowledge).

The information society label is misleading in another respect as well, as the project itself recognizes. For purposes of governance, the focus is less on information than it is on frameworks for interpreting information. The first report of the project makes this point explicit in its illuminating essay on the informa-

119 Quoted in the *New York Times*, March 23, 1993, A19.

tion society concept. "The focus," it states, "is not so much on the management of information, as on management of the frameworks within which information is interpreted."[120]

This distinction is so abstract that we may not immediately realize its full implications. But it is this distinction that lies at the heart of the Governance project. In the context of the project, the term "information society" should not be understood merely as referring to new ways of managing information but as referring to new ways of perceiving the world, thinking about it and interpreting its meaning.

The Deeper Ambiguity

Once we recognize that the information society concept focuses on frameworks for interpretation, rather than on information itself, we are then free to confront its deeper ambiguities. Even a casual reading of the project's deliberations reveals that it is hunting bigger game than the management of information. Something so limited in scope as the management of information could not conceivably have the large effects the project is looking for. And the ambitions of the project are large: it is seeking nothing less than a decisive transformation in governance from its present state of semi-paralysis and low public esteem to a state of high effectiveness and renewed public confidence. Reinventing government, if it can be done at all, is not going to be done by juggling information more cleverly.

Here, then, is the deeper ambiguity of the project. What the project's information society concept is really about is an ambitious effort to reframe the vast network of assumptions undergirding both the organization of government and government's relations with the citizenry. These assumptions are being undermined by a vast cultural shift that is unfolding in all of the advanced industrial democracies. What the Governance project is doing is strategically selecting some of the new concepts the

120 Rosell, Steven A., et al., *Governing In An Information Society* (Montreal: Institute for Research on Public Policy, 1992), 33.

cultural shift is generating, and applying them to government. The process of selection is, however, a prickly task because the cultural shift is so sprawling and amorphous.

The Critique of Modernity

The cultural shift is unfolding both at the level of ideas and of institutions. At the level of ideas, it takes the form of a sweeping critique of modernity. What generally is meant by this vague word "modernity" is a constellation of values, concepts, assumptions and modes of thought that began to emerge in the 17th century, became further elaborated in the 18th and 19th centuries, and grew rigid and doctrinaire in the 20th century. Only now is the modernity paradigm beginning to lose some of its credibility and power, being slowly displaced by a new constellation of ideas whose shape and form is not yet clearly discernible.

One quick way to grasp the modernity paradigm is to think of it as a series of distinctions that, after the Enlightenment, crystallized the intellectual framework of the West for controlling knowledge and organizing action. All of us, born in this century, have learned to live and work in a world dominated by an inherited division of effort between scientific and non-scientific forms of knowledge, between value and fact, between the individual and the society, between the professional and the amateur, between government and the private sector, between labour and capital, between city and country, between the secular and the divine, between one profession and another, one nation state and another, and so on.

Sociologist Anthony Giddens characterizes the rise of modernity as representing one of the few real discontinuities in human history, in terms of the pace of change wrought by technology, the scope of change that affected the entire world, and the nature of modern institutions, which transformed traditional ways of life into the nationalized, urbanized, industrialized societies of today.[121] We live our lives, and do our work, wholly immersed in

121 Ibid., 6.

the modern world: it is as familiar to us as the houses we inhabit and the streets we walk. To the extent that this still dominant mode of thought is being challenged and replaced by other frameworks for interpretation, we find ourselves entering a strange and unfamiliar new world.

The strategy of the Governance project is to begin to map that new world. It is doing so

- by identifying those trends that signal a change in one or another vulnerable part of the modernity paradigm;
- by critiquing the most crippling flaws in the existing framework;
- by seeking to replace its defective parts with assumptions, and methods of organization, better suited to solving the problems that governments must address.

In this effort, the Governance project is not alone. It is, in fact, part of a vast intellectual enterprise that cuts across many different fields. The various efforts to reform modernity have many names. "Information society" is just one of them. "Post-industrial" is another. "Post-structural" and "postmodern" are others. For more than a century now, seminal thinkers from many disciplines have questioned the fundamental assumptions of the modern era. They have challenged virtually every aspect of the frameworks of thought underlying the modern sciences, the professions, the humanities and the arts. It was Nietzsche who is generally acknowledged to have initiated the postmodern critique. Since then, a small army of thinkers from fields as diverse as philosophy, literary criticism, sociology, history, political science, anthropology and the physical sciences have deconstructed one or another facet of modernity with their own critiques.

So diverse is this enterprise, that each school of thought attacks a different aspect of modernity. Max Weber, one of the early sociological critics of modernity, attacked what he called the process of rationalization: the tendency of "instrumental reason" to dominate all forms of modern life, ultimately creating, he believed, an "iron cage" civilization stuffed with "heartless experts" and "spineless pleasure seekers."[122] The philosopher Jean-Francois Lyotard, who has written extensively about postmodernity, attacks modernity's "metanarrative" of progress, and the claims of science to be a superior path to knowledge.[123]

The anthropologist Clifford Geertz attacks one of modernity's most subtle assumptions. As Geertz wryly notes, anthropology long has been dominated by a "me-anthropologist-you-native" framework. That framework, he argues, now is yielding to a new way of thinking, in which the information content remains constant (he is the anthropologist and his informant is the native), but the mode of interpreting the relationship has shifted. Geertz says that he has stopped thinking about the relationship in a way that suggests a vast social distance between anthropologist and subject, with the anthropologist occupying the high-status, disinterested observer role and the informant reduced to an impersonal object of study. Even more fundamentally, the me-anthropologist-you-native framework suggests a sharp, virtually unbridgeable gap between the observer and the object of observation, which a closer examination shows to be arbitrary and profoundly ideological: its purpose is to preserve distance, preserve superiority in status, preserve a conception of social science that has proven not to be very productive or insightful.[124]

The cumulative effect of these, and many other, critiques of modernity is a powerful one: it is transforming the way we think about the world and everything in it. Its implications for governance are all-embracing.

But the critique of modernity has not gone smoothly. Few critics agree with one another. All are pursuing different agendas. Some are so hostile to modernity that they reject it in all of its

---

122 Quoted in Daniel Yankelovich et al., *The World at Work* (New York: Octagon Press, 1985), 40-3.

123 See, for example, Jean Francois Lyotard, *The Post Modern Condition: a Report on Knowledge* (Minneapolis: University of Minnesota Press, 1984).

124 Geertz, Clifford, "Blurred Genres: the Refiguration of Social Thought" in *Critical Theory Since 1965*, Hazard Adams and Leroy Seattle, eds. (Tallahassee: Florida State University Press).

forms – rationality, logic, truth, reality, science, order). Out goes the baby along with the bath water. Other critics pursue a vaguely "new age" line of thought, blurring the hard edges of modernity in a cloud of semi-mystical emanations. The Governance project is typical of yet another school of critics who seek to preserve and expand the immense benefits of modernity, while softening its excesses and correcting some of its more mechanistic tendencies.

Members of the various schools of thought have mounted heated attacks against each other, filling the air with controversy and making it almost impossible to develop a reasoned perspective about the true defects, and glories, of modernity. The result has been a mixed blessing. Today, postmodern thinking is a potpourri of creative ideas, destructive ideologies, strident arguments, brilliant insights, prejudices, pretentiousness, vendettas and obscurantisms. In Gertrude Himmelfarb's scathing words, "The beasts of modernism have mutated into the beasts of postmodernism – relativism into nihilism, amorality into immorality, irrationality into insanity...."[125] The postmodern movement is, at once, a source of immense intellectual energy and, at the same time, a colossal intellectual mess.

To succeed, the Governance project must exercise great judiciousness in selecting usable ideas from the vast storehouse of postmodern thought. "Great ideas," Alfred North Whitehead once observed, "often enter reality in strange guises and with disgusting alliances." The same insight is conveyed in cruder form by an old joke. A farmer is seen to be digging furiously into a huge pile of horse manure that towers above his head. When a bewildered observer asks why he is digging, the farmer replies, in some exasperation: "Because there's a pony under all this horseshit." For officials wrestling with the day-to-day problems of governance, the challenge is to be able to extricate the pony. The first of these is the attempt to manage complexity by means of compartmentalization: the work of government is done through a variety of agencies and departments neatly compartmentalized, each

125 Himmelfarb, Gertrude, *On Looking into the Abyss* (New York: Alfred A. Knopf, 1994), 6.

from the other, on organizational charts that seem logical, but rarely mirror the reality with which they must cope. The second defect is the tendency to objectify relationships in a manner that distances the people in government from those they serve. These two defects feed on each other, almost guarantying in advance that government will be both inefficient and offensive to the citizenry. Finally, I will suggest several ways in which the information society framework can help to overcome these defects.

The First Defect: Compartmentalization

Perhaps the most distinctive feature (and crippling defect) of modernity is its mode of imposing order on the chaos of experience. Over scores of years, one institution after another has developed an ingrained habit of compartmentalizing, dividing and subdividing all aspects of reality, according to certain logical principles, in order to maximize their control over their environment.

In Western civilization, the process of logical categorization can be traced all the way back to Aristotle but, in the modern era, it has been extended systematically to institutions and to the life world (*lebenswelt*), as well as to ideas. In its advanced form, this is the process that Max Weber feared would lead to an iron cage of rigid and destructive compartmentalization. Today, rationalization takes the form of inexorably greater bureaucratization, specialization, regulation, computerization, abstraction and manipulation of the public and of the political process.

The rationalizing of virtually every aspect of life world is, of course, a fundamental phenomenon of contemporary existence. From childhood on, all of us internalize this feature of the modern framework so thoroughly that we often are unaware of the automatic ways in which we compartmentalize reality in order to deal with it. Unfortunately, reality doesn't always cooperate. On some issues, it stubbornly refuses to reflect the neatness of the categories we bring to the task of apprehending it.

We can see this process of categorizing reality being applied in every issue that involves governance. Some issues fit into the bureaucratic boxes that government creates, but the most important ones do not. They are too sprawling to fit.

The best way to grasp the harm this defect causes is to look at a specific issue. Consider, for example, the emerging threat to our societies of class warfare. This threat is implicit in one of the Governance project's scenarios. It is as applicable to the United States as it is to Canada, and is, I believe, the most likely outlook for the future of both nations, unless the two societies actively intervene to change the flow of history.

In this scenario, the private sector has succeeded in creating a reasonably strong economy accompanied, however, by high unemployment and exceptionally high frustration levels for the majority of the work force. There are enough good, full-time, full-benefit jobs for the highly skilled and/or well educated minority (about 40 per cent of the work force), but not for the 60 per cent majority who lack either a four-year college education, or those specialized skills that happen to be in demand at the moment. As a consequence, the incomes of all but the top tier stagnate or deteriorate. Among the majority, expectations are lowered. Political resentment grows. The underclass swells. The gap between rich and poor widens. Social cleavages, crime and social pathology grow ever more serious, threatening to undermine political stability, even though the economy flourishes according to the familiar standards of GDP growth and return on capital.

This scenario need not be imagined for a remote future. It already is happening. In the emerging global economy, the class warfare scenario is a far more likely outcome than it would have been in the more autonomous, less interdependent economies of the past. The brutal fact is that, in today's global economy, employers can grow and be profitable by restructuring their operations so as to be less dependent on large numbers of full-time, full-benefit, locally recruited employees. They systematically can reduce their own work force, utilize the work forces of other nations, and organize their work in such a way that much of it can be done by a contingent labour force, a labour force that does not have to be paid benefits, and that does not have to be granted even the most limited job security.

With modern technology, it is possible today, in any one nation, to achieve economic growth by employing only a fraction of the total number of people who are seeking jobs. The result either is high unemployment, as we are seeing in Europe, or the steady substitution of low-wage, low-benefit jobs for high-wage, high-benefit jobs, as we are seeing in the United States. At some point, when the public's frustration level reaches a critical mass, the issue will cease to be an economic one and will become political. In our two societies, at present, we are just beginning to see this happen.

If this process accelerates, it will be an enormous setback for our societies. One of the great achievements of the post-World War II era was the creation of a two-track economy: not only could people with a college education make a good living, but so could people without a college education. This was a political accomplishment of the first order: it led not only to prosperity, but also to a conviction of rightness, fairness and legitimacy. It was this two-track economy that made us into middle-class societies, with home ownership in the United States reaching the 70 per cent level. If the trends I have been describing continue and even accelerate, our societies will grow ever more divided and embittered, fanning the flames of demagogy.

There can be no more urgent task for leadership and governance than to slow, stop and reverse these trends. And there can be no better test of the merits of the Governance project than to ask whether its master concept, the concept of the "information society," gives leaders a more effective strategy to accomplish this goal than do existing governance strategies.

One approaches a problem like the threat of class warfare with the utmost respect for its complexity. It is unyielding to conventional approaches. The right framework can be decisive: a relevant framework can bring success, while an obtuse framework almost guarantees failure. Unfortunately, the existing policy framework is of the obtuse kind: where it should be revealing solutions, it obscures them; where it should be focusing on the critical factors, it deflects and divides attention.

When we look at what needs to be done to head off class warfare, we immediately see the irrelevance of the old framework. The knowledge base, and the governance institutions that must deal with it, have been compartmentalized in a highly dysfunctional manner. On the institutional front, work is separated from education. Education is divided from training. Academic education is divided from vocational education. Higher education is divided from lower. Labour is divided from management. White-collar work is divided from blue-collar work. Business is divided from government. To reverse the class warfare trend, we need policies that blur and loosen up all of these dichotomies, rather than treat them as if they were engraved in stone.

On the knowledge front, the situation is even worse. In all but the most advanced policy think tanks, the relevant professions of economics, politics and sociology are divided from each other as separate disciplines, each one jealously guarding its own narrow preserve, each armed with its own methodology, sub-culture and metanarrative.

In summary, while the reality of the class warfare threat cuts across many disciplines, requires bold acts of political will and moral vision, and demands a unified institutional effort to deal with it, the existing policy framework fragments and dissipates the knowledge base, lacks moral vision, and undercuts the unity of institutional action. The knowledge base needed to devise strategies to combat class warfare is fragmented in ways that ravage the integrity of the issue. And the bureaucratic institutions needed to counter the trend are too rigidly compartmentalized to take effective action.

The dysfunctionality of the existing framework does not, of course, guarantee that the new information framework will succeed any better in assisting political leadership to head off destructive class warfare. But it has a reasonable chance of doing so for two reasons: one negative, the other positive.

The negative reason is that it is not burdened with the rigidities of the existing framework. The new information framework still is in the process of emerging but, to judge from the general direction in which it is developing, it is seeking actively to correct the dysfunctions of the old framework. Thus, in its general tendencies, hierarchies are flattened, teams work across organizational and institutional boundaries, education and training are seen as aspects of a single whole, work and education are more closely integrated, business and government seek new forms of partnership rather than persisting in destructive adversarial relations, information is disseminated more widely, and vision, informed by ethical values, is understood to be more important to the advancement of human purpose than technical reason. Every one of these characteristics, and many more, remove obstacles from governance initiatives to counter class warfare.

On the positive side of the ledger, the grounds for hope are even greater. When one steps back from all of the institutional obstacles imposed by the existing framework, the problems that are leading to class warfare do not seem insurmountable. While, technically, it may be possible for the economy to grow without good jobs for the bulk of the work force, such a result is unacceptable morally and politically. When leaders ask what kinds of proactive initiatives they can take to reproduce the post-war equivalent of the two-track system (when those without a college education also could make a good living), there are some obvious answers that can serve as a useful point of departure for policy and vision.

While our society, at present, suffers from a paucity of good jobs for those who seek them, it does not lack vast areas of unmet needs. Potentially, there are tens of millions of jobs needed to provide better child care service, home care for the aged and the infirm, training for the millions who are functionally illiterate or whose job skills need to be upgraded, support systems for the homeless and for those excluded from mainstream society, as well as jobs renewing the nation's infrastructure. And, for many of these tasks, people do not have to be at the cutting edge of advanced technology.

In our mixed economies, there is plenty of precedent for government to seek to compensate for market failure. Also, opinion polls show that while the public (at least in the United States) distrusts government's social agenda (on the rational grounds that government hasn't learned how to cope with social problems very well), it does support a proactive government in the economic arena. There is virtual consensus that market solutions should have priority but, that when these fail, government must step in. For the public, the issue is not ideological but pragmatic. The public mandate is: Do whatever it takes to make the economy work to provide good jobs for all who seek them, and who have the skills and motivation to do them well.

There almost is no end to the jobs one can imagine that, if filled, would enhance our nation's quality of life, as well as directly benefit those who fill them. Where imagination is lacking is in addressing the problem of how to match unfilled needs with jobs for people who want to work. This failure of the political imagination is directly traceable to the existing framework. The professionals trained within it simply do not think in these terms; they have what the late Herman Kahn aptly called a "trained incapacity" to do so. But the bolder thinkers in our societies, who are at home with the new information framework, would not shrink from such a task.

The Second Defect: Objectification

The second defect in the day-to-day operating framework of modern governments, takes its toll on the bond that binds leaders to voters, government to citizens. It distorts that bond, making leaders less effective than they should be, and citizens less responsive, and responsible, than they should be.

This characteristic long has been familiar to both Marxist and non-Marxist philosophical critics of modernism, who refer to it as the process of objectifying relationships inappropriately. Marx associated this characteristic that he called "reification" with capitalism, but most post-Marxist philosophers have generalized its application to all aspects of modern life. At this late date in the 20th century, it is clear that they are correct. Objectification is not confined to the capitalist system of organizing the economy or to the government-citizen relationship: it is omnipresent in our culture. When the surgeon thinks of the suffering patient as the "infarction in Room 379," when the giant corporation thinks of its employees as "labour," when scientists think of their subjects as "the control group," we know that objectification is operative. In everyday life, this process of depersonalizing relationships is so automatic and omnipresent that we take it in stride. It annoys us, but we shrug it off as part of the price we pay for living in a complex technological society. We remain unaware of how deeply destructive it is.

Clifford Geertz was noting this defect, in his own field of anthropology, when he referred to the "me-anthropologist-you-native" framework. In that example, the existing framework automatically converts the subject of study into an *object* of study, distancing the social scientist and colouring every aspect of discourse between social scientist and subject.

These distortions take a particularly heavy toll in the political and governmental domain. In effect, they create an invisible barrier between government and citizens. Government officials come to see themselves as elites who "do things for" the people. And "the people," placed in the role of those for whom things are done, grow passive and unrealistically demanding. The relationship inevitably deteriorates, with people constantly nagging at government about their rights, while government officials, tiring of the unreasonableness of incessant public demands, respond by becoming more secretive, cunning and manipulative. A vicious circle is set in motion that erodes our democratic institutions.

This defect, as it applies to the government-citizen relationship, has been noted and diagnosed in several different ways. David Mathews, President of the Kettering Foundation and former Cabinet member in the United States government, has been studying the relationship between government and citizens for many years. In his recent work, he identifies this framework defect with the growth of professionalism. The American public, he notes, may like and admire individual professionals (their own doctor, congressperson, or kids' teachers), but they are in revolt against professionalism as a doctrine.

Professionalism developed in the United States in the 1890s and early 1900s. As it did so, it drew heavily upon the growing prestige of science as a privileged and superior method for gaining knowledge. It internalized many aspects of the culture of science, including the high value placed on objectivity, instrumental reason, the rigid separation of fact from value, and the distancing of scientifically minded professionals from the "objects" of their study. Mathews observes that, as professionalism evolved to its present advanced state, the distancing effect between professionals and the public has grown more pronounced. Presently, he states, the relationship of professionals to the public:

> grows out of a conviction that the public is deficient and that what the public lacks can only be supplied by the professional.... From within the professional paradigm, there is no other way to understand the public than as a passive mass.... Citizens couldn't be anything other than various kinds of clients: patients, consumers, readers. So the world of citizens – the public world – faded from view. The term public lost much of its original meaning....[126]

In my own work, in the field of public opinion, I have attributed the growing gap between leaders and the public to the dominance of what I call the *Culture of Technical Control*. This is the trend, in our culture, to seek to gain ever greater control over all aspects of our life by technical means, and that results in creeping expertism. In my book, *Coming to Public Judgment*, I advanced the thesis that the Culture of Technical Control is "undermining

---

126 Mathews, David, *Professionalism and Public Life* (unpublished manuscript), 7.

the country's ability to reach agreement between the public and the experts on the serious problems that beset the society."[127]

While David Mathews emphasizes one destructive form of the Culture of Technical Control (its distorting effects on professionalism), I emphasize another one that manifests itself constantly in the field of public opinion research. Virtually all studies of public opinion find a huge gap between the views of the public and the views of experts and leaders on the vital issues of our times. There is an almost unbridgeable chasm separating elites from the public. We are accustomed to looking back at traditional society, with its wide social distance between the classes, while congratulating ourselves on our classlessness and equality. But, in actuality, the distance between our elites and the general public today is probably as great as it was in French society just prior to the French Revolution.

Today, that distance is not social: we have achieved a somewhat more social equality. That distance is a matter of belonging to two different worlds: the world of professionals, experts and policy elites who manage, through countless conferences and workshops and meetings, to carry on a spirited dialogue among themselves, and the world of the general public, which lies in a region so far beyond the policy world as to inhabit a different universe. A great invisible wall divides the two worlds, a wall that is bad for democracy.

The most harmful effect of that wall is to cause the public to persist in a state of raw opinion. My book, *Coming to Public Judgment*, develops the all-important distinction between "raw opinion" and "public judgment." Raw opinion is opinion on an issue that is formed before the public has had the opportunity to deliberate it, and to grasp its full implications. Inconveniently, people do hold strong opinions on subjects about which they know nothing, and to which they have devoted little or no thought. Typically, such opinions are highly volatile, changing

---

127 Daniel Yankelovich, *Coming to Public Judgment: Making Democracy Work in a Complex World* (Syracuse, NY: Syracuse University Press, 1991), 8-9ff.

from day to day, and full of internal contradictions. The surest sign of raw opinion is when people are unaware of the consequences of their own views. For example, at the present time, the majority of voters in the United States hold favourable opinions about various health care reforms that would, if enacted, produce the very effects they most dread: impersonal care accompanied by higher taxes and less real decision making on their own part. This is raw opinion.

On some issues, however, the public's views have evolved from raw opinion into more thoughtful judgment. Typically, this evolution requires a complex process of deliberation that unfolds through a number of stages. One knows that public judgment has been reached on an issue when, on probing, peoples' opinions are found to be firm rather than volatile, self-consistent rather than contradictory and, most importantly, self-conscious, thoughtful and responsible about consequences. For example, if people did form firm, unshakable, positive opinions on plans for health care reform, in full consciousness of their costs and trade-offs, and if these views did not conflict with their other opinions and values, that would be a sign of public judgment rather than of raw opinion.

What is the implication of this discussion for the Governance project? If we give this concept too literal a meaning, it would seem to imply that the best way to overcome the policy maker-public gap, and to help the public move from raw opinion to public judgment, would be to share more information with the public. But such an inference would be a huge mistake.

Sharing more information with the public is what our societies have been doing for the past four or five decades, through the mass media. Today, the public is bombarded with vastly greater quantities of information than in the past. But, significantly, this has not closed the gap, or moved the public further along the journey from mass opinion to public judgment. In a study of public opinion in the United States, conducted in 1989, political scientist Michael Kagay and a co-author measured the public's current knowledge of politics and civic affairs, and compared it to their level of knowledge 40 years earlier. The authors were disappointed to find that the public's knowledge levels were hardly different than in the 1950s. As one of them commented, "It is hard to imagine, if this is the level of information citizens bring to politics, that they have enough context to make informed political decisions."[128]

It is to avoid inferences of this sort, which place an exaggerated value on conveying information, that I have focused on the objectification defect of the existing framework. We need to recognize that the true problem is not a lack of information. Rather, the problem lies in the tendency of governments to objectify themselves and, in so doing, to distance themselves from ordinary citizens. It lies in the tendency of governments to assume airs of superiority because they have more information, and to treat people as objects for spinmeisters to manipulate, rather than as citizens whose values and points of view carry as much weight as their own. Once we recognize this, we can begin to see a solution to the problem of a distorted relationship between government and citizens.

The solution is more genuine dialogue, not more information. Information is an aspect of dialogue, but not its essential feature. To illustrate, in President Clinton's forays into so-called "town meetings," we have the form of dialogue, but rarely the substance. If, in one of these pseudo town meetings, the President transmits information to citizens and the citizens in turn seize the opportunity to urge the President to pay more attention to their own special interests (more money for disabled veterans, or drug treatment centers, or flood victims), it is highly unlikely that genuine dialogue is taking place. In these town meetings, the President of the United States and ordinary citizens are seen and heard addressing each other, but just because information is transmitted or because a special interest is urged by an individual rather than by an organized group, doesn't constitute dialogue.

The philosopher Martin Buber observed that in the I-thou form of dialogue, both parties (the I and the thou) are changed,

---

128 Ibid., 47.

and changed forever. In these town meetings, neither side has truly listened to or understood the standpoint of the other with any of the depth needed to achieve what Buber had in mind. Neither side has changed in any essential way.

The key point here is that dialogue is the single, most powerful tool governments possess for helping citizens to navigate the difficult journey from raw opinion to public judgment. It can do so by engaging citizens in a deliberative process that is focused on shaping policies that are consonant with peoples' values, rather than policies and programs that violate their values. For example, most of the health care reform plans under discussion in the United States feature some variant of managed care, where physician services inevitably become more impersonal in the interests of controlling costs. But, on health care, preserving and enhancing personal care is the average American's most deeply cherished value. Dialogue between citizens and government about this value, what it is worth to people to preserve, and about how much impersonality they are willing to accept for the sake of cost savings – they are willing to accept some – would give Americans the impetus to engage the issue deliberatively, and move closer to public judgment.

Genuine dialogue does, sometimes, take place in our societies. It takes place among elites who have established many excellent fora for encouraging exchanges among equals. It also takes place among citizen groups who engage each other in serious conversation. But it doesn't take place between the two strata, for the simple reason that the existing framework has objectified them as two strata rather than as a single indivisible whole, some of whom happen to work for the government.

Implications for Leadership

Implicit in this discussion of the new information society framework are some far-reaching implications for styles of leadership. These cannot be developed properly at the end of a long paper, but a brief comment may be in order.

The style of leadership, most consonant with the evolving new framework, is one in which leaders:

- resonate well with citizens' values and share many of those same values;
- possess the strong moral convictions that citizens aspire to even if they do not always live up to them;
- possess the ability to listen creatively to what people really mean, even when people are inarticulate in expressing their meaning;
- possess the ability to highlight the value content of alternative policy proposals, as distinct from their technical, bureaucratic, administrative content;
- respond to citizens as equals;
- give citizens the opportunity to deliberate alternative choices on important issues, rather than trying to sell them a single prepackaged choice;
- possess the communication skills (and patience) needed to help citizens make the journey from raw opinion to public judgment;
- empower average people to take moral responsibility for the consequences of their opinions;
- endow difficult policy choices with moral vision as well as pragmatic feasibility.

There are numerous other leadership qualities implied by the new framework. But these are sufficient to suggest both the continuities with traditional styles of leadership and the differences.

One of the fears expressed by elites, deeply immersed in the culture of modernism, is that this style of leadership is "wimpy;" a conception of the leader as discussion moderator. And it is true that prominent among the many mistaken interpretations of new leadership styles is the view that leadership involves a form of participative democracy, in which everyone has a voice and a vote. Organizations that have experimented with this approach quickly learn to abandon it as unwieldy and ineffective.

In any practical model of leadership, responsibility for ultimate decision making falls on the leader. In Harry Truman's unambiguous phrase, "The buck stops here." Leaders who guide people to work their own way through thorny issues, rather than adopting a "we know best" posture, and who create the conditions for dialogue, rather than imposing their own views and values on the citizenry, are not abdicating their responsibility for making the hard decisions. On the contrary, they are ensuring that their decisions, once made, will reflect the true convictions of the citizenry, as well as their own best judgment.

The essence of the leadership style implicit in the new framework is not that it is more democratic in the sense of shared decision-making, but that it is more democratic in the process that leads up to the final decision.[129]

Summary

To summarize the highly compressed argument I have sought to develop in this paper, I am concerned that the great promise of the Governance project can be blunted by a misunderstanding that will surely confuse outsiders and may even confuse the Project participants themselves.

The participants are searching the crowded cupboard of postmodernist thought for new insights that will help them overcome the obsolete features of government in the interests of restoring legitimacy to governance and regaining the confidence of citizens. They are correct, I believe, in their assumption that the postmodern critique harbours the kind of revitalizing insights they seek. But they are mistaken, I have argued in this paper, in identifying these liberating insights with something called the "information society." At best, this label is a misnomer; at worst, it is terribly misleading. Information is a minor part of the treasure they seek. Indeed, among the worst features of modernity are its unrealistic assumptions about the nature and power of information.

---

129 I am indebted to my wife, Mary K. Yankelovich, for her thinking on the leadership implications of the new information society framework.

The true object of the search into postmodern thought is to liberate the modernist world view from a deeply embedded distortion that has long undermined the work of government as well as other institutions; an unwitting tendency to objectify the *lebenswelt* and then to compartmentalize it by categorizing human experience into a series of oversimplified dichotomies (e.g., fact vs. value, economics vs. politics, scientific vs. nonscientific modes of knowing). These dichotomies illustrate what Alfred North Whitehead has called "fallacies of misplaced concreteness" whereby, to put it bluntly, one mistakes high abstractions for hard facts.

This inbuilt tendency of modernity guarantees that information will be misinterpreted, overvalued and misapplied – the more information received and the more quickly it travels, the greater the likelihood of misuse. Therefore, to identify the liberating change it seeks as the "information society" will cause the project to be just enough off target to jeopardize the potential value of its work.

These are, admittedly, subtle and elusive matters, difficult to apply to the day-to-day problems of government. But if they weren't subtle and elusive, they would not have been neglected for over two hundred years. For the Governance project, this is the pony hidden under the vast pile of horseshit that constitutes the present state of postmodernist thought.

Glossary of Acronymns

ADM	Assistant/Associate Deputy Minister
AFTA	Americas Free Trade Agreement
CEU	Commission of the European Union
CIAR	Canadian Institute for Advanced Research
CIDA	Canadian International Development Agency
ESOP	Employee Stock Ownership Plan
GERD	gross expenditure on Research and Development
GNP	gross national product
ICT	information and communications technologies
IDRC	International Development Research Centre
IMF	International Monetary Fund
IT	information technology
MERIT	Maastricht Economic Research Institute on Innovation and Technology (Netherlands)
NIE	Newly Industrialized Economy
OECD	Organization for Economic Cooperation and Development
PR	public relations
R&D	Research and Development
SPRU	Science Policy Research Unit (University of Sussex, England)